Java™ 2 For Dummies®

Cheat Sheet

Java Keywords

Keyword	What It Does
abstract	Indicates that the details of a class, a method, or an interface are given elsewhere in the code.
boolean	Indicates that a value is either true or false.
break	Jumps out of a loop or switch.
byte	Indicates that a value is an 8-bit whole number.
case	Introduces one of several possible paths of execution in a switch statement.
catch	Introduces statements that are executed when something interrupts the flow of execution in a try clause.
char	Indicates that a value is a character (a single letter, digit, punctuation symbol, and so on) stored in 16 bits of memory.
class	Introduces a class — a blueprint for an object.
const	You can't use this word in a Java program. The word has no meaning. Because it's a keyword, you can't create a const variable.
continue	Forces the abrupt end of the current loop iteration and begins another iteration.
default	Introduces a path of execution to take when no case is a match in a switch statement.
do	Causes the computer to repeat some statements over and over again (for instance, as long as the computer keeps getting unacceptable results).
double	Indicates that a value is a 64-bit number with one or more digits after the decimal point.
else	Introduces statements that are executed when the condition in an if statement isn't true.
extends	Creates a *subclass* — a class that reuses functionality from a previously defined class.
final	Indicates that a variable's value cannot be changed, that a class's functionality cannot be extended, or that a method cannot be overridden.
finally	Introduces the last will and testament of the statements in a try clause.
float	Indicates that a value is a 32-bit number with one or more digits after the decimal point.
for	Gets the computer to repeat some statements over and over again (for instance, a certain number of times).
goto	You can't use this word in a Java program. The word has no meaning. Because it's a keyword, you can't create a goto variable.
if	Tests to see if a condition is true. If it's true, the computer executes certain statements; otherwise, the computer executes other statements.
implements	Reuses the functionality from a previously defined interface.
import	Enables the programmer to abbreviate the names of classes defined in a package.
instanceof	Tests to see if a certain object comes from a certain class.
int	Indicates that a value is a 32-bit whole number.

(continued)

Java™ 2 For Dummies®

Java Keywords (continued)

Keyword	What It Does
interface	Introduces an interface, which is like a class, only less specific. (Interfaces are used in place of the confusing multiple-inheritance feature that's in C++.)
long	Indicates that a value is a 64-bit whole number.
native	Enables the programmer to use code that was written in another language (one of those awful languages other than Java).
new	Creates an object from an existing class.
package	Puts the code into a *package* — a collection of logically related definitions.
private	Indicates that a variable or method can be used only within a certain class.
protected	Indicates that a variable or method can be used in subclasses from another package.
public	Indicates that a variable, class, or method can be used by any other Java code.
return	Ends execution of a method; possibly returns a value to the calling code.
short	Indicates that a value is a 16-bit whole number.
static	Indicates that a variable or method belongs to a class, rather than to any object created from the class.
strictfp	Limits the computer's ability to represent extra large or extra small numbers when the computer does intermediate calculations on float and double values.
super	Refers to the superclass of the code in which the word *super* appears.
switch	Tells the computer to follow one of many possible paths of execution (one of many possible cases), depending on the value of an expression.
synchronized	Keeps two threads from interfering with one another.
this	A self-reference — refers to the object in which the word *this* appears.
throw	Creates a new exception object; indicates that an exceptional situation (usually something unwanted) has occurred.
throws	Indicates that a method or constructor may pass the buck when an exception is thrown.
transient	Indicates that, if and when an object is serialized, a variable's value doesn't need to be stored.
try	Introduces statements that are watched (during runtime) for things that can go wrong.
void	Indicates that a method doesn't return a value.
volatile	Imposes strict rules on the use of a variable by more than one thread at a time.
while	Repeats some statements over and over again (as long as a condition is still true).

Hungry Minds™

For Dummies: Bestselling Book Series for Beginners

 ™

References for the Rest of Us!®

BESTSELLING BOOK SERIES

Are you intimidated and confused by computers? Do you find that traditional manuals are overloaded with technical details you'll never use? Do your friends and family always call you to fix simple problems on their PCs? Then the For Dummies® computer book series from Hungry Minds, Inc. is for you.

For Dummies books are written for those frustrated computer users who know they aren't really dumb but find that PC hardware, software, and indeed the unique vocabulary of computing make them feel helpless. For Dummies books use a lighthearted approach, a down-to-earth style, and even cartoons and humorous icons to dispel computer novices' fears and build their confidence. Lighthearted but not lightweight, these books are a perfect survival guide for anyone forced to use a computer.

> *"I like my copy so much I told friends; now they bought copies."*
>
> **— Irene C., Orwell, Ohio**

> *"Quick, concise, nontechnical, and humorous."*
>
> **— Jay A., Elburn, Illinois**

> *"Thanks, I needed this book. Now I can sleep at night."*
>
> **— Robin F., British Columbia, Canada**

Already, millions of satisfied readers agree. They have made For Dummies books the #1 introductory level computer book series and have written asking for more. So, if you're looking for the most fun and easy way to learn about computers, look to For Dummies books to give you a helping hand.

Hungry Minds™

Java™ 2

FOR

DUMMIES®

Java™ 2

FOR DUMMIES®

by Barry Burd

Hungry Minds™

Best-Selling Books • Digital Downloads • e-Books • Answer Networks • e-Newsletters • Branded Web Sites • e-Learning

New York, NY ◆ Cleveland, OH ◆ Indianapolis, IN

Java 2™ For Dummies®

Published by
Hungry Minds, Inc.
909 Third Avenue
New York, NY 10022
www.hungryminds.com
www.dummies.com

Library of Congress Control Number: 00-111129

ISBN: 0-7645-0765-6

Printed in the United States of America

10 9 8 7 6 5 4 3 2 1

1B/SR/QZ/QR/IN

Distributed in the United States by Hungry Minds, Inc.

Distributed by CDG Books Canada Inc. for Canada; by Transworld Publishers Limited in the United Kingdom; by IDG Norge Books for Norway; by IDG Sweden Books for Sweden; by IDG Books Australia Publishing Corporation Pty. Ltd. for Australia and New Zealand; by TransQuest Publishers Pte Ltd. for Singapore, Malaysia, Thailand, Indonesia, and Hong Kong; by Gotop Information Inc. for Taiwan; by ICG Muse, Inc. for Japan; by Intersoft for South Africa; by Eyrolles for France; by International Thomson Publishing for Germany, Austria and Switzerland; by Distribuidora Cuspide for Argentina; by LR International for Brazil; by Galileo Libros for Chile; by Ediciones ZETA S.C.R. Ltda. for Peru; by WS Computer Publishing Corporation, Inc., for the Philippines; by Contemporanea de Ediciones for Venezuela; by Express Computer Distributors for the Caribbean and West Indies; by Micronesia Media Distributor, Inc. for Micronesia; by Chips Computadoras S.A. de C.V. for Mexico; by Editorial Norma de Panama S.A. for Panama; by American Bookshops for Finland.

For general information on Hungry Minds' products and services please contact our Customer Care Department within the U.S. at 800-762-2974, outside the U.S. at 317-572-3993 or fax 317-572-4002.

For sales inquiries and reseller information, including discounts, premium and bulk quantity sales, and foreign-language translations, please contact our Customer Care Department at 800-434-3422, fax 317-572-4002, or write to Hungry Minds, Inc., Attn: Customer Care Department, 10475 Crosspoint Boulevard, Indianapolis, IN 46256.

For information on licensing foreign or domestic rights, please contact our Sub-Rights Customer Care Department at 212-884-5000.

For information on using Hungry Minds' products and services in the classroom or for ordering examination copies, please contact our Educational Sales Department at 800-434-2086 or fax 317-572-4005.

For press review copies, author interviews, or other publicity information, please contact our Public Relations Department at 317-572-3168 or fax 317-572-4168.

For authorization to photocopy items for corporate, personal, or educational use, please contact Copyright Clearance Center, 222 Rosewood Drive, Danvers, MA 01923, or fax 978-750-4470.

Hungry Minds™ is a trademark of Hungry Minds, Inc.

About the Author

Dr. Barry Burd received an M.S. degree in Computer Science at Rutgers University and a Ph.D. in Mathematics at the University of Illinois. As a teaching assistant in Champaign-Urbana, Illinois, he was elected five times to the university-wide List of Teachers Ranked as Excellent by their Students.

Since 1980, Dr. Burd has been a professor in the Department of Mathematics and Computer Science at Drew University in Madison, New Jersey. When he's not lecturing at Drew University, Dr. Burd leads training courses for professional programmers in business and industry. He has lectured at conferences in the United States, Europe, Australia, and Asia. He is the author of several articles and books, including *JSP: JavaServer Pages,* published by Hungry Minds, Inc.

Dr. Burd lives in Madison, New Jersey, with his wife and two children. In his spare time, he enjoys being a workaholic.

Dedication

for

Harriet, Sam, and Jennie,

Sam and Ruth,

Abram and Katie, Benjamin and Jennie,

and Basheva

Author's Acknowledgments

Thanks.

-Barry Burd

Publisher's Acknowledgments

We're proud of this book; please send us your comments through our Hungry Minds Online Registration Form located at www.dummies.com.

Some of the people who helped bring this book to market include the following:

Acquisitions, Editorial, and Media Development

Project Editor: Paul Levesque

Acquisitions Editor: Jill Byus Schorr

Copy Editor: Rebecca Huehls

Technical Editor: Namir Shammas

Editorial Manager: Constance Carlisle

Permissions Editor: Laura Moss

Media Development Specialist: Travis Silvers

Media Development Coordinator: Marisa Pearman

Media Development Manager: Laura Carpenter

Media Development Supervisor: Richard Graves

Editorial Assistant: Amanda Foxworth

Production

Project Coordinator: Maridee Ennis

Layout and Graphics: Amy Adrian, Gabrielle McCann, Jacque Schneider, Betty Schulte, Brian Torwelle, Julie Trippetti, Jeremey Unger

Proofreaders: Laura Albert, John Bitter, Valery Bourke, Angel Perez, Dwight Ramsey, Marianne Santy, TECHBOOKS Production Services

Indexer: TECHBOOKS Production Services

General and Administrative

Hungry Minds, Inc.: John Kilcullen, CEO; Bill Barry, President and COO; John Ball, Executive VP, Operations & Administration; John Harris, Executive VP and CFO

Hungry Minds Technology Publishing Group: Richard Swadley, Senior Vice President and Publisher; Mary Bednarek, Vice President and Publisher, Networking; Walter R. Bruce III, Vice President and Publisher; Joseph Wikert, Vice President and Publisher, Web Development Group; Mary C. Corder, Editorial Director, Dummies Technology; Andy Cummings, Publishing Director, Dummies Technology; Barry Pruett, Publishing Director, Visual/Graphic Design

Hungry Minds Manufacturing: Ivor Parker, Vice President, Manufacturing

Hungry Minds Marketing: John Helmus, Assistant Vice President, Director of Marketing

Hungry Minds Production for Branded Press: Debbie Stailey, Production Director

Hungry Minds Sales: Michael Violano, Vice President, International Sales and Sub Rights

◆

The publisher would like to give special thanks to Patrick J. McGovern, without whom this book would not have been possible.

◆

Contents at a Glance

Cartoons at a Glance

By Rich Tennant

page 321

page 309

page 9

page 233

page 63

page 137

Cartoon Information:
Fax: 978-546-7747
E-Mail: richtennant@the5thwave.com
World Wide Web: www.the5thwave.com

Table of Contents

Introduction

Java is good stuff. I've been using it for years. I like Java because it's very orderly. Almost everything follows simple rules. The rules can seem intimidating at times, but this book is here to help you figure them out. So, if you want to use Java and want an alternative to the traditional techie, soft-cover book, then sit down, relax, and start reading *Java 2 For Dummies*.

How to Use This Book

I wish I could say, "Open to a random page of this book and start writing Java code. Just fill in the blanks and don't look back." In a sense, this is true. You can't break anything by writing Java code, so you're always free to experiment.

But I'll be honest. If you don't understand the bigger picture, writing a program is difficult. That's true with any computer programming language — not just Java. If you're typing code without knowing what it's about, and the code doesn't do exactly what you want it to do, then you're just plain stuck.

So, in this book, I divide Java programming into manageable chunks. Each chunk is (more or less) a chapter. You can jump in anywhere you want — Chapter 5, Chapter 10, or wherever. You can even start by poking around in the middle of a chapter. I've tried to make the examples interesting without making one chapter depend on another. When I use an important idea from another chapter, I include a note to help you find your way around.

In general, my advice is as follows:

- If you already know something, don't bother reading about it.
- If you're curious, don't be afraid to skip ahead. You can always sneak a peek at an earlier chapter if you really need to do so.

Conventions Used in This Book

Almost every technical book starts with a little typeface legend, and *Java 2 For Dummies* is no exception. What follows is a brief explanation of the typefaces used in this book.

- New terms are set in *italics*.

- If you need to type something that's mixed in with the regular text, the characters you type appear in bold. For example: Type **java** at the command prompt.

- You'll also see this `computerese` font. I use computerese for Java code, filenames, Web page addresses (URLs), on-screen messages, and other such things. Also, if something you need to type is really long, it appears in computerese font on its own line (or lines).

- There are certain things that you'll change when you type them on your own computer keyboard. For instance, I may ask you to type

    ```
    public class Anyname
    ```

    which means you should type **public class** and then some name that you make up on your own. Words that you need to replace with your own words are set in `italicized computerese`.

What You Don't Have to Read

Pick the first chapter or section that has material you don't already know and start reading there. Of course, you may hate making decisions as much as I do. If so, here are some guidelines you can follow:

- If you already know what kind of an animal Java is and know that you want to use Java, then skip Chapter 1 and go straight to Chapter 2. Believe me, I won't mind.

- If you already know how to get a Java program running, then skip Chapter 2 and start with Chapter 3.

- If you write programs for a living but use any language other than C or C++, then start with Chapter 2 or 3. When you reach Chapters 5 and 6, you'll probably find them to be easy reading. When you get to Chapter 7, it'll be time to dive in.

- If you write C (not C++) programs for a living, start with Chapters 3 and 4 but just skim Chapters 5 and 6.

- If you write C++ programs for a living, then glance at Chapter 3, skim Chapters 4 through 6, and start reading seriously in Chapter 7. (Java is a bit different from C++ in the way it handles classes and objects.)

- If you write Java programs for a living, then come to my house and help me write *Java 2 For Dummies*, 2nd Edition.

If you want to skip the sidebars and the Technical Stuff icons, then please do. In fact, if you want to skip anything at all, feel free.

Foolish Assumptions

In this book, I make a few assumptions about you, the reader. If one of these assumptions is incorrect, then you're probably okay. If all these assumptions are incorrect . . . well, buy the book anyway.

- ✔ **I assume that you have access to a computer.** Here's good news. You can run the code in this book on almost any computer. The only computers you can't use to run this code are ancient things that are more than six years old (give or take a few years). Occasionally I'm lazy and lapse into Microsoft Windows terminology, but that's only because so many people run Windows.

  Java's so versatile that it runs on just about anything. (Yes, it even runs on PDAs and some household appliances.) In Chapter 2, you can find instructions for downloading Java onto your favorite machine.

- ✔ **I assume that you can navigate through your computer's common menus and dialog boxes.** You don't have to be a Windows, Unix, or Macintosh power user, but you should be able to start a program, find a file, put a file into a certain directory . . . that sort of thing. Most of the time, when you practice the stuff in this book, you are typing code on your keyboard, not pointing and clicking your mouse.

  On those rare occasions when you need to drag and drop, cut and paste, or plug and play, I guide you carefully through the steps. But your computer may be configured in any of several billion ways, and my instructions may not quite fit your special situation. So, when you reach one of these platform-specific tasks, try following the steps in this book. If the steps don't quite fit, consult a book with instructions tailored to your system.

- ✔ **I assume that you can think logically.** That's all there is to programming in Java — thinking logically. If you can think logically, then you've got it made. If you don't believe that you can think logically, then read on. You may be pleasantly surprised.

- ✔ **I make very few assumptions about your computer programming experience (or your lack of such experience).** In writing this book, I've tried to do the impossible. I've tried to make the book interesting for experienced programmers, yet accessible to people with little or no programming experience. This means that I don't assume any particular programming background on your part. If you've never created a loop or indexed an array, that's okay.

  On the other hand, if you've done these things (maybe in Visual Basic, COBOL, or C++), you'll discover some interesting plot twists in Java. The developers of Java took the best ideas in object-oriented programming, streamlined them, reworked them, and reorganized them into a sleek, powerful way of thinking about problems. You'll find many new, thought-provoking features in Java. As you learn about these features, many of them will seem very natural to you. One way or another, you'll feel good about using Java.

How This Book Is Organized

This book is divided into subsections, which are grouped into sections, which come together to make chapters, which are lumped finally into six parts. (When you write a book, you get to know your book's structure pretty well. After months of writing, you find yourself dreaming in sections and chapters when you go to bed at night.) The parts of the book are listed here.

Part 1: Getting Started

This part is your complete executive briefing on Java. It includes a "What is Java?" chapter and a complete set of instructions on installing and running Java. It also has a jump-start chapter — Chapter 3. In this chapter, you visit the major technical ideas, and dissect a simple program.

Part II: Writing Your Own Java Programs

Chapters 4 through 6 cover the basic building blocks. These chapters describe the things you need to know so you can get your computer humming along.

If you've written programs in Visual Basic, C++, or another language, some of the material in Part II may be familiar to you. If so, you can skip some sections or read this stuff quickly. But don't read too quickly. Java is a little different from some other programming languages, especially in the things described in Chapter 4.

Part III: Working with the Big Picture: Object-Oriented Programming

Part III has some of my favorite chapters. This part covers the all-important topic of object-oriented programming. In these chapters, you find out how to map solutions to big problems. (Sure, the examples in these chapters aren't big, but the examples involve big ideas.) In bite-worthy increments, you learn to design classes, reuse existing classes, and construct objects.

Have you read any of those books that explain object-oriented programming in vague, general terms? I'm very proud to say that *Java 2 For Dummies* isn't like that. In this book, each concept is illustrated with a simple-yet-concrete program example.

Part IV: Savvy Java Techniques

If you've tasted some Java and want more, you can find what you need in this part of the book. This part's chapters are devoted to details — the things you don't see when you first glance at the material. So, after you've read the earlier parts and written some programs on your own, you can dive in a little deeper by reading Part IV.

Part V: The Part of Tens

The Part of Tens is a little Java candy store. In the Part of Tens, you can find lists — lists of tips, resources, and all kinds of interesting goodies.

Part VI: Appendix

The appendix describes the material that's on the CD-ROM. This material includes all the sample code from the book, available for copying, tinkering, and running. The CD also includes some super-useful software and more chapters about programming in Java.

(Yes, this book has only one appendix. At one point in this book's development, there was another appendix. But the appendix became too large, so we had to have it removed. It was an emergency procedure. Fortunately, I'm covered by author's insurance.)

Bonus Chapters on the CD-ROM!

You've read the *Java 2 For Dummies* book, seen the *Java 2 For Dummies* movie, worn the *Java 2 For Dummies* T-shirt, and eaten the *Java 2 For Dummies* candy. What more is there to do?

That's easy. Just pop in the book's CD-ROM, and you can find three additional chapters:

- In Bonus Chapter A, you handle button clicks, keystrokes, and other such things. You find out about one additional Java language feature (something like a Java class), called an *interface*.

> ✔ In Bonus Chapter B, you deal with Java applets. You put applets on Web pages, draw things, and make things move. A visitor to your site fills out a small form.

> ✔ In Bonus Chapter C, you see an example of Java database handling. The example takes you from start to finish — from establishing a connection and creating a table, to adding rows and making queries.

Note: For you Web fanatics out there, you can also read the bonus chapters on the Web at `www.dummies.com/extras/Java2/`.

Icons Used in This Book

If you could watch me write this book, you'd see me sitting at my computer, talking to myself. I say each sentence in my head. Most of the sentences are muttered several times. When I have an extra thought, a side comment, something that doesn't belong in the regular stream, I twist my head a little bit. That way, whoever's listening to me (usually nobody) knows that I'm off on a momentary tangent.

Of course, in print, you can't see me twisting my head. I need some other way of setting a side thought in a corner by itself. I do it with icons. When you see a Tip icon or a Remember icon, you know that I'm taking a quick detour.

Here's a list of icons that I use in this book.

A tip is an extra piece of information — something helpful that the other books may forget to tell you.

Everyone makes mistakes. Heaven knows that I've made a few in my time. Anyway, when I think people are especially prone to make a mistake, I mark it with a Warning icon.

Question: What's stronger than a Tip, but not as strong as a Warning?

Answer: A Remember icon.

Occasionally I run across a technical tidbit. The tidbit may help you understand what the people behind the scenes (the people who developed Java) were thinking. You don't have to read it, but you may find it useful. You may also find the tidbit helpful if you plan to read other (more geeky) books about Java.

I use this icon to point out stuff that's on the CD (obviously) and how that stuff is useful.

Where to Go from Here

If you've gotten this far, then you're ready to start reading about Java. Think of me (the author) as your guide, your host, your personal assistant. I do everything I can to keep things interesting and, most importantly, help you understand. If you like what you read, then send me a note. My e-mail address, which I created just for comments and questions about this book, is Java2ForDummies@BurdBrain.com.

Part I
Getting Started

In this part . . .

Become acquainted with Java. Learn what Java is all about, and why you do (or don't) want to use Java. If you've heard things about Java and aren't sure what they mean, the material in this part can help you. If you're staring at your computer, wondering how you're going to get a Java program running, this part has the information you need. Maybe you've told people that you're a Java expert, and now you need to do some serious bluffing. If so, then this part of the book is your crash course in Java. (Of course, if the word *bluffing* describes you accurately, then you may also want to pick up a copy of *Ethics For Dummies*.)

Chapter 1

All About Java

Say what you want about computers. As far as I'm concerned, computers are good for just two simple reasons:

- ✔ **When computers do work, they feel no resistance, no stress, no boredom, and no fatigue.** Computers are our electronic slaves. I have my computer working 24/7 doing calculations for SETI@home — the search for extraterrestrial intelligence. Do I feel sorry for my computer because it's working so hard? Does the computer complain? Will the computer report me to the National Labor Relations Board? No.

  I can make demands, give the computer its orders, and crack the whip. Do I (or should I) feel the least bit guilty? Not at all.

- ✔ **Computers move ideas, not paper.** Not long ago, when you wanted to send a message to someone, you hired a messenger. The messenger got on his or her horse and delivered your message personally. The message was on paper, parchment, a clay tablet, or whatever physical medium was available at the time.

  This whole process seems wasteful now, but that's only because you and I are sitting comfortably at the dawn of the electronic age. The thing is that messages are ideas. Physical things like ink, paper, and horses have little or nothing to do with real ideas. These physical things are just temporary carriers for ideas (temporary because people used them to carry ideas for several centuries). But, in truth, the ideas themselves are paperless, horseless, and messengerless.

  So the neat thing about computers is that they carry ideas efficiently. They carry nothing but the ideas, a couple of photons, and a little electrical power. They do this with no muss, no fuss, and no extra physical baggage.

When you start dealing efficiently with ideas, something very nice happens. Suddenly, all the overhead is gone. Instead of pushing paper and trees, you're pushing numbers and concepts. Without the overhead, you can do things much faster and do things that are far more complex than ever before.

What You Can Do with Java

It would be so nice if all this complexity were free but, unfortunately, it isn't. Someone has to think hard and decide exactly what the computer will be asked to do. After that thinking is done, someone has to write a set of instructions for the computer to follow.

Given the current state of affairs, you can't write these instructions in English or any other language that people speak. Science fiction is filled with stories about people who say simple things to robots and get back disastrous, unexpected results. English and other such languages are unsuitable for communication with computers for several reasons:

- **An English sentence can be misinterpreted.** "Chew one tablet three times a day until finished."
- **It's difficult to weave a very complicated command in English.** "Join flange A to protuberance B, making sure to connect only the outermost lip of flange A to the larger end of the protuberance B, while joining the middle and inner lips of flange A to grommet C."
- **An English sentence has lots of extra baggage.** "Sentence has unneeded words."
- **English is difficult to interpret.** "As part of this Publishing Agreement between Hungry Minds, Inc. ('HMI') and the Author ('Barry Burd'), HMI shall pay the sum of one-thousand-two-hundred-fifty-seven dollars and sixty-three cents ($1257.63) to the Author for partial submittal of *Java 2 For Dummies* ('the Work')."

To tell a computer what to do, you have to speak a special language and write terse, unambiguous instructions in that language. A special language of this kind is called a *computer programming language*. A set of instructions, written in such a language, is called a *program*. When they're looked at as a big blob, these instructions are called *software* or *code*. Here's what code looks like when it's written in Java:

```java
public class PayBarry
{
    public static void main(String args[])
    {
        double checkAmount = 1257.63;
        System.out.print("Pay to the order of ");
        System.out.print("Dr. Barry Burd ");
        System.out.print("$");
```

```
        System.out.println(checkAmount);
    }
}
```

Why You Should Use Java

It's time to celebrate! You've just picked up a copy of *Java 2 For Dummies*, and you're reading Chapter 1. At this rate, you'll be an expert Java programmer in no time at all, so rejoice in your eventual success by throwing a big party.

To prepare for the party, I'll bake a cake. I'm lazy, so I'll use a ready-to-bake cake mix. Let's see . . . add water to the mix, then add butter and eggs . . . Hey, wait! I just looked at the list of ingredients. What's MSG? And what about propylene glycol? That's used in antifreeze, isn't it?

I'll change plans and make the cake from scratch. Sure, it's a little harder. But that way, I get exactly what I want.

Computer programs work the same way. You can use somebody else's program, or you can write your own. If you use somebody else's program, then you use whatever you get. When you write your own program, you can tailor the program especially for your needs.

Writing computer code is a big, worldwide industry. Companies do it, freelance professionals do it, hobbyists do it, all kinds of people do it. A typical big company has teams, departments, and divisions that write programs for the company. But you can write programs for yourself or someone else, for a living or for fun. In a recent estimate, the number of lines of code written each day by programmers in the United States alone exceeds the number of methane molecules on the planet Jupiter.* Take almost anything that can be done with a computer. With the right amount of time, you can write your own program to do it. (Of course, the "right amount of time" may be very long, but that's not the point. Many interesting and useful programs can be written in hours or even minutes.)

* I made up this fact all by myself.

Getting Perspective: Where Java Fits In

Here's a brief history of modern computer programming:

➤ **1954-1957: FORTRAN is developed.**

FORTRAN was the first modern computer programming language. For scientific programming, FORTRAN is a real racehorse. Year after year,

FORTRAN is a leading language among computer programmers through-out the world. A well-known computer scientist, Tony Hoare, once said, "I don't know what the language of the year 2000 will look like, but I know it will be called FORTRAN."

✔ **1959: COBOL is created.**

The letter *B* in COBOL stands for *Business,* and business is just what COBOL is all about. The language's primary feature is the processing of one record after another, one customer after another, or one employee after another.

Within a few years after its initial development, COBOL became the most widely used language for business data processing. Even today, COBOL represents a large part of the computer programming industry.

✔ **1972: Dennis Ritchie at AT&T Bell Labs develops the C programming language.**

The look and feel that you see in this book's examples come from the C programming language. Code written in C uses curly braces, if state-ments, for statements, and so on.

In terms of power, you can use C to solve the same problems that you can solve by using FORTRAN, Java, or any other modern programming language. (You can write a scientific calculator program in COBOL, but doing that sort of thing would feel really strange.) The difference between one programming language and another isn't power. The difference is ease and appropriateness of use. That's where the Java language excels.

✔ **1986: Bjarne Stroustrup (again at AT&T Bell Labs) develops C++.**

Unlike its C language ancestor, the language C++ supports object-oriented programming. This represents a huge step forward.

✔ **May 23, 1995: Sun Microsystems releases its first official version of the Java programming language.**

Java improves upon the concepts in C++. Unlike C++, Java is streamlined for use on the World Wide Web. Java's "Write Once, Run Anywhere" phi-losophy makes the language ideal for distributing code across the Internet.

In addition, Java is a great general-purpose programming language. With Java, you can write windowed applications, build and explore databases, control handheld devices, and more. Within five short years, the Java programming language has 2.5 million developers worldwide. (I know. I have a commemorative T-shirt to prove it.)

✔ **November 2000: The College Board announces that, starting in the year 2003, the Computer Science Advanced Placement exams will be based on Java.**

Wanna know what that snot-nosed kid living down the street is going to be learning in high school next year? You guessed it — Java.

Chapter 2

Running Canned Java Programs

In This Chapter

▶ Setting up your computer to run Java

▶ Running text-based programs

▶ Running window-based programs

▶ Running Java applets

*T*he best way to learn Java is to do Java. When you're "doing" Java, you're writing, testing, and running your own Java programs. This chapter prepares you by having you run other people's programs.

Downloading and Installing the Java Software Development Kit (SDK)

First you need some Java development software. You can choose from several products. In fact, you may already have one of these products on your own computer. If you don't, you can download the basic software by visiting a Sun Microsystems Web site. The product you want to download is known by a few different names. It's called the Java Development Kit (JDK), the Java 2 Software Development Kit (SDK), and the Java 2 Standard Edition (J2SE).

The CD-ROM has trial versions of two cool Java Development Environments — JBuilder from Borland and Kawa from Allaire.

Java development environments

You may be familiar with development environments for other programming languages. In a typical development environment you have several windows — a window for editing code, a window for displaying the result of running code, a window for debugging, and a window that displays the parts of your program. Some fancier development environments, such as the Borland JBuilder development environment shown here, have drag-and-drop panels so that you can design your graphical interface visually.

Plenty of development environments for Java exist. Some of the more popular products include Microsoft Visual J++, Borland JBuilder, Visual Café, and IBM WebSphere. Each environment offers its own special features and has its own special quirks. To help you learn real Java (not quirky Java), this book avoids any discussion of the development environments and focuses on the most basic tools — freeware tools and tools that you already have on your computer. With these tools, you can learn Java, unhindered by the eccentricities of a glitzy environment.

After you're comfortable with plain old Java, you may want to try some of the Java development environments. If you do, the techniques in this book can help you work in those environments.

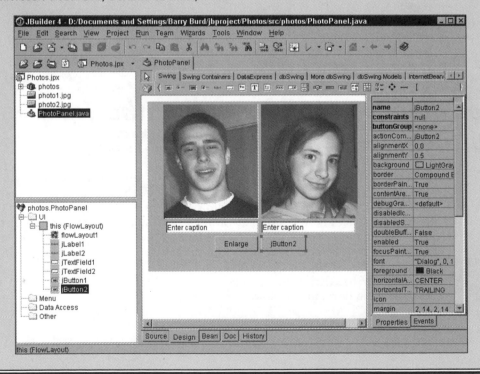

Downloading the software you need

You can download the Java Software Development Kit from a Sun Microsystems Web site. Just follow these steps:

1. **Visit** www.javasoft.com.

2. **On the Web page's left margin, click the Products & APIs link.**

3. **On the Products and APIs page, look for the latest Java 2 Standard Edition.**

   Depending on what Sun Microsystems has cooking when you visit the Web site, you may find variations on the simple Java 2 Standard Edition link. You may see the word *Platform* and the acronyms JDK, SDK, and J2SE (which are all fine). You also see version numbers, such as 1.3 and 1.4. You want the highest version number that's available at the Web site.

   Avoid the Enterprise Edition unless you have special reason to download it. You also want to avoid JRE links, because they lead to the software for running existing Java programs, not the software for writing new Java programs.

   In locating the proper link, you may end up moving from page to page. If, as you move, you notice a link to something called the API documentation, make a mental note of the link's location.

   You may find more than one way to reach the download page with the latest Java 2 Standard Edition, so don't be afraid to poke around at the Javasoft Web site. If you don't like losing your place as you explore, try NetCaptor, which is a multitabbed Web browser that's included on this book's CD-ROM.

4. **Clink the link corresponding to your computer's operating environment (also know as an operating system).**

   Your choices include Windows, Linux, and Solaris.

   If your favorite operating environment isn't Windows, Linux, or Solaris, don't despair. Visit java.sun.com/cgi-bin/java-ports.cgi for a list of vendors that have converted Java to other environments.

5. **Do whatever you normally do with license agreements.**

   I won't be the one to tell you not to bother reading it.

6. **Click the link or button to start the download.**

   The Web site offers both FTP and HTTP downloads. The difference isn't terribly important. If your system supports FTP, FTP is a bit faster and more reliable.

   As you begin downloading the software, note the directory on your hard drive where the software is being deposited.

7. **Find a link to the API documentation for the version of Java that you just downloaded.**

   The Java language has a built-in feature for creating consistent, nicely formatted documentation in Web page format. As a Java programmer, you won't survive without a copy of the API documentation by your side. You can bookmark the documentation at the Javasoft site and revisit the site whenever you need to look up something. But in the long run (and in the not-so-long run), you can save time by downloading your own copy of the API docs. See Chapter 4 for more about the API.

8. **Download the API documentation.**

Like so many other downloads, the Java API documentation comes in a compressed file format. If you're a Windows user and choose the ZIP format, you need an unzipping program. The best zip/unzip program ever created is ZipMagic from Ontrack Software. A copy of ZipMagic is on this book's CD-ROM.

Installing the software

After you download the Java Software Development Kit, you're ready to install the kit on your computer. Of course, you can do this nine hundred different ways, depending on your operating system, the names of directories on your hard drive, the wind velocity, and other factors. The following steps offer some guidelines:

1. **Find the file that you downloaded.**

   The file has a name like `j2sdk-1_3-blah-blah.exe`. The exact name depends on the operating system you're using, the version number that Sun has reached with Java, and whatever naming conventions the people at Sun have changed since the week this book was written.

   One way or another, the file that you downloaded is executable, which means that it's a program that you can run, probably by double-clicking its icon.

2. **Run the file that you downloaded.**

   If you're a Windows user, choose Start⇨Run and then browse for the name of the file that you downloaded. Whether or not you're a Windows user, you can run the file by double-clicking an icon, typing the name of the file, or doing any of the other things your system makes available to you for running executable files.

   When the installation starts, it'll probably offer you the option of installing the SDK in the default directory or in a different directory that you specify. You've probably read other people's advice about sticking with the default directory that the installation offers to you. As far as I'm concerned, you can follow that advice or ignore it. Either way, make sure to note the name of the directory that the SDK is using for its install directory. This piece of information comes in handy when you configure your system for Java. (See the next section.) Unless the people at Sun shift gears suddenly, the default directory is something like \jdk1.4.

3. **Enjoy the splash screens that you see while the software is being installed.**

Configuring your system

After the bare-bones SDK installation is finished, you can configure your operating system to make the SDK software run seamlessly. More specifically, your computer's operating system needs to know two things: where to find the Java SDK that you've just installed and where you plan to put the Java programs that you're going to write.

To remind your system where the SDK is installed, you set something called a PATH variable, which is a piece of information that your computer's operating system stores. The way you set the PATH variable depends on which system you're using. A few hints and pointers follow in the next few steps:

1. **Figure out where the SDK software has been installed.**

   The installation created a brand-new directory on your hard drive. You see this directory's name pass by when the SDK installs itself (refer to Step 2 in the previous section).

   Because I'm not sitting in front of your computer screen right now, I can only guess what the new SDK directory's name is. Perhaps the directory's name is c:\jdk1.4. If so, then that directory has a subdirectory named c:\jdk1.4\bin. Whatever it's named on your computer, I call this the "Java bin" directory.

2. **Add the Java bin directory to your system's PATH.**

   The Java bin directory contains executable files that you'll be running frequently. To make running these files easy no matter where you are in your system's directory hierarchy, you need to add the name of the Java bin directory to your system's PATH variable.

   On Windows NT or 2000:

   a. Choose Start⇨Settings⇨Control Panel⇨System.

   b. On Windows NT, select the Environment tab; on Windows 2000, select the Advanced tab. Then click the Environment Variables button.

   c. In the Environment Variables window, find the PATH variable, as shown in Figure 2-1.

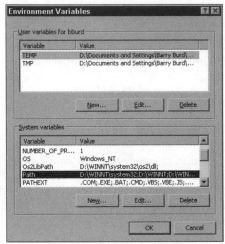

Figure 2-1:
The
Environment
Variables
window in
Windows
2000.

  d. At the end of the current PATH, add a semicolon, followed by the
     name of your Java bin directory. After making the change, your
     PATH may look something like this:

```
PATH=C:\WINNT\system32;C:\WINNT;c:\jdk1.4\bin
```

  e. Click Apply, Set, OK, and whatever other affirming options your
     system offers to you.

In Windows NT or 2000, the change described above doesn't affect any
command prompt windows that are already open. You should close any
command prompt windows after you follow the above steps. Then, when
you open a brand-new command prompt window, the change of PATH
will have taken effect. (For more details on command prompt windows,
see the section, "The command prompt window," later in this chapter.)

On Windows XP:

  a. Choose Start⇨Settings⇨Control Panel⇨Performance &
     Maintenance⇨System.

  b. Follow the instructions above for Windows 2000 (starting with
     item b).

On Windows 95 or 98:

  a. Choose Start⇨Run.

  b. In the Run field, type **sysedit**.

     This step starts the Windows System Configuration Editor. The
     Editor looks a lot like Windows Notepad, but the Editor automati-
     cally opens files that control some of the features in your operating
     environment.

c. In the System Configuration Editor, open the AUTOEXEC.BAT window. (See Figure 2-2.)

d. The AUTOEXEC.BAT window may have lots of text in it (or it may have very little). If you can, find a line that starts with the word *PATH* or the words *SET PATH*. At the end of that line, add a semicolon followed by the name of your Java bin directory. After making the change, your PATH may look something like this:

```
PATH C:\WINDOWS\system;C:\WINDOWS;c:\jdk1.4\bin
```

Your AUTOEXEC.BAT window may not contain any lines beginning with PATH or SET PATH. If that's the case, just make a new blank line in the AUTOEXEC.BAT window and type the text shown above. (When you type the text, replace `c:\jdk1.4\bin` with the name of your Java bin directory. See Step 1.) If typing a new line in your AUTOEXEC.BAT file causes any trouble down the road, you may need individual counseling. Find a computer geek in your neighborhood and tell him or her about your situation.

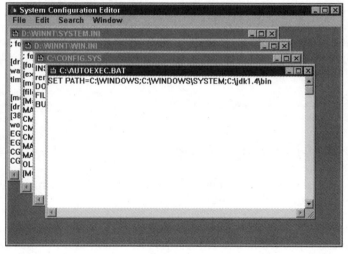

Figure 2-2:
Use the
System
Configur-
ation Editor
to open the
AUTOEXEC.
BAT
window.

e. From the System Configuration Editor main menu, choose File⇨Save.

f. Close the System Configuration Editor.

g. Restart your computer.

On Windows Me:

a. Choose Start⇨Programs⇨Accessories⇨System Tools⇨System Information.

With any luck, the Microsoft Help and Support window appears.

b. In the Microsoft Help and Support window, choose Tools⇨System Configuration.

c. On the Environment tab, select PATH and then click the Edit button.

d. At the end of the current PATH, add a semicolon followed by the name of your Java bin directory.

e. Click Apply, Set, OK, or whatever you need to click until your computer is happy with the change.

f. Close the Microsoft Help and Support window.

g. Restart your computer.

Okay, you've set your PATH variable. Now what? The next thing you do is to tell your system where you plan to put your Java programs. To do this, you set something called a CLASSPATH variable.

The good news is, after you've followed the instructions to set the PATH variable (earlier in this section), then setting the CLASSPATH is the same story all over again. In fact, it's even easier, because you don't have to know the name of any directories. Just follow the steps described above for setting a variable on your particular operating system. When you get to the point where you're actually filling in a value for the CLASSPATH, make sure the value contains a single dot (that's right, a period).

```
c:\jdk\classes;.
```

What have you done?

By following the steps in this section, you've placed three important things on your computer's hard drive:

- ✔ **The javac program (more formally known as the *Java compiler*).** The Java compiler translates code from something that humans can type and understand to something that's too dense for humans to deal with. Only computers can interpret the translated (compiled) version of the code.

- ✔ **A program named *java* (more formally known as the *Java Virtual Machine*).** Henceforth, whenever you issue the java command, you tell the computer to run a Java program. In all likelihood, this Java program will be one that you've written on your own!

- ✔ **A copy of the Java API documentation.** You'll be glad you have this.

Running Your First Text-Based Program

In this section, you run a Java program that computes the monthly payment on a home mortgage. You lift the program right off this book's CD-ROM (or type the program yourself, if you want) and follow some nice, neat instructions to get the program running on your computer.

Putting the program file where it belongs

You need a directory on your hard drive to store this section's mortgage program as well as all the Java programs that you write on your own. You can give your directory any name you want but, in this book, I call it the JavaPrograms directory. So, the next step is to place the mortgage program in your JavaPrograms directory.

To find the mortgage program on this book's CD-ROM, visit the CD-ROM's Author directory, find the Chapter02 subdirectory, and look for the file named MortgageText.java. Copy this file from the CD-ROM to your JavaPrograms directory.

The command prompt window

The mortgage program that you run in this section displays its wares in your computer's *command prompt window.* Normally, the command prompt window is a place where geeks type cryptic instructions for the computer to follow. For instance, instead of clicking the Outlook Express icon, you can go to your command prompt window and type this command:

```
cd C:\Program Files\Outlook Express
msimn
```

When you do this, Outlook Express opens its own beautiful-looking window on your screen.

The mortgage program doesn't open its own window. While it runs, anything you type appears in the command prompt window along with anything that the mortgage program displays. (See Figure 2-3.) A program that operates completely in the command prompt window is called a *text-based program.*

Figure 2-3:
The text-
based
mortgage
program.

```
D:\WINNT\system32\cmd.exe                                              _ □ ×

C:\JavaPrograms>java MortgageText
How much are you borrowing?          100000.00
What's the interest rate?            7.00
How many years are you taking to pay? 15

Your monthly payment is              $897.77

C:\JavaPrograms>
```

If you're not familiar with your friend the command prompt window, you
should check it out right away. Table 2-1 explains how.

Table 2-1	Finding Your System's Command Prompt Window
If Your Operating System Is	**Do This**
Windows NT	Choose Start⇨Programs⇨Command Prompt
Windows 2000	Choose Start⇨Programs⇨Accessories⇨ Command Prompt
Windows 95 or 98	Choose Start⇨Programs⇨MS-DOS Prompt
Windows Me	Choose Start⇨Programs⇨Accessories⇨ MS-DOS Prompt
Windows XP	Choose Start⇨All Programs⇨Accessories⇨ Command Prompt
Linux	Click the icon that looks like a computer monitor

If you're using a Macintosh, you can ignore all these instructions about the
command prompt window. Instead, you drag a file with the .java extension,
and drop the file onto the javac icon. Then, if you're using Apple's MRJ
(Macintosh Runtime for Java), you drag a file with the .class extension, and
drop the file onto the JBindery icon.

Actually, as you run the mortgage program, you see three things in the command prompt window:

✔ **The command that you type.** This command starts running the mortgage program.

✔ **Messages and results that the mortgage program sends to you.** Messages include things like How much are you borrowing? Results
include lines like Your monthly payment is $897.77.

✔ **Responses that you give to the mortgage program while it runs.** If you
type **100000.00** in response to the program's question about how much
you're borrowing, you see that number echoed on the screen.

In Windows 2000 and a few other operating systems, you can't always get rid of the command prompt window by clicking the regular close button in the corner of the window. If the close button doesn't work, you can usually get rid of a command problem window by typing **exit** in the window and then pressing Enter.

Compiling and running your text-based program

Running a Java text-based program is easy. Here's how you do it:

1. **Make sure you've followed the instructions at the beginning of this chapter for installing the Java SDK.**

   Thank goodness! You don't have to follow those instructions more than once.

2. **Make sure you've placed a copy of the program that you want to run in your JavaPrograms directory.**

   For instance, you can copy MortgageText.java from this book's CD-ROM to the JavaPrograms directory on your hard drive. For details, see the section, "Putting the program file where it belongs," later in this chapter.

3. **Open your computer's command prompt window.**

   You don't know how? Don't fret. Refer to Table 2-1 for details.

4. **In the command prompt window, go to your JavaPrograms directory.**

   If you're a Windows user and have created a JavaPrograms directory on your C: drive, then type the following in the command prompt window:

   ```
   c:
   cd JavaPrograms
   ```

   Press the Enter key after each line that you type. After you've done this, your screen displays the name of the directory that you've reached, C:\JavaPrograms>. (See Figure 2-4.)

Figure 2-4:
Moving to
your Java-
Programs
directory.

```
D:\WINNT\system32\cmd.exe                                    _ □ ✕
Microsoft Windows 2000 [Version 5.00.2195]
(C) Copyright 1985-1999 Microsoft Corp.

D:\>c:

C:\>cd JavaPrograms

C:\JavaPrograms>_
```

Peeking into the Java compiler

The letter *c* in the javac command stands for *compile.* When you type the javac command, you run the Java compiler.

A *compiler* translates code from one form to another. For instance, if you look inside the MortgageText.java file, you see code like this:

```
import java.io.*;
import
  java.text.NumberFormat;
public class MortgageText {
    public static void
  main(String args[]) throws
  IOException
```

Although this code isn't easy reading, it certainly uses letters and other characters that English-speaking people can understand. This file, MortgageText.java, is what you have before you've done any compiling — before you run javac.

When you run javac, the computer takes your file and translates it into something called *byte-code.* The newly created bytecode file is automatically given a name like MortgageText.class. (After running javac, you can look for the new .class file in your JavaPrograms directory.) Unlike the original .java file, the new .class file has no recognizable characters in it and isn't suitable for human consumption. Instead, the .class file is streamlined so that the computer can carry out your program's commands quickly and easily.

In the way that it compiles code, Java represents a strict departure from most other programming languages. When you compile a program in another language (COBOL or C++, for instance), you create a file that can be run on only one operating system. For example, if you compile a C++ program on a Windows computer and then move the translated file to a Unix computer, the Unix computer treats the translated file as pure garbage. The Unix computer can't interpret any of the instructions in the translated file. This is bad for many reasons. One of the most striking reasons is that you can't send this kind of code over the World Wide Web and expect anyone with a different kind of computer to be able to run the code.

But with Java, you can take a bytecode file you created with a Windows computer, copy the bytecode to who-knows-what kind of computer, and then run the bytecode with no trouble at all. That's one of the many reasons why Java has become popular so quickly. This outstanding feature, the ability to run code on many different kinds of computers, is called *portability.*

By typing **c:** you make sure that you're working on the C: drive. Then, by typing **cd JavaPrograms**, you place yourself squarely in the JavaPrograms directory. (In this context, the letters *cd* stand for *change directory.*)

5. **Compile the program by typing the javac command plus your program's filename.**

For example, to compile the mortgage program, just type the following in your command prompt window:

```
javac MortgageText.java
```

If all goes well, your computer responds with very little fanfare. Instead of displaying a bunch of happy-looking messages, your computer just puts the name of your JavaPrograms directory in the command prompt window again. (See Figure 2-5.)

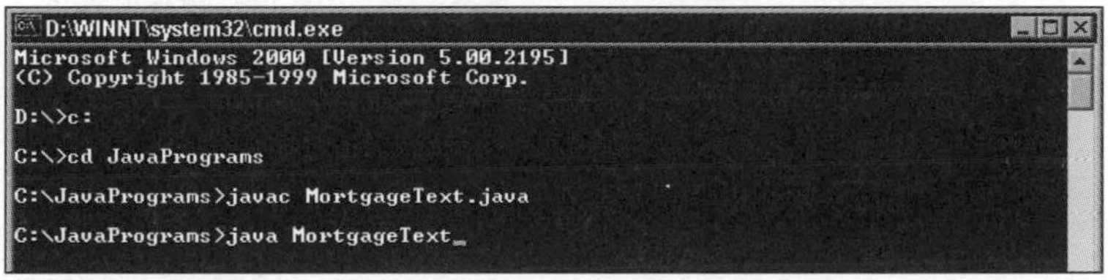

Figure 2-5:
Using the
javac and
java
commands.

```
D:\WINNT\system32\cmd.exe                                    _ □ ✕
Microsoft Windows 2000 [Version 5.00.2195]
(C) Copyright 1985-1999 Microsoft Corp.

D:\>c:

C:\>cd JavaPrograms

C:\JavaPrograms>javac MortgageText.java

C:\JavaPrograms>java MortgageText_
```

If all doesn't go well, don't panic. Refer to Table 2-2 for help.

Table 2-2	Troubleshooting the javac Command
Symptom	*What To Try*
Your computer thinks that the javac command doesn't exist.	Make sure you've installed the Java SDK (in this chapter, see the first section, "Downloading and Installing the Java Software Development Kit (SDK)").
	Make sure you've set your system's PATH variable correctly (also in the first section of this chapter).
	Check the spelling of javac.
Your computer shows you a Usage message, along with lots of options (see Figure 2-6).	Check your javac command line. Excluding any prompts that your system displays, the command line should include the javac command, the filename, and nothing more (`javac MortgageText.java`, for example). (Refer to Figure 2-5.)
	Make sure you included the .java file extension (all lowercase letters) at the end of the filename.

(continued)

Table 2-2 *(continued)*

Symptom	What To Try
Your computer thinks the file that you want to compile doesn't exist. (For instance, you see the message `error: cannot read: MortgageText.java`.)	Make sure that you're working in the JavaPrograms directory.
	Make sure that the file is in your JavaPrograms directory. (If you're trying to compile `MortgageText.java`, is there a file with that name in your JavaPrograms directory?)
	Check the spelling of the filename in the javac command against the actual filename in your directory. (If you're trying to compile `MortgageText.java`, did you spell this filename exactly the same way when you typed the javac command?)
You see one or more caret symbols (^) and a count of the number of errors (Figure 2-7).	Make sure the capitalization of the filename in your command matches the filename in your JavaPrograms directory. (If you're working with a file named `MortgageText.java`, then in your javac command, the `M` in `Mortgage` and the `T` in `Text` should be capitalized. No other letters should be capitalized.)
	Did you type the file yourself instead of copying a file from the book's CD-ROM? If so, you may have made some typos. Try copying the file directly from the CD-ROM.

6. **Run the program by typing the java command and then the name of your program (without the file extension).**

To run the `MortgageText.java` program, just type the following in your command prompt window:

```
java MortgageText
```

With any luck, the computer responds by asking you `How much are you borrowing?` You can respond by typing a number (like **100000.00**) and then pressing Enter. After you press Enter, the computer asks you another question (refer to Figure 2-3). When you're done answering the questions, the computer displays a monthly mortgage payment amount. Disclaimer: Your local mortgage company will charge you much more than the amount that my Java program calculates.

If you have problems using the java command to run a program, check Table 2-3 for some troubleshooting tips.

Figure 2-6: The javac Usage message.

```
D:\WINNT\system32\cmd.exe
C:\JavaPrograms>javac
Usage: javac <options> <source files>
where possible options include:
  -g                         Generate all debugging info
  -g:none                    Generate no debugging info
  -g:{lines,vars,source}     Generate only some debugging info
  -O                         Optimize; may hinder debugging or enlarge class file

  -nowarn                    Generate no warnings
  -verbose                   Output messages about what the compiler is doing
  -deprecation               Output source locations where deprecated APIs are us
ed
  -classpath <path>          Specify where to find user class files
  -sourcepath <path>         Specify where to find input source files
  -bootclasspath <path>      Override location of bootstrap class files
  -extdirs <dirs>            Override location of installed extensions
  -d <directory>             Specify where to place generated class files
  -encoding <encoding>       Specify character encoding used by source files
  -source <release>          Provide source compatibility with specified release
  -target <release>          Generate class files for specific VM version
  -help                      Print a synopsis of standard options

C:\JavaPrograms>_
```

Figure 2-7: Running javac can generate an error like this.

```
D:\WINNT\system32\cmd.exe
Microsoft Windows 2000 [Version 5.00.2195]
(C) Copyright 1985-1999 Microsoft Corp.

C:\JavaPrograms>javac MortgageText.java
MortgageText.java:9: cannot resolve symbol
symbol  : class BufferedReade
location: class MortgageText
        BufferedReade keyboard =
        ^
1 error

C:\JavaPrograms>
```

Table 2-3	Troubleshooting the java Command
Symptom	*What To Try*
You get a `NoClassDefFoundError`.	Make sure that you're working in your JavaPrograms directory. (See Step 4 above.)
	Make sure that your JavaPrograms directory contains a .class file (for example, `MortgageText.class`).
	Make sure you successfully compiled the .java file using the javac command (see Step 5 of the instructions in this section for the correct use of the javac command). You have to do this before you can use the java command.
	Make sure the spelling and capitalization of the filename in your javac command matches the filename in your JavaPrograms directory. (If you started with `MortgageText.java`, did you type **MortgageText** exactly the same way when you typed the javac command?)
	Make sure you typed a name *without* a file extension. (For example, to use the java command, you type **MortgageText**, not **MortgageText.java** or **MortgageText.class**.)
You get a NumberFormatException	I'm assuming that you're running the MortgageText program. When asked for the mortgage's principle, interest rate or duration in years, you may have typed a number in the wrong format. Make sure the numbers you enter have nothing but digits and decimal points in them. The program doesn't like commas, dollar signs, or blank spaces. For the number of years, your number shouldn't even have a decimal point.

For some versions of the Java SDK (most notably, some versions for the Linux platform) the java command has an addclasspath option. If you have trouble running your code, check the documentation for this addclasspath option.

When you type the java command in your command prompt window, you're really telling the computer to run its Java Virtual Machine program. The Java Virtual Machine serves as an intermediary — an interpreter between the run-anywhere bytecode and your machine's own system. The Java Virtual Machine that's on your computer runs on only one operating system — whatever system is on your computer. If you run Windows, then the software for your Java Virtual Machine is specific to Windows. So, when your computer runs the Virtual Machine, the Virtual Machine can take the bytecode you feed to it and interpret the bytecode for your own Windows system.

Running a GUI on Its Own

In the previous section, you go through all the steps for compiling and running a text-based Java program. The text-based program is in a file named MortgageText.java. In this section, you go through the same steps for a GUI. The new GUI program is in a file named MortgageWindow.java. The term *GUI* stands for *Graphical User Interface*. It's the term used for a program that displays windows, buttons, and other nice-looking stuff. GUI programs are good because, unlike text-based programs, they don't look like they're running on your grandparents' computers.

An ugly rumor is going around that Java can display buttons and other graphical objects only in connection with Web pages. That rumor is completely untrue. Starting at your command prompt window, you can get Java to open dialog boxes, pull-down menus, and other impressive-looking things. Here's how you do it:

1. **Make sure the .java file that you want to run is in your JavaPrograms directory.**

   To use my example, copy MortgageWindow.java from this book's CD-ROM to your hard drive's JavaPrograms directory. (Even if you've already copied MortgageText.java, you should go back and copy this new file, MortgageWindow.java.) For details, see the section, "Putting the program file where it belongs."

2. **Use the javac command to compile the program.**

   For the MortgageWindow example, in your command prompt window, type the command

   ```
   javac MortgageWindow.java
   ```

   If your computer hardly responds (just pauses for a minute, and then spits back another copy of the command prompt), then your attempt to compile was successful. If not (that is, if you get error messages), then go back and read some of the material in the previous section, "Running Your First Text-Based Program."

   When you use the javac command, include the .java extension in the filename that follows the command.

   On some systems, the case of letters in the javac command matters. Because the file you're trying to compile is named MortgageWindow. java, the command `javac mortgagewindow.java` (without capitalization) won't work.

3. **Use the java command to run the program.**

   If you are running the MortgageWindow example, then type the following command in your command prompt window:

   ```
   java MortgageWindow
   ```

   When you do this, the MortgageWindow program should start running. The program displays a window like the one shown in Figure 2-8. In the window, you can experiment and type your own values for the principal, the interest rate, and the number of years of the loan. Whenever you change a value, the program responds instantly by updating the value in the Payment field.

Figure 2-8:
A window
from the
Mortgage-
Window
program.

Mortgage Payment Calculator	
Principal $	100000.00
Rate (%)	7.00
Years	15
Payment $	897.77

If you run into trouble with this step, see the hints in Table 2-3.

When you use the java command, don't include the file extension (.java) with the name that follows the command.

Running a GUI on a Web Page (Your First Java Applet)

Java's big splash onto the scene came in the mid-1990s. The people at Sun Microsystems had managed to work Java programs into Web pages, and the results were dazzling. The infusion of Java into the Web was powerful, efficient, portable, and secure. The trick was to create a part of a program, called an *applet,* and to display the applet inside a rectangle on the Web page.

An applet can have many of the features that you'd find in any ordinary GUI program. You can have buttons, pull-down gizmos, and other fun stuff. You can even have an applet open its own floating window (but, in practice, this is seldom done).

This section shows you how to put an applet on your Web page. The applet you use as an example is one from this book's CD-ROM.

Getting an applet running

The steps you follow to run an applet are a bit different from the steps you take to run any other kind of Java program. Here's what you do:

1. **Make sure the applet program you want to use is in your hard drive's JavaPrograms directory.**

   For the example, copy `MortgageApplet.java` from this book's CD-ROM to your hard drive's JavaPrograms directory.

   For details, see the section, "Putting the program file where it belongs."

   If you're keeping score, `MortgageApplet.java` is the third Java program in this chapter. The first, `MortgageText.java`, is a text-based program. The second, `MortgageWindow.java` is a GUI. This third program, `MortgageApplet.java`, is a Web page applet.

2. **Use the javac command to compile the program.**

   If you're using the MortgageApplet example, in your command prompt window, type the command

   ```
   javac MortgageApplet.java
   ```

   If you run into any trouble at this point, refer to Table 2-2.

   Elsewhere in this chapter, I tell you to run the java command after you run the javac command, but in those sections, you aren't running applets. Don't issue the command `java MortgageApplet`. To find out how to trigger an applet, read on.

3. **Make sure that an .htm or .html file for your applet is in the JavaPrograms directory.**

   To use the example, copy `MortageApplet.html` from this book's CD-ROM to your hard drive's JavaPrograms directory.

   To get an applet running you need two files — a compiled Java program and an .html file (a *HyperText Markup Language* file). An .html file is a Web page — the kind of file you normally visit on the World Wide Web. You don't have to compile the .html file. Just leave it in your JavaPrograms directory.

4. **Visit your .html file with your favorite Web browser.**

   Open a Web browser (Internet Explorer, Netscape Navigator, or any of the other products that are recovering from the Browser Wars of the late 1990s). In the browser's Address field (or Location field), type the name of the .html file that you copied in Step 3. Make sure to type the file's full path name, including the hard drive letter (if you're a Windows user), and the name of the subdirectory containing the file. (See Figure 2-9.)

Figure 2-9:
Visiting your
.html file
with a Web
browser.

After pressing Enter, you should see a new Web page containing the mortgage applet in the Web browser window. (See Figure 2-10.) If you don't, then check some of the troubleshooting hints in Table 2-4.

Figure 2-10:
The
mortgage
applet
appears in
your
browser
window.

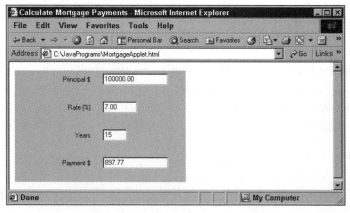

You don't need an Internet connection to visit a Web page that's already on your local hard drive.

The mortgage applet takes up a 300-x-200-pixel rectangle in your browser window. The rest of the window is blank (because I didn't put any other distracting stuff in the `MortgageWindow.html` file).

Table 2-4	Troubleshooting the Display of an Applet
Symptom	*What To Try*
A `Web page not found` error message appears	Make sure the .html file is in your JavaPrograms directory (for example `MortgageApplet.html`).
	Check the filename that you've typed in your Web browser's Address field. If you think the filename is correct, try another way of visiting the .html file with your browser. For instance, from your browser's menu bar, choose File⇨Open and then browse to the .html file on your hard drive.
Your browser displays a blank page or a page with an empty rectangle in it. (The browser was unable to load the compiled applet.)	Make sure your JavaPrograms directory contains the appropriate .class file (such as `MortgageApplet.class`). If not, look for the .class file in another directory on your hard drive. (You couldn't have put the file in the wrong directory, so the file must have walked to the wrong directory on its own!) If you can't find the required .class file on your hard drive, run javac to create a .class file (see Step 2 of the instructions in this section).
	Make sure that the two files (such as `MortgageApplet.html` and `MortgageApplet.class`) are in the same directory on your hard drive.
	Check your browser's settings to make sure that the displaying of Java applets is enabled.

When you write your own Java applets, you'll repeat Steps 2 and 4 over and over again. (Type some code, compile the code, and then visit the Web page. Change the code that you've typed, compile again, and then visit the Web page again. And so on.) When you do this, you may find your Web browser stubbornly refusing to load your modified applet's code. Time after time, you'll click the Refresh or Reload button, only to see a display of your original, unchanged Java applet. You may think you're going crazy, but you're not.

Java's built-in security mechanisms are keeping your browser from replacing your previously loaded applet code. To override the security, try holding down the Control key while you click the Refresh button. If that doesn't work, try holding down the Shift key while you click the Refresh button. Then, if all else fails, close your Web browser and start the browser running again. That'll fix the problem.

Creating an .html file

Whenever you create a Java applet, you need an .html file for testing the applet in a Web browser. The file you need is a simple one-liner. You can type it in your sleep. For instance, the file `MortgageApplet.html` that you can copy from this book's CD-ROM has this single line in it. (See Listing 2-1.)

Listing 2-1:   The MortgageApplet.html file

```
<applet code="MortgageApplet" width=300 height=200></applet>
```

To create this file from scratch, open your favorite text editor, type the line shown above, and then save the file as `MortgageApplet.html` in your JavaPrograms directory. For some explicit hints on using text editors, see the next section, "Typing Your Own Code."

When you type the line in Listing 2-1, you must remember to capitalize `MortgageApplet` exactly as it's shown in the listing. Alternate capitalizations cause nothing but problems. In general, the name and capitalization of the stuff in double quotes must exactly match the name of the .class file in your JavaPrograms directory.

When you write a Java program, a bunch of names have to match up with one another. The name in Listing 2-1 has to be the same as the .class filename, and that name has to be the same as a name inside the `MortgageApplet.java` file. If you peek inside the file `MortgageApplet.java`, you can see the words `class MortgageApplet`, with that exact spelling and capitalization, near the very top of the file.

Your .html file can have any name, as long as the name ends in either .html or .htm. This is good news, because it means you can reuse an .html file to test new applets. For instance, to test an applet named `ForeclosureApplet`, just replace `code="MortgageApplet"` with `code="ForeclosureApplet"` in the line shown in Listing 2-1. You don't have to rename the .html file.

You can even test two applets in one .html file. To do this, place the code for the second applet's .html file in your existing `MortgageApplet.html` file. (See Listing 2-2.)

Listing 2-2:   A page with two applets

```
<applet code="MortgageApplet" width=300 height=200></applet>
<applet code="ForeclosureApplet" width=300 height=200>
</applet>
```

When you do this, your Web browser displays two rectangles, each with its own applet. (See Figure 2-11.)

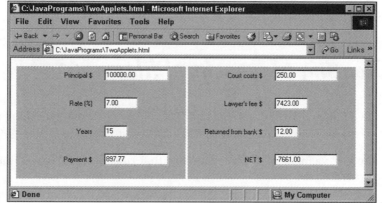

Figure 2-11: Two applets on one Web page.

When you're typing your HTML code, it helps to know a little bit about the code itself. Here is some useful info:

- ✔ **The stuff inside a pair of angle brackets (< >) is called an HTML *tag*.** So the file MortgageApplet.html (Listing 2-1) has two tags in it. The first tag (<applet . . .) is called an applet *start tag*. The second tag (</applet>) is known as an applet *end tag*.

- ✔ **Each equal sign inside the applet start tag is part of a *field*.**

- ✔ **The field code="MortgageApplet" points to the Java code that you're planning to run.** Sometimes, you see a code field with something like MortgageApplet.class in it. The extra .class file extension is okay, but any extension other than .class (like MortgageApplet.java) causes problems.

- ✔ **The width and height fields tell your Web browser how big the applet should be in pixels.** Remember that the mortgage applet appears in a rectangular area on your Web page.

- ✔ **Although you don't always need an end tag, add one anyway.** In this example, the applet end tag seems redundant. After all, the start tag ends with a close angle bracket (>), so what more do you need? The reason the end tag seems useless is because the mortgage applet is so simple. In a more elaborate example, the end tag can be very useful.

With a simple example like the mortgage applet, Internet Explorer lets you leave off the applet end tag. But Netscape Navigator isn't so forgiving, so don't get in the habit of omitting the end tag.

If you ever find yourself in a spot where you need your .html file and your Java .class file to be in two different directories, look up the applet tag field that goes by the name *codebase*. With the codebase field, you can put the .html file and the .class file in two different directories.

A complete reference guide for HTML, called HTMLib, is on this book's CD-ROM. For details, see the appendix.

Creating bigger .html files

The file `MortgageApplet.html` (Listing 2-1) is a bare-bones .html file. If you've had any formal training in HTML, or if you've read anything about good HTML coding, you've probably been brainwashed on the importance of including all the official, standardized tags in your HTML page. In truth, a complete, valid .html document — one that runs on any Java-enabled browser in the universe — looks like the document in Listing 2-3.

Listing 2-3:   A complete .html document

```
<!DOCTYPE HTML PUBLIC
    "-//W3C//DTD HTML 3.2 Final//EN">
<html>
    <head>
        <title>Calculate Mortgage Payments</title>
    </head>
    <body>
        <applet code="MortgageApplet"
            width=300 height=200></applet>
    </body>
</html>
```

Ultimately, your degree of fussiness about HTML coding depends on the kind of work you're doing. If you're writing code for the Queen of England, or for WeArePerfectInEveryWay.com, then you probably want to use the best possible HTML code. On the other hand, if you're testing applets to learn Java or posting curiosities on your family's personal Web site, then you can get away with a single line like the one in `MortgageApplet.html` (Listing 2-1).

The World Wide Web has some nice resources on the proper (and improper) coding of HTML documents. To check the correctness of your HTML code, visit `www.htmlhelp.com/tools/validator/`. Or, for a list of options that you can use to check your HTML code, visit `www.awpa.asn.au/html/validate.html`.

This book's CD-ROM has a free copy of CSE HTML Validator Lite. If you're concerned about the correctness of your HTML code, you can use this program to check your work.

Typing Your Own Code

When you create your own Java program, you type code into a .java file. If the program that you're creating is an applet, you type code into two files — a .java file and an .html file. To type your own code, use a text editor that doesn't add formatting to your text.

If you're a Windows user, Notepad will do the trick. (Choose Start⇨ Programs⇨Accessories⇨Notepad.) If you don't do Windows, look for the plainest vanilla editor that's available on the system.

If the file you're creating has a Java program in it, then you must follow the Java file-naming conventions. Here are the conventions:

✔ The filename has to be `SomethingOrOther.java`. In the name, the .java file extension must have all lowercase letters.

✔ If the file has something called a public class in it, then the `SomethingOrOther` in `SomethingOrOther.java` must be the same as the name of the public class. (Chapter 3 explains what a class looks like.) For instance, if the stuff in the file starts with the words `public class MyFirstProgram`, then your filename must be `MyFirstProgram.java`. Even the capitalization in `MyFirstProgram.java` has to be the same as the capitalization in `public class MyFirstProgram`.

In Windows, Notepad's standard Save As dialog box has a charming feature that appends the .txt file extension to any brand-new filename. This means, when you think you're saving a file named `ForeclosureApplet.java`, you're really saving `ForeclosureApplet.java.txt`. This feature can drive you crazy until you get used to it (and even after you become used to it). To keep the Save As dialog box from adding the extra .txt extension, put the entire filename in double quote marks. (See Figure 2-12.)

Don't use a word processor (like Microsoft Word) to compose your .java or .html file. Word processors add bold, italics, and other junk to your file, even though they may not show the junk in their so-called WYSIWYG windows (What You See Is What You Get).

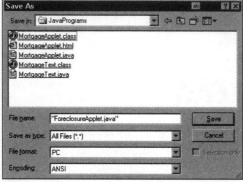

Figure 2-12:
Keep
Windows
from adding
the .txt
extension to
your
filename.

This book's CD-ROM has a copy of TextPad, a super-duper text editor. TextPad's outstanding features include color highlighting for Java programs, a button to view your work in a Web browser, and tools to help you compile and run your Java code.

Chapter 3

Using the Basic Building Blocks

*1*t's three in the morning. I'm dreaming about the history course that I failed in high school. The teacher is yelling at me, "You have two days to study for the final exam, but you won't remember to study. You'll forget and feel guilty, guilty, guilty."

Suddenly, the phone rings. I'm awakened abruptly from my deep sleep. (Sure, I disliked dreaming about the history course, but I like being awakened even less.) At first, I drop the telephone on the floor. After fumbling to pick it up, I issue a grumpy, "Hello, who's this?" A voice answers, "I'm a reporter from *The New York Times*. I'm writing an article about Java and I need to know all about the programming language in five words or less. Can you explain it?"

My mind is too hazy. I can't think. So I say anything that comes to my mind, and then go back to sleep.

Come morning, I hardly remember the conversation with the reporter. In fact, I don't remember how I answered the question. Did I tell the reporter where he could put his article about Java?

I put on my robe and rush to the front of my house's driveway. As I pick up the morning paper, I glance at the front page and see the two-inch headline:

Burd calls Java "A Great Object-Oriented Language"

The winding road from FORTRAN to Java

Back in the mid-1950s, a team of people created a programming language named FORTRAN. It was a good language, but it was based on the idea that you should issue direct, imperative commands to the computer. "Do this, computer. Then do that, computer." (Of course, the commands in a real FORTRAN program were much more precise than "Do this" or "Do that.")

In the years that followed, many new computer languages were developed, and many of the languages copied the FORTRAN "Do this/Do that" model. One of the more popular "Do this/Do that" languages went by the one-letter name *C*. Of course, the "Do this/Do that" camp had some renegades. In languages named SIMULA and Smalltalk, programmers moved the imperative "Do this" commands into the background and concentrated on descriptions of data. In these languages, you didn't come right out and say, "Print a list of delinquent accounts." Instead, you began by saying "This is what it means to be an account. An account has a name and a balance." Then you said, "This is how you ask an account if it's delinquent." Suddenly, the data became king. An account was a thing that had a name, a balance, and a way of telling you if it was delinquent or not.

Languages that focus first on the data are called *object-oriented* programming languages. These object-oriented languages make excellent programming tools. Here's why:

✔ Thinking first about the data makes you a good computer programmer.

✔ You can extend and reuse the descriptions of data over and over again. When you try to teach old FORTRAN programs new tricks, however, the old programs show how brittle they are. They break.

In the 1970s, object-oriented languages like SIMULA and Smalltalk became buried in the computer hobbyist magazine articles. In the meantime, languages based on the old FORTRAN model were multiplying like rabbits.

So in 1986, a fellow named Bjarne Stroustrup created a language named *C++*. The C++ language became very popular because it mixed the old C language terminology with the improved object-oriented structure. Many companies turned their backs on the old FORTRAN/C programming style and adopted C++ as their standard.

But C++ had a flaw. Using C++, you could bypass all the object-oriented features and write a program by using the old FORTRAN/C programming style. When you started writing a C++ accounting program, you could take either fork in the road.

✔ You could start by issuing direct "Do this" commands to the computer, saying the mathematical equivalent of "Print a list of delinquent accounts, and make it snappy."

✔ Alternatively, you could take the object-oriented approach, and begin by describing what it means to be an account.

Some people said that C++ offered the best of both worlds, but others argued that the first world (the world of FORTRAN and C) shouldn't be part of modern programming. If you gave a programmer an opportunity to write code either way, the programmer would too often choose to write code the wrong way.

So in 1995, James Gosling of Sun Microsystems created the language named *Java*. In creating Java, Gosling borrowed the look and feel of C++. But Gosling took most of the old "Do this/Do that" features of C++ and threw them in the trash. Then he added features that made the development of objects smoother and easier. All in all, Gosling created a language whose object-oriented philosophy is pure and clean. When you program in Java, you have no choice but to work with objects. That's the way it should be.

Object-Oriented Languages

Java is object-oriented. What does that mean? Unlike languages such as FORTRAN, which focus on giving the computer imperative "Do this/Do that" commands, object-oriented languages focus on data. Of course, object-oriented programs still tell the computer what to do. You start, however, by organizing the data, and the commands come later.

Object-oriented languages are better than "Do this/Do that" languages because they organize data in a way that lets people do all kinds of things with it. To modify the data, you can build on what you already have, rather than scrap everything you've done and start over each time you need to do something new. Although computer programmers are generally smart people, they took awhile to figure this out. For the full history lesson, see the sidebar, "The winding road from FORTRAN to Java" (but I won't make you feel guilty if you don't read it).

Objects and Their Classes

In an object-oriented language, you use objects *and* classes to organize your data.

Imagine that you're writing a computer program to keep track of the houses in a new real-estate development. The development (still under construction) is a condominium. The houses differ only slightly from one another. Each house has a distinctive siding color, an indoor paint color, a kitchen cabinet style, and so on. In your object-oriented computer program, each house is an object.

But objects aren't the whole story. Although the houses differ slightly from one another, all the houses share the same list of characteristics. For instance, each house has a characteristic known as "siding color." Each house has another characteristic known as "kitchen cabinet style." In your object-oriented program, you need a master list containing all the characteristics that a house object can possess. This master list of characteristics is called a *class*.

So there you have it. Object-oriented programming is misnamed. It should really be called "programming with classes and objects."

Now notice that I put the word *classes* first. How dare I do this! Well, maybe I'm not so crazy. Think again about a housing development that's under construction. Somewhere on the lot, in a rickety trailer parked on bare dirt, is a master list of characteristics known as a blueprint. An architect's blueprint is like an object-oriented programmer's class. A blueprint is a list of characteristics that each house will have. The blueprint says, "siding." The actual house object has gray siding. The blueprint says, "kitchen cabinet." The actual house object has Louis XIV kitchen cabinets.

The analogy doesn't end with lists of characteristics. Another important parallel exists between architects' blueprints and object-oriented programmers' classes. A year after you create the blueprint, you use it to build ten houses. It's the same with classes and objects. First, the programmer writes code to describe a class. Then when the program runs, the computer creates objects from the (blueprint) class.

So that's the real relationship between classes and objects. The programmer defines a class, and from the class definition, the computer makes individual objects.

What's So Good about an Object-Oriented Language?

Based on the previous section's story about home building, imagine that you have already written a computer program to keep track of the building instructions for houses in a new development. Then, the big boss decides on a modified plan — a plan in which half the houses will have three bedrooms, and the other half will have four.

If you used the old FORTRAN/C style of computer programming, your instructions would look like this:

```
Dig a ditch for the basement.
Lay concrete around the sides of the ditch.
Put two-by-fours along the sides for the basement's frame.
...
```

This would be like an architect creating a long list of instructions instead of a blueprint. To modify the plan, you would have to sort through the list to find the instructions for building bedrooms. To make things worse, the instructions could be scattered among pages 234, 324, 287, 394-410, 739, 10, and 2. If the builder had to decipher other peoples' complicated instructions, the task would be ten times harder.

Starting with a class, however, is like starting with a blueprint. If someone decides to have both three- and four-bedroom houses, you can start with a blueprint called the "house blueprint" that has a ground floor and a second floor, but has no indoor walls drawn on the second floor. Then, you make two more second-floor blueprints — one for the three-bedroom house and another for the four-bedroom house. (You name these new blueprints the "three-bedroom house blueprint" and the "four-bedroom house blueprint.")

Your builder colleagues are amazed with your sense of logic and organization, but they have concerns. They pose a question. "You called one of the blueprints the 'three-bedroom house blueprint.' How can you do this if it's a blueprint for a second floor, and not for a whole house?"

You smile knowingly and answer, "The three-bedroom house can say, 'For info about the lower floors, see the original house blueprint.' That way, the three-bedroom house blueprint describes a whole house. The four-bedroom house blueprint can say the same thing. With this setup, we can take advantage of all the work we already did to create the original house blueprint and save lots of money."

In the language of object-oriented programming, the three- and four-bedroom house classes are *inheriting* the features of the original house class. You can also say that the three- and four-bedroom house classes are *extending* the original house class. (See Figure 3-1.)

The original house class is called the *superclass* of the three- and four-bedroom house classes. In that vein, the three- and four-bedroom house classes are *subclasses* of the original house class. Put another way, the original house class is called the *parent class* of three- and four-bedroom house classes. The three- and four-bedroom house classes are *child classes* of the original house class. (See Figure 3-1.)

Needless to say, your home-builder colleagues are jealous. A crowd of home-builders is mobbing around you to hear about your great ideas. So, at that moment, you drop one more bombshell: "By creating a class with subclasses, we can reuse the blueprint in the future. If someone comes along and wants a five-bedroom house, we can extend our original house blueprint by making a five-bedroom house blueprint. We'll never have to spend money for an original house blueprint again."

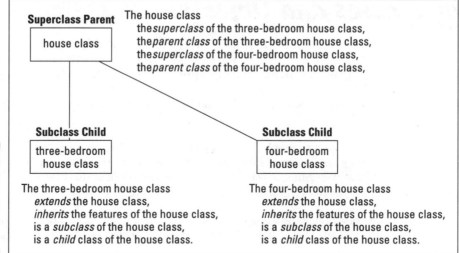

Figure 3-1: Terminology in object-oriented programming.

Superclass Parent

house class

The house class
 the *superclass* of the three-bedroom house class,
 the *parent class* of the three-bedroom house class,
 the *superclass* of the four-bedroom house class,
 the *parent class* of the four-bedroom house class,

Subclass Child

three-bedroom house class

Subclass Child

four-bedroom house class

The three-bedroom house class
 extends the house class,
 inherits the features of the house class,
 is a *subclass* of the house class,
 is a *child* class of the house class.

The four-bedroom house class
 extends the house class,
 inherits the features of the house class,
 is a *subclass* of the house class,
 is a *child* class of the house class.

"But," says a colleague in the back row, "what happens if someone wants a different first-floor design? Do we trash the original house blueprint, or start scribbling all over the original blueprint? That'll cost big bucks, won't it?"

In a confident tone you reply, "We don't have to mess with the original house blueprint. If someone wants a Jacuzzi in his living room, we can make a new, small blueprint describing only the new living room and call this the 'Jacuzzi-in-living-room house blueprint.' Then, this new blueprint can refer to the original house blueprint for info on the rest of the house (the part that's not in the living room)." In the language of object-oriented programming, the Jacuzzi-in-living-room house blueprint still *extends* the original house blueprint. The Jacuzzi blueprint is still a subclass of the original house blueprint. In fact, all the terminology about superclass, parent class, and child class still applies. The only thing that's new is that the Jacuzzi blueprint *overrides* the living room features in the original house blueprint.

In the days before object-oriented languages, the programming world experienced a crisis in software development. Programmers wrote code, then discovered new needs, and then had to trash their code and start from scratch. This happened over and over again, because the code the programmers were writing couldn't be reused. Object-oriented programming changed all this for the better (and, as Burd said, Java is "A Great Object-Oriented Language").

Refining Your Understanding of Classes and Objects

When you program in Java, you work constantly with classes and objects. These two ideas are really important. That's why, in this chapter, I hit you over the head with one analogy after another about classes and objects.

Close your eyes for a minute, and think about what it means for something to be a chair. . . .

A chair has a seat, a back, and legs. Each seat has a shape, a color, a degree of softness, and so on. These are the properties that a chair possesses. What I've just described is "chairness" — the notion of something's being a chair. In object-oriented terminology, I'm describing the chair class.

Now peek over the edge of this book's margin, and take a minute to look around your room. (If you're not sitting in a room right now, then fake it.)

Several chairs are in the room, and each chair is an object. Each of these objects is an example of that ethereal thing called the "chair class." So that's how it works — the class is the idea of "chairness," and each individual chair is an object.

A class isn't quite a collection of things. Instead, a class is the idea behind a certain kind of thing. When I talk about the class of chairs in your room, I'm talking about the fact that each chair has legs, a seat, colors, and so on. The colors may be different for different chairs in the room, but that doesn't matter. When you talk about a class of things, you're focusing on the properties that each of the things possesses.

It makes sense to think of an object as being a concrete instance of a class. In fact, the official terminology is consistent with this thinking. If you write a Java program in which you define a Chair class, then each actual chair (the chair you're sitting on, the empty chair right next to you, and so on) is called an *instance* of the Chair class.

Here's another way to think about a class. Imagine a table displaying all three of your bank accounts. (See Table 3-1.)

Table 3-1	A Table of Accounts	
Account Number	*Type*	*Balance*
16-13154-22864-7	Checking	174.87
1011 1234 2122 0000	Credit	-471.03
16-17238-13344-7	Savings	247.38

Think of the table's column headings as a class, and think of each row of the table as an object. The table's column headings describe the Account class.

According to the table's column headings, each account has an account number, a type, and a balance. Rephrased in the terminology of object-oriented programming, each object in the Account class (that is, each instance of the Account class) has an account number, a type, and a balance. So, the bottom row of the table is an object with account number *16-17238-13344-7*. This same object has type *Savings* and has balance *247.38*. If you opened a new account, you would have another object, and the table would grow an additional row. The new object would be an instance of the same Account class.

Speaking the Java Language

If you try to picture in your mind the whole English language, what do you see? Maybe you see words, words, words. (That's what Hamlet saw.) Looking at the language under a microscope, you see one word after another. The bunch-of-words image is fine, but if you step back a bit, you may see two other things:

 ✔ The language's grammar

 ✔ Thousands of expressions, sayings, idioms, and historical names

The first category (the grammar) includes rules like, "The verb agrees with the noun in number and person." The second category (expressions, sayings, and stuff) includes knowledge like, "Julius Caesar was a famous Roman emperor, so don't name your son Julius Caesar, unless you want him to get beat up every day after school."

The Java programming language has all the aspects of a spoken language like English. Java has words, grammar, commonly used names, stylistic idioms, and other such things.

The grammar and the common names

The people at Sun Microsystems who created Java thought of Java as coming in two parts. Just as English has its grammar and commonly used names, the Java programming language has its specification (its grammar) and its Application Programming Interface (its commonly used names). Whenever I write Java programs, I keep two important pieces of documentation — one for each part of the language — on my desk:

 ✔ **The Java Language Specification:** This includes rules like, "Always put an open parenthesis after the word *for*" and "Use an asterisk to multiply two numbers."

 ✔ **The Application Programming Interface:** Java's *Application Programming Interface (API)* contains thousands of tools that were added to Java after the language's grammar was defined. These tools range from the commonplace to the exotic. For instance, the tools include a routine named *pow* that can raise 5 to the 10th power for you. A more razzle-dazzle tool (named *Frame*) displays a window on your computer's screen. Other tools listen for the user's button clicks, query databases, and do all kinds of useful things.

 You can download the Language Specification, the API documents, and all the other Java documentation (or view the documents online) by visiting `www.javasoft.com/j2se/1.3/docs.html`. (And, by the way, these documents are moving targets. If this Internet address is out of date by the time you read this book, don't blame me!)

The first part of Java, the Language Specification, is relatively small. That doesn't mean you won't take plenty of time learning how to use the rules in the language specification. Other programming languages, however, have double, triple, or ten times the number of rules.

The second part of Java — the API — can be intimidating because it's so large. The API contains at least 4,000 tools and keeps growing with each new Java language release. Pretty scary, eh? Well, the good news is, you don't have to memorize anything in the API. Nothing. None of it. You can look up the stuff you need to use in the documentation and ignore the stuff you don't need. What you use often, you'll remember. What you don't use often, you'll forget (like any other programmer).

To help you use, ignore, remember, and forget things in the Java API, I've included some advice about reading and understanding the API documentation in Chapter 4.

No one learns all there is to know about the Java API. If you're a Java programmer who frequently writes programs that open new windows, then you know how to use the API Frame class. If you seldom write programs that open windows, then the first few times you need to create a window, you can look up the Frame class in the API documentation. My guess is, if you took a typical Java programmer and kept that programmer from looking up anything in the API documentation, the programmer would be able to use less than 2 percent of all the tools in the Java API.

In a way, nothing about the Java language API is special. Whenever you write a Java program — even the smallest, simplest Java program — you're creating a class that's on par with any of the classes defined in the official Java API. The API is just a set of classes and other tools that were created by ordinary programmers who happen to work at Sun Microsystems. Unlike the tools that you create yourself, the tools in the API are distributed with every version of Java. (I'm assuming that you, the reader, are not a member of the Java team at Sun Microsystems. But then, with a fine book like *Java 2 For Dummies*, one never knows.)

The folks at Sun don't keep the Java programs in the official Java API a secret. If you want, you can look at all these programs. When you install Java on your computer, the installation puts a file named `src.jar` on your hard drive. Find `src.jar` and rename the file to `src.zip`. Then open the file with your favorite unzipping program. There, before your eyes, is all the Java API code.

The words in a Java program

A hard-core Javateer will say that the Java programming language has two different kinds of words: keywords and identifiers. This is true. But the bare truth, without any other explanation, is sometimes misleading. So let's dress up the truth a bit and think in terms of three kinds of words: keywords, identifiers that ordinary programmers like you and me create, and identifiers from the API.

The differences among these three kinds of words are similar to the differences among words in the English language. In the sentence "Sam is a person," the word *person* is like a Java keyword. No matter who uses the word *person*, the word always means roughly the same thing. (Sure, you can think of bizarre exceptions in English usage, but please don't.)

The word *Sam* is like a Java identifier, because Sam is a name for a particular person. Words like *Sam, Dinswald,* and *McGillimaroo* don't come prepacked with meaning in the English language. These words apply to different people depending on the context and become names when parents pick one for their newborn kid.

Now consider the sentence "Julius Caesar is a person." If you utter this sentence, then you're probably talking about the fellow who ruled Rome until the Ides of March. Although the name *Julius Caesar* isn't hard-wired into the English language, almost everyone uses the name to refer to the same person. If English were a programming language, then the name *Julius Caesar* would be an API identifier.

So here's how I, in my own mind, divide the words in a Java program into categories:

✔ **Keywords:** A *keyword* is a word that has its own special meaning in the Java programming language, and that meaning doesn't change from one program to another. Examples of keywords in Java include *if, else* and *do.* The Cheat Sheet in the front of this book has a complete list of Java keywords.

  The people at Sun Microsystems, who have the final say on what constitutes a Java program, have created all of Java's keywords. Thinking about the two parts of Java, which I discuss in "The grammar and the common names" section earlier in this chapter, the Java keywords belong solidly to the Language Specification.

✔ **Identifiers:** An *identifier* is a name for something. The identifier's meaning can change from one program to another, but some identifiers' meanings tend to change more than others.

  • **Identifiers created by you and me:** As a Java programmer (yes, even as a novice Java programmer), you create new names for classes and other things that you describe in your programs. Of course, you may name something Prime, and the guy writing code two cubicles down the hall can name something else Prime. That's okay, because Java doesn't have a predetermined meaning for the word *Prime*. In your program, you can make Prime stand for the Federal Reserve's prime rate. And the guy down the hall can make Prime stand for the "bread, roll, preserves, and prime rib." A conflict doesn't arise, because you and your coworker are writing two different Java programs.

• **Identifiers from the API:** The people at Sun Microsystems have created names for many things and thrown at least 4,000 of these names into the Java API. The API comes with each version of Java, so these names are available to anyone who writes a Java program. Examples of such names are String, Integer, Window, Button, TextField, and File.

Strictly speaking, the meanings of the identifiers in the Java API are not cast in stone. Although you can make up your own meanings for the words like *Button* or *Window,* this isn't a good idea. If you did, you would confuse the dickens out of other programmers, who are used to the standard API meanings for these familiar identifier names. But even worse, when your code assigns a new meaning to an identifier like Button, you lose any computational power that was created for the identifier in the API code. The programmers at Sun Microsystems did all the work writing Java code to handle buttons. If you assign your own meaning to the word *Button,* you're turning your back on all the progress made in creating the API.

Checking Out Java Code for the First Time

The first time you look at somebody else's Java program, you tend to feel a bit queasy. The realization that you don't understand something (or many things) in the code can make you nervous. I've written hundreds (maybe thousands) of Java programs, but I still feel insecure when I start reading someone else's code.

The truth is, learning about a Java program is a bootstrapping experience. First you gawk in awe of the program. Then you run the program to see what it does. Then you stare at the program for a while, or read someone's explanation of the program and its parts. Then you gawk a little more and run the program again. Eventually, you come to terms with the program. (Don't believe the wise guys who say they never go through these steps. Even the experienced programmers approach a new project slowly and carefully.)

In Listing 3-1, you get a blast of Java code. (Like all novice programmers, you're expected to gawk humbly at the code.) Hidden in the code, I've placed some important ideas, which I explain in detail in the next section. These ideas include the use of classes, methods, and Java statements.

Listing 3-1:   The simplest Java program

```
class Displayer
{
    public static void main(String args[])
```

(continued)

Listing 3-1: *(continued)*

```
    {
        System.out.println("You'll love Java!");
    }
}
```

You can scoop the code of Listing 3-1 right from this book's CD-ROM. Or, if you're in a pioneering mood, you can skip the CD-ROM and type the code right into your favorite text-editing program. (If you're a Windows user, Notepad works just fine.) After you save the code in a file on your hard drive, run the program. (In Chapter 2, you can find the steps for running a stand-alone, text-based Java program.) A screen like the one shown in Figure 3-2 appears.

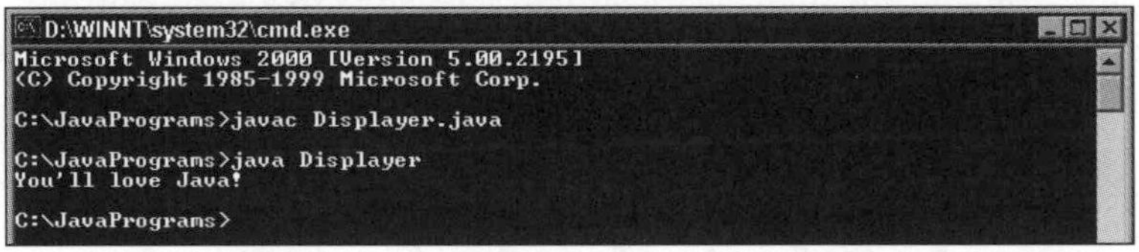

Figure 3-2:
Running the
program in
Listing 3-1.

```
D:\WINNT\system32\cmd.exe
Microsoft Windows 2000 [Version 5.00.2195]
(C) Copyright 1985-1999 Microsoft Corp.

C:\JavaPrograms>javac Displayer.java

C:\JavaPrograms>java Displayer
You'll love Java!

C:\JavaPrograms>
```

When you run the program from Listing 3-1, the computer displays the words You'll love Java! on the screen. Now I admit that writing and running a Java program is a lot of work just to get the words You'll love Java! to appear on somebody's computer screen, but every endeavor has to start somewhere.

In the next section, you do more than just run the program and admire the program's output. After you read the next section, you'll actually understand what makes the program in Listing 3-1 work.

Understanding the Simple Java Program

This section presents, explains, analyzes, dissects, and otherwise demystifies the Java program in Listing 3-1.

The Java class

Java is an object-oriented programming language so, in Java, your primary goal is to describe classes and objects. (If you're not convinced about this, read the first few sections in this chapter.)

On those special days when I'm feeling sentimental, I tell people that Java is more pure in its object-orientation than most other so-called object-oriented languages. I say this because, in Java, you can't do anything until you've created a class of some kind. It's like being on Jeopardy; hearing Alex Trebec say, "Let's go to a commercial;" and then interrupting him by saying, "I'm sorry, Alex. You can't issue an instruction without putting your instruction inside a class."

In Java, the entire program is a class. I wrote the program, so I get to make up a name for my new class. I chose the name *Displayer,* because the program displays a line of text on the computer screen. That's why the code in Listing 3-1 starts with `class Displayer`. (See Figure 3-3.)

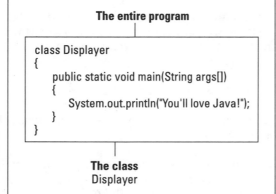

The entire program

```
class Displayer
{
    public static void main(String args[])
    {
        System.out.println("You'll love Java!");
    }
}
```

The class
Displayer

Figure 3-3:
A Java
program is
a class.

The first word in Listing 3-1, the word *class*, is a Java keyword. (See the section, "The words in a Java program," earlier in this chapter.) No matter who writes a Java program, the word *class* is always used the same way. On the other hand, the word *Displayer* in Listing 3-1 is an identifier. I made up the word *Displayer* while I was writing this chapter. The word *Displayer* is the name of a particular class — the class that I'm creating by writing this program.

The Java programming language is *case-sensitive.* This means that, if you change a lowercase letter in a word to an uppercase letter, you change the word's meaning. Changing case can make the entire word go from being meaningful to being meaningless. In the first line of Listing 3-1, you can't replace *class* with *Class.* If you do, the whole program stops working.

The Java method

You're working as an auto mechanic in an upscale garage. Your boss, who's always in a hurry and has a habit of running words together, says,

"FixTheAlternator on that junkyOldFord." Mentally, you run through a list of tasks. "Drive the car into the bay, lift the hood, get a wrench, loosen the alternator belt," and so on. Three things are going on here:

- ✔ **You have a name for the thing you're supposed to do.** The name is FixTheAlternator.

- ✔ **In your mind, you have a list of tasks associated with the name FixTheAlternator.** The list includes "Drive the car into the bay, lift the hood, get a wrench, loosen the alternator belt," and so on.

- ✔ **You have a grumpy boss who's telling you to do all this work.** Your boss gets you working by saying, "FixTheAlternator." In other words, your boss gets you working by saying the name of the thing you're supposed to do.

In this scenario, using the word *method* wouldn't be a big stretch. You have a method for doing something with an alternator. Your boss calls that method into action, and you respond by doing all the things in the list of instructions that you've associated with the method.

If you believe all that (and I hope you do), then you're ready to read about Java methods. In Java, a *method* is a list of things to do. Every method has a name, and you tell the computer to do the things in the list by using the method's name in your program.

I've never written a program to get a robot to fix an alternator. But, if I did, the program may include a FixTheAlternator method. The list of instructions in my FixTheAlternator method would look something like the text in Listing 3-2.

Listing 3-2:   A method declaration

```
void FixTheAlternator()
{
    DriveInto(car, bay);
    Lift(hood);
    Get(wrench);
    Loosen(alternatorBelt);
    ...
}
```

Somewhere else in my Java code (somewhere outside of Listing 3-2), I need an instruction to call my FixTheAlternator method into action. The instruction to call the FixTheAlternator method into action may look like the line in Listing 3-3.

Listing 3-3:   A method call

```
FixTheAlternator(junkyOldFord);
```

Don't scrutinize Listings 3-2 and 3-3 too carefully. All the code in Listings 3-2 and 3-3 is fake! I made up this code so that it looks a lot like real Java code, but it's not real. What's more important, the code in Listings 3-2 and 3-3 isn't meant to illustrate all the rules about Java. So, if you have a grain of salt handy, take it with Listings 3-2 and 3-3.

Now that you have a basic understanding of what a method is and how it works, you can dig a little deeper into some useful terminology:

✔ If I'm being lazy, I refer to the code in Listing 3-2 as a *method*. If I'm not being lazy, I refer to this code as a *method declaration*.

✔ The method declaration in Listing 3-2 has two parts. The first line (the part with the name *FixTheAlternator* in it) is called a *method header*. The rest of Listing 3-3 (the part surrounded by curly braces) is a *method body*.

✔ The term *method declaration* distinguishes the list of instructions in Listing 3-2 from the instruction in Listing 3-3, which is known as a *method call*.

A *method's declaration* tells the computer what will happen if you call the method into action. A *method call* (a separate piece of code) tells the computer to actually call the method into action. A method's declaration and the method's call tend to be in different parts of the Java program.

The main method in a program

Figure 3-4 has a copy of the code from Listing 3-1. The bulk of the code contains the declaration of a method named *main*. (Just look for the word *main* in the code's method header.) For now, don't worry about the other words in the method header — the words *public, static, void, String,* and *args.* I explain these words in the next several chapters.

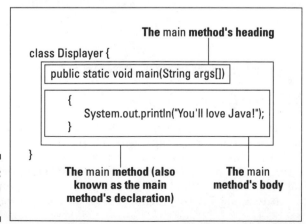

Figure 3-4: The main method.

The main **method's heading**

```
class Displayer {

    public static void main(String args[])

    {
        System.out.println("You'll love Java!");
    }

}
```

The main **method (also known as the main method's declaration)**   The main method's body

Like any Java method, the main method is a recipe.

```
How to make biscuits:
    Heat the oven.
    Roll the dough.
    Bake the rolled dough.
```

or

```
How to follow the main instructions for a Displayer:
    Print "You'll love Java!" on the screen.
```

The word *main* plays a special role in Java. In particular, you never write code that explicitly calls a main method into action. The word *main* is the name of the method that is called into action automatically when the program begins running.

So look back at Figure 3-2. You type **java Displayer** in the command prompt window to run the Displayer program. When the Displayer program runs, the computer automatically finds the program's main method and executes any instructions inside the method's body. In the Displayer program, the main method's body has only one instruction. That instruction tells the computer to print You'll love Java! on the screen. So in Figure 3-2, you type **java Displayer**, and the computer responds immediately with the words You'll love Java!

None of the instructions in a method are executed until the method is called into action. But, if you give a method the name *main,* then that method is called into action automatically.

Almost every computer programming language has something akin to Java's methods. If you've worked with other languages, you may remember things like subprograms, procedures, functions, subroutines, subprocedures, or PERFORM statements. Whatever you call it in your favorite programming language, a method is a bunch of instructions collected together and given a new name.

How you finally tell the computer to do something

Buried deep in the heart of Listing 3-1 is the single line that actually issues a direct instruction to the computer. The line, which is highlighted in Figure 3-5, tells the computer to display the words You'll love Java! in the command prompt window (refer to Figure 3-2). This line is known as a statement. In Java, a *statement* is a direct instruction that tells the computer to do something (for example, display this text, put 7 in that memory location, make a window appear).

```
class Displayer
{
    public static void main(String args[])
    {
        System.out.println("You'll love Java!");
    }
}
```

A statement (a call to the
System.out.println **method)**

Figure 3-5:
A Java
statement.

Of course, Java has different kinds of statements. A method call, which I introduce in "The Java method" section earlier in this chapter, is one of the many kinds of Java statements. Listing 3-3 shows you what a method call looks like, and Figure 3-5 also contains a method call that looks like this:

```
System.out.println("You'll love Java!");
```

When the computer starts executing this statement, the computer calls a method named *System.out.println* into action. (Yes, in Java, a name can have dots in it. The dots mean something, but I won't open that can of worms until Chapter 7.)

Figure 3-6 illustrates the System.out.println situation. Actually, two methods play active roles in the running of the Displayer program. Here's how they work:

✔ **There's a declaration for a main method.** I wrote the main method myself. This main method is called automatically whenever I start running the Displayer program.

✔ **There's a call to the System.out.println method.** The method call for the System.out.println method is the only statement in the body of the main method. In other words, calling the System.out.println method is the only thing on the main method's to-do list.

The declaration for the System.out.println method is buried inside the official Java API. For a refresher on the Java API, see the sections, "The grammar and the common names" and "The words in a Java program," earlier in this chapter.

When I say things like "System.out.println is buried inside the API," I'm not doing justice to the API. True, you can ignore all the nitty-gritty Java code inside the API. All you need to remember is that System.out.println is defined somewhere inside that code. But I'm not being fair when I make the API code sound like something magical. The API is just another bunch of Java code. The statements in the API that tell the computer what it means to carry out a call to System.out.println look a lot like the Java code in Listing 3-1.

In Java, each statement (like the highlighted line in Figure 3-5) ends with a semicolon. Other lines in Figure 3-5 don't end with semicolons, because the other lines in Figure 3-5 aren't statements. For instance, the method header (the line with the word *main* in it) doesn't directly tell the computer to do anything. The method header announces, "Just in case you ever want to do main, the next few lines of code tell you how you'll do it."

Every complete Java statement ends with a semicolon.

Curly braces

Long ago, or maybe not so long ago, your schoolteachers told you how useful outlines are. With an outline, you can organize thoughts and ideas, you can help people see forests instead of trees, and you can generally show that you're a member of the Tidy Persons Club. Well, a Java program is like an outline. The program in Listing 3-1 starts with a big heading line that says, "Here comes a class named *Displayer*." After that first big heading is a subheading that announces, "Here comes a method named *main*."

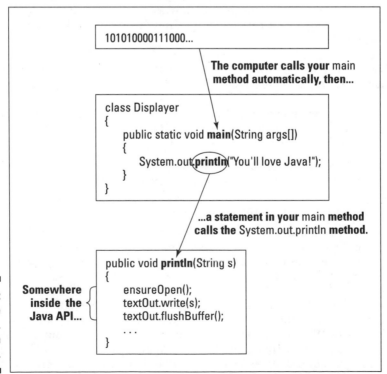

Figure 3-6:
Calling the System.out.println method.

Now, if a Java program is like an outline, why doesn't a program look like an outline? What takes the place of the Roman numerals, capital letters, and other things? The answer is twofold:

- ✔ In a Java program, curly braces enclose meaningful units of code.
- ✔ You, the programmer, can (and should) indent lines so that other programmers can see the outline form of your code at a glance.

In an outline, everything is subordinate to the item in Roman numeral I. In a Java program, everything is subordinate to the top line — the line with the word *class* in it. To indicate that everything else in the code is subordinate to this class line, you use curly braces. Everything else in the code goes inside these curly braces. (See Listing 3-4.)

Listing 3-4:   Curly braces for a Java class

```
class Displayer
{

    public static void main(String args[])
    {
        System.out.println("You'll love Java!");
    }
}
```

In an outline, some stuff is subordinate to a capital letter A item. In a Java program, some lines are subordinate to the method header. To indicate that something is subordinate to a method header, you use curly braces. (See Listing 3-5.)

Listing 3-5:   Curly braces for a Java method

```
class Displayer
{

    public static void main(String args[])
    {                                                    //Open!
        System.out.println("You'll love Java!");
    }                                                    //Close!
}
```

In an outline, some items are at the bottom of the food chain. In the Displayer class, the corresponding line is the line that begins with System.out.println. Accordingly, this System.out.println line goes inside all the other curly braces and is indented more than anything else.

You should never lose sight of the fact that a Java program is, first and foremost, an outline.

If you put curly braces in the wrong places or omit curly braces where the braces should be, then your program probably won't work at all. If your program works, it'll probably work incorrectly.

If you don't indent lines of code in an informative manner, your program will still work correctly, but neither you nor any other programmer will be able to figure out what you were thinking when you wrote the code.

If you're one of those visual thinkers, you should picture outlines of Java programs in your head. One friend of mine visualizes an actual numbered outline morphing into a Java program. (See Figure 3-7.) Another person, who shall remain nameless, uses more bizarre imagery. (See Figure 3-8.)

When you put two slashes in your Java code, anything after the slashes (on the same line of code) is treated as a comment. A comment is informative text for fellow programmers to read. So, in Listing 3-5, the computer doesn't try to make sense of the text Open! or Close! To create a comment that spans more than one line of code, start the comment with a slash followed by a star /*, and end the comment with star followed by a slash */.

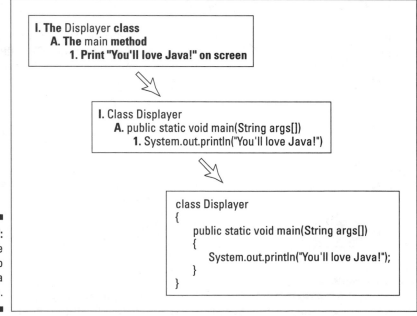

Figure 3-7:
An outline
turns into
a Java
program.

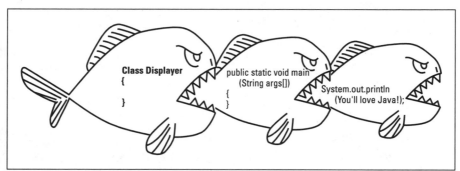

Figure 3-8:
A class is
bigger than
a method; a
method is
bigger than
a statement.

Part II
Writing Your Own Java Programs

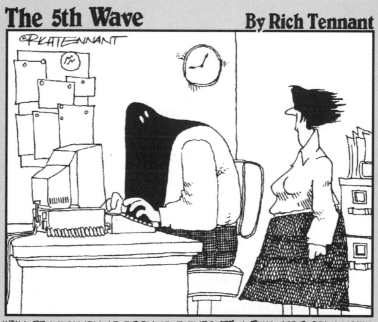

The 5th Wave   By Rich Tennant

"I'LL BE WITH YOU AS SOON AS I EXECUTE A FEW MORE COMMANDS."

In this part . . .

In this part, you dig in and get dirty by writing some programs and finding out what Java really feels like. Some of the stuff in this part is specific to Java, but lots of the material is just plain old, generic computer programming. This part concentrates on details — details about data, logic, and program flow. After you've read this part and practiced some of the techniques, you can write all kinds of interesting Java programs.

Chapter 4

Making the Most of Variables and Their Values

*T*he following conversation (between Van Doren and Philbin) never took place:

> *Charles:* A sea squirt eats its brain, turning itself from an animal into a plant.
>
> *Regis:* Is that your final answer, Charles?
>
> *Charles:* Yes, it is.
>
> *Regis:* How much money do you have in your account today, Charles?
>
> *Charles:* I have fifty dollars and twenty-two cents in my checking account.
>
> *Regis:* Well, you better call the IRS, because I'm putting another million dollars in your account. What do you think of that, Charles?
>
> *Charles:* I owe it all to honesty, diligence, and hard work, Regis.

Some aspects of this dialogue can be represented in Java by a few lines of code.

Varying a Variable

No matter how you acquire your million dollars, you can use a variable to tally your wealth. The code is shown in Listing 4-1.

Listing 4-1:   Using a variable

```
amountInAccount = 50.22;
amountInAccount = amountInAccount + 1000000.00;
```

The code in Listing 4-1 makes use of the amountInAccount variable. A *variable* is a placeholder. You can stick a number like 50.22 into a variable. After you've placed a number in the variable, you can change your mind and put a different number into the variable. (That's what varies in a variable.) Of course, when you put a new number in a variable, the old number is no longer there. If you didn't save the old number somewhere else, the old number is gone.

Figure 4-1 gives a "before and after" picture of the code in Listing 4-1. After the first statement in Listing 4-1 is executed, the variable amountInAccount has the number 50.22 in it. Then, after the second statement of Listing 4-1 is executed, the amountInAccount variable suddenly has 1000050.22 in it. When you think about a variable, picture a place in the computer's memory where wires and transistors store 50.22, 1000050.22, or whatever. In the left-hand side of Figure 4-1, imagine that the box with the number 50.22 in it is surrounded by millions of other such boxes.

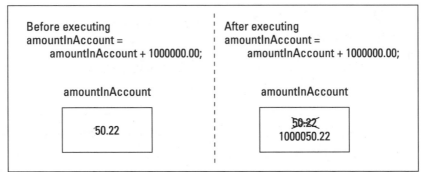

Figure 4-1:
A variable
(before and
after).

Now you need some terminology. The thing stored in a variable is called a *value.* A variable's value can change during the run of a program (when Regis gives you a million bucks, for instance). The value stored in a variable isn't necessarily a number. (You can, for instance, create a variable that always stores a letter.) The kind of value stored in a variable is variable's *type.* (You can read more about types in the next section.)

A subtle, almost unnoticeable difference exists between a variable and a variable's *name.* Even in formal writing, I often use the word *variable* when I mean *variable name.* Strictly speaking, amountInAccount is a variable name, and all the memory storage associated with amountInAccount (including the type that amountInAccount has and whatever value amountInAccount currently represents) is the variable itself. If you think this distinction between *variable* and *variable name* is too subtle for you to worry about, join the club.

Every variable name is an identifier — a name that you can make up in your own code. (See Chapter 3.) In preparing Listing 4-1, I made up the name *amountInAccount*.

Before the sun sets on Listing 4-1, you need to notice one more part of the listing. The listing has 50.22 and 1000000.00 in it. Anybody in his or her right mind would call these things "numbers" but, in a Java program, it helps to call these things *literals*.

And what's so literal about 50.22 and 1000000.00? Well, think about the variable amountInAccount in Listing 4-1. The variable amountInAccount stands for 50.22 some of the time, but it stands for 1000050.22 the rest of the time. You could sort of use the word *number* to talk about amountInAccount. But really, what amountInAccount stands for depends on the fashion of the moment. On the other hand, 50.22 literally stands for the value $50^{22}/_{100}$.

A variable's value changes; a literal's value doesn't.

Assignment Statements

Statements like the ones in Listing 4-1 are called *assignment statements*. In an assignment statement, you assign a value to something. In many cases, this "something" is a variable.

You should get into the habit of reading assignment statements from right to left. For instance, the first line in Listing 4-1 says,

```
                        "Assign 50.22 . . .

amountInAccount    =    50.22;

. . . to the
amountInAccount
variable."
```

The second line in Listing 4-1 is just a bit more complicated. Reading the second line from right to left, you get

```
                        "Add 1000000.00 to the value that's
                        already in the amountInAccount
                        variable . . .

amountInAccount    =    amountInAccount + 1000000.00;

. . . and make
that number
(1000050.22) be
the new value of the
amountInAccount variable."
```

In an assignment statement, the thing being assigned a value is always on the left side of the equal sign.

Understanding the Types of Values That Variables May Have

Have you seen the TV commercials that make you think you're flying around among the circuits inside a computer? Pretty cool, eh? These commercials show zeros and ones sailing by, because zeros and ones are the only things computers can really deal with. When you think a computer is storing the letter *J*, the computer is really storing 01001010. Everything inside the computer is a sequence of zeros and ones. As every computer geek knows, a zero or one is called a *bit*.

Now it turns out that the sequence 01001010, which stands for the letter *J*, can also stand for the number 74. The same sequence can also stand for $1.0369608636003646 \times 10^{-43}$. In fact, if the bits are interpreted as screen pixels, the same sequence can be used to represent the dots shown in Figure 4-2. The meaning of 01001010 depends on the way the software interprets this sequence of zeros and ones.

Figure 4-2:
An extreme
close-up of
eight black-
and-white
screen
pixels.

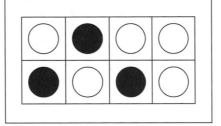

So how do you tell the computer what 01001010 stands for? The answer is in the concept called *type*. The type of a variable is the range of values that the variable is permitted to store.

I copied the lines from Listing 4-1 and put them into a complete Java program. The program is in Listing 4-2. When I run the program in Listing 4-2, I get the output shown in Figure 4-3.

Listing 4-2: A program uses amountInAccount

```
public class Millionaire
{
    public static void main(String args[])
```

```
{
    double amountInAccount;

    amountInAccount = 50.22;
    amountInAccount = amountInAccount + 1000000.00;

    System.out.print("You have $");
    System.out.print(amountInAccount);
    System.out.println(" in your account.");
}
}
```

Figure 4-3:
Running the
program in
Listing 4-2.

```
C:\JavaPrograms>java Millionaire
You have $1000050.22 in your account.
C:\JavaPrograms>
```

In Listing 4-2, look at the first line in the body of the main method.

```
double amountInAccount;
```

This line is called a *variable declaration*. Putting this line in your program is like saying "I'm declaring my intention to have a variable named amountInAccount in my program." This line reserves the name *amountInAccount* for your use in the program.

In this variable declaration, the word *double* is a Java keyword. This word *double* tells the computer what kinds of values you intend to store in amountInAccount. In particular, the word *double* stands for numbers between -1.8×10^{308} and 1.8×10^{308}. (These are enormous numbers with 308 zeros before the decimal point. Only the world's richest people write checks with 308 zeros in them. The second of these numbers is pronounced "one-point-eight gazazzo-zillion-kaskillion." The number 1.8×10^{308}, a constant defined by the International Bureau of Weights and Measures, is the number of eccentric computer programmers between Sunnyvale, California, and the M31 Andromeda Galaxy.)

More important than the humongous range of the double keyword's numbers is the fact that a double value can have digits beyond the decimal point. After you declare amountInAccount to be of type double, you can store all sorts of numbers in amountInAccount. You can store 50.22, 0.02398479, or –3.0. In Listing 4-2, if I hadn't declared amountInAccount to be of type double, then I may not have been able to store 50.22. Instead, I would have had to store plain old 50, without any digits beyond the decimal point.

Digits beyond the decimal point

Java has two different types that have digits beyond the decimal point: type double and type float. So what's the difference? When you declare a variable to be of type double, you're telling the computer to take up 64 bits of memory to store the variable's values. When you declare a variable to be of type float, you use only 32 bits of memory.

In Listing 4-2, the number 50.22 takes up 64 bits of precious random access memory. Is this a big waste? Well, you could change Listing 4-2 and declare amountInAccount to be of type float.

```
float amountInAccount;
```

Surely, 32 bits are enough to store a small number like 50.22. Well, they are and they aren't. You could easily store 50.00 with only 32 bits. Heck, you could store 50.00 with only 6 bits. The size of the number doesn't matter. It's the accuracy that matters. In a 64-bit double variable, you're using most of the bits to store stuff beyond the decimal point. To store the .22 part of 50.22, you need more than the measly 32 bits that you get with type float.

Do you really believe what you just read — that it takes more than 32 bits to store .22? To help convince you, I made a few changes to the code in Listing 4-2. I made amountInAccount be of type float, and the output I got was

```
You have $1000050.25 in
  your account.
```

Compare this with the output in Figure 4-3. When I switch from type double to type float, Charles has an extra three cents in his account. By changing to the 32-bit float type, I've clobbered the accuracy in the amountInAccount variable's hundredths place. That's bad.

Another difficulty with float values is purely cosmetic. Look again at the literals, 50.22 and 1000000.00, in Listing 4-2. The Laws of Java say that literals like these take up 64 bits each. This means that, if you declare amountInAccount to be of type float, you're going to run into trouble. You'll have trouble stuffing those 64-bit literals into your little 32-bit amountInAccount variable. To compensate, you can switch from double literals to float literals by adding an F to each double literal, but a number with an extra F at the end looks funny.

```
float amountInAccount;
    amountInAccount = 50.22F;
    amountInAccount =
amountInAccount +
1000000.00F;
```

To experiment with numbers, visit babbage.cs.qc.edu/courses/cs341/I EEE-754.html. The page takes any number you enter and shows you how the number would be represented as 32 bits and as 64 bits.

Another type — type float — also allows you to have numbers after the decimal point, but this type isn't as accurate. (See the sidebar, "Digits beyond the decimal point," for the full story.) Don't sweat the choice between float and double. For most programs, just use double.

The last three statements in Listing 4-2 use a neat formatting trick. You want to display several different things on a single line on the screen. You put these things in separate statements. All but the last of the statements are calls to System.out.print. (The last statement is a call to System.out.println.) Calls to System.out.print display text on part of a line and then leave the cursor at the end of the current line. After executing System.out.print, the cursor is still at the end of the same line, so the next System.out.*whatever* can continue printing on that same line. With several calls to print capped off by a single call to println, the result is just one nice-looking line of output (refer to Figure 4-3).

A call to System.out.print writes some things and leaves the cursor sitting at the end of the line of output. A call to System.out.println writes things and then finishes the job by moving the cursor to the start of a brand new line of output.

Numbers without Decimal Points

"In 1995, the average family had 2.3 children."

At this point, a wise guy always remarks that no real family has exactly 2.3 children. Clearly, whole numbers have a role in this world. So in Java, you can declare a variable to store nothing but whole numbers. Listing 4-3 shows a program that uses whole number variables.

Listing 4-3:   Using the int type

```
public class ElevatorFitter
{
    public static void main(String args[])
    {
        int weightOfAPerson;
        int elevatorWeightLimit;
        int numberOfPeople;

        weightOfAPerson = 150;
        elevatorWeightLimit = 1400;
        numberOfPeople =
            elevatorWeightLimit/weightOfAPerson;

        System.out.print("You can fit ");
        System.out.print(numberOfPeople);
        System.out.println(" people on the elevator.");
    }
}
```

The story behind the program in Listing 4-3 takes some heavy-duty explaining. So here goes:

You have a hotel elevator whose weight capacity is 1,400 pounds. One weekend, the hotel hosts the Brickenchicker family reunion. In a certain branch of the Brickenchicker family are identical dectuplets (ten siblings, all with the same physical characteristics). Normally, each of the Brickenchicker dectuplets weighs exactly 145 pounds. But on Saturday the family has a big catered lunch and, because lunch included strawberry shortcake, each of the Brickenchicker dectuplets now weighs 150 pounds. Immediately after lunch, all ten of the Brickenchicker dectuplets arrive at the elevator at exactly the same time. (Why not? All ten of them think alike.) So the question is, how many of the dectuplets can fit on the elevator?

Now remember, if you put one ounce more than 1,400 pounds of weight on the elevator, then the elevator cable will break, plunging all dectuplets on the elevator to their sudden (and costly) deaths.

The answer to the Brickenchicker riddle (the output of the program of Listing 4-3) is shown in Figure 4-4.

Figure 4-4:
Save the
Bricken-
chickers.

```
C:\JavaPrograms>java ElevatorFitter
You can fit 9 people on the elevator.

C:\JavaPrograms>
```

At the core of the Brickenchicker elevator problem, you've got whole numbers — numbers with no digits beyond the decimal point. When you divide 1,400 by 150, you get 9⅓, but you shouldn't take the ⅓ seriously. No matter how hard you try, you can't squeeze an extra 50 pounds worth of Brickenchicker dectuplet onto the elevator. This fact is reflected nicely in Java. In Listing 4-3, all three variables (weightOfAPerson, elevatorWeightLimit, and numberOfPeople) are of type int. An int value is a whole number. When you divide one int value by another (as you do with the slash in Listing 4-3), you get another int. When you divide 1,400 by 150, you get 9 — not 9⅓. You see this in Figure 4-4. Taken together, the following statements put the number 9 on the computer screen:

```
numberOfPeople =
    elevatorWeightLimit/weightOfAPerson;

System.out.print(numberOfPeople);
```

Variations on a Theme

Look back at Listing 4-3. In that listing are three variable declarations — one for each of the program's three int variables. I could have done the same thing with just one declaration.

```
int weightOfAPerson, elevatorWeightLimit, numberOfPeople;
```

Four ways to store whole numbers

Java has four different types of whole numbers. The types are called *byte, short, int,* and *long.* The difference among the four types is the number of bits used to store a value. A byte variable takes up 8 bits, a short variable takes 16 bits, an int takes 32, and a long takes 64 bits.

Unlike the complicated story about the accuracy of types float and double, the only thing that matters when you choose among the whole number types is the size of the number you're trying to store. If you want to use numbers larger than 127, don't use byte.

Most of the time, you'll use int. But if you need to store numbers larger than 2147483647, then forsake int in favor of long. (A long number can be as big as 9223372036854775807.) For the whole story, see Table 4-1.

You can always combine declarations this way, whether they're int, double, or any other type. The way you choose is just a matter of personal style.

If two variables have completely different types, you can't create both variables in the same declaration. For instance, to create an int variable named *weightOfFred* and a double variable named *amountInFredsAccount,* you need two separate variable declarations.

You can give variables their starting values in a declaration. In Listing 4-3 for instance, one declaration can replace the several lines in the main method (all but the calls to print and println).

```
int weightOfAPerson=150, elevatorWeightLimit=1400,
    numberOfPeople=elevatorWeightLimit/weightOfAPerson;
```

When you do this, you don't say that you're assigning values to variables. The pieces of the declarations with equal signs in them aren't really called assignment statements. Instead, you say that you're *initializing* the variables. Believe it or not, keeping this distinction in mind is helpful. For one thing, you can drag a declaration with its initialization outside of a method, as shown in the following code:

```
public class ElevatorFitterNew
{
    static int weightOfAPerson=150, elevatorWeightLimit=1400;
    static int numberOfPeople=
                elevatorWeightLimit/weightOfAPerson;

    public static void main(String args[])
    {
        System.out.print("You can fit ");
```

```
        System.out.print(numberOfPeople);
        System.out.println(" people on the elevator.");
    }
}
```

You can't do the same thing with assignment statements. In fact, you can't drag any statements outside any methods. (Even though a variable declaration ends with a semicolon, a variable declaration isn't considered to be a statement. Go figure!)

The advantage of putting a declaration outside a method is explained in Chapter 10. While you wait impatiently to reach that chapter, notice how I added the word *static* to each declaration that I pulled out of the main method. I had to do this because the main method's header has the word *static* in it. Not all methods are static. In fact, most methods aren't static. But, whenever you pull a declaration out of a static method, you have to add the word *static* at the beginning of the declaration. All the mystery surrounding the word *static* is resolved in Chapter 10.

The Atoms: Java's Primitive Types

The words *int* and *double,* described in the previous sections, are examples of *primitive types* (also known as *simple* types) in Java. The Java language has exactly eight primitive types. As a newcomer to Java, you can pretty much ignore all but four of these types. (As programming languages go, Java is nice and compact that way.) The complete list of primitive types is in Table 4-1.

Table 4-1	Java's Primitive Types		
Type Name	*Storage*	*What a Literal Looks Like*	*Range of Values*
Whole Number Types			
byte	8 bits	(byte)42	−128 to 127
short	16 bits	(short)42	−32768 to 32767
int	32 bits	42	−2147483648 to 2147483647
long	64 bits	42L	−9223372036854775808 to 9223372036854775807

Type Name	Storage	What a Literal Looks Like	Range of Values
Decimal Number Types			
float	32 bits	42.0F	-3.4×10^{38} to 3.4×10^{38}
double	64 bits	42.0	-1.8×10^{308} to 1.8×10^{308}
Character Type			
char	16 bits	'A'	Thousands of characters, glyphs, and symbols
Logical Type			
boolean		true	true, false

The types you shouldn't ignore are int, double, char, and boolean. Earlier sections in this chapter cover the int and double types. So this section covers char and boolean types.

The char type

There was a time, not so long ago, when people thought computers were only for doing big number-crunching calculations. Nowadays, with word processors, nobody thinks that way anymore. So, if you haven't been in a cryogenic freezing chamber for the last 20 years, you know that computers store letters, punctuation symbols, and other characters.

The Java type that's used to store characters is called *char*. Listing 4-4 has a simple program that uses the char type. The output of the program of Listing 4-4 is shown in Figure 4-5.

Listing 4-4:   Using the char type

```
public class CharDemo
{
   public static void main(String args[])
   {
      char myLittleChar, myBigChar;
      myLittleChar = 'b';
      myBigChar = Character.toUpperCase(myLittleChar);
      System.out.println(myBigChar);
   }
}
```

Figure 4-5:
An exciting
run of the
program of
Listing 4-4.

```
C:\JavaPrograms>java CharDemo
B
C:\JavaPrograms>_
```

In Listing 4-4, the first assignment statement stores the letter *b* in the variable myLittleChar. In the statement, notice how *b* is surrounded by single quote marks. In Java, every char literal starts and ends with a single quote mark.

In a Java program, single quote marks surround the letter in a char literal.

In the second assignment statement of Listing 4-4, the program calls an API method whose name is Character.toUpperCase. (For an introduction to the Java API, see Chapter 3.) The Character.toUpperCase method does just what its name suggests — the method produces the uppercase equivalent of the letter *b*. This uppercase equivalent (the letter *B*) is assigned to the myBigChar variable, and the B that's in myBigChar is printed on the screen.

If you're tempted to write the following statements,

```
char myLittleChars;
myLittleChars = 'barry';   //Don't do this
```

then please resist the temptation. You can't store more than one letter at a time in a char variable, and you can't put more than one letter between a pair of single quotes. If you're trying to store words or sentences (not just single letters), then you need to use something called a *String*. For a look at Java's String type, see the section, "The Molecules and Compounds: Reference Types," later in this chapter.

If you're used to writing programs in other languages, you may be aware of something called the ASCII Character Encoding. Most languages use ASCII; Java uses Unicode. In the old ASCII representation, each character takes up only 8 bits, but in Unicode, each character takes 16 bits. Whereas ASCII stores the letters of the familiar Roman (English) alphabet, Unicode has room for characters from all the world's languages. The only problem is, some of the API methods are geared specially toward the 16-bit code. Occasionally, this bites you in the back. If you're using a method to write Hello on the screen and H e l l o shows up instead, check the method's documentation for mention of Unicode characters.

It's worth noticing that the two methods, Character.toUpperCase and System.out.println, are used quite differently in Listing 4-4. The method Character.toUpperCase is called as part of assignment statement, but the method System.out.println is called on its own. To learn more about this, see Chapter 7.

The boolean type

A variable of type boolean stores one of two values — true or false. The use of a boolean variable is demonstrated in Listing 4-5. The output of the program in Listing 4-5 is shown in Figure 4-6.

Listing 4-5:   Using the boolean type

```
public class ElevatorFitter2
{
    public static void main(String args[])
    {
        int weightOfAPerson;
        int elevatorWeightLimit;
        int numberOfPeople;
        boolean allTenOkay;

        System.out.println("True or False?");
        System.out.println("You can fit all ten of the");
        System.out.println("Brickenchicker dectuplets");
        System.out.println("on the elevator:");
        System.out.println();

        weightOfAPerson = 150;
        elevatorWeightLimit = 1400;
        numberOfPeople =
            elevatorWeightLimit/weightOfAPerson;

        allTenOkay = numberOfPeople>=10;
        System.out.println(allTenOkay);
    }
}
```

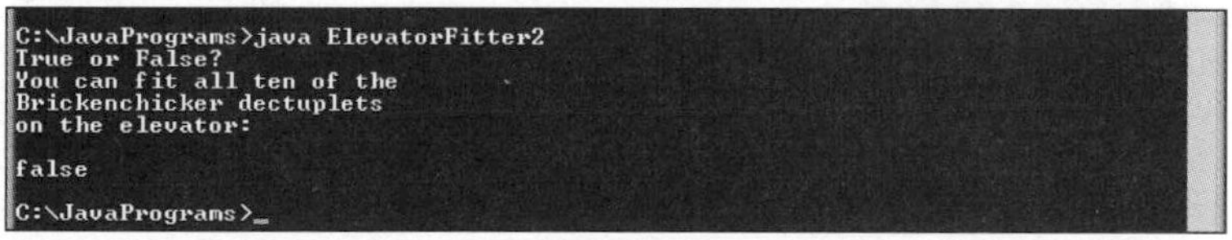

Figure 4-6:
The
Bricken-
chicker
dectuplets
strike again.

```
C:\JavaPrograms>java ElevatorFitter2
True or False?
You can fit all ten of the
Brickenchicker dectuplets
on the elevator:

false

C:\JavaPrograms>_
```

In Listing 4-5, the allTenOkay variable is of type boolean. To find a value for the allTenOkay variable, the program checks to see if numberOfPeople is greater than or equal to ten. (The symbols >= stand for "greater than or equal to.")

At this point, becoming fussy about terminology pays. Any part of a Java program that has a value is called an *expression*. If you write

```
weightOfAPerson = 150;
```

then 150 is an expression (an expression whose value is the quantity 150). If you write

```
numberOfeggs = 2 + 2;
```

then 2 + 2 is an expression (because 2 + 2 has the value 4). If you write

```
numberOfPeople =
        elevatorWeightLimit/weightOfAPerson;
```

then elevatorWeightLimit/weightOfAPerson is an expression. (The value of the expression elevatorWeightLimit/weightOfAPerson depends on whatever values the variables elevatorWeightLimit and weightOfAPerson have when the statement with the expression in it is executed.)

Any part of a Java program that has a value is called an expression.

In Listing 4-5, the code `numberOfPeople>=10` is an expression. The expression's value depends on the value stored in the numberOfPeople variable. But, as we all know from seeing the strawberry shortcake at the Brickenchicker family's catered lunch, the value of numberOfPeople is not greater than or equal to ten. This makes the value of `numberOfPeople>=10` to be false. So, in the statement in Listing 4-5 in which allTenOkay is assigned a value, the allTenOkay variable is assigned a false value.

The Molecules and Compounds: Reference Types

By combining simple things, you get more complicated things. That's the way it always goes. Take some of Java's primitive types, whip them together to make a primitive type stew, and what do you get? A more complicated type called a *reference type*.

The program in Listing 4-6 uses reference types. Figure 4-7 shows you what happens when you run the program in Listing 4-6.

Listing 4-6:   Using reference types

```java
import java.awt.*;

public class ShowAFrame
{
    public static void main(String args[])
    {
        String myTitle;
        Frame f;
        myTitle = "Blank Frame";
        f = new Frame();
        f.setTitle(myTitle);
        f.setSize(200,200);
        f.show();
    }
}
```

Figure 4-7:
An empty
frame.

The program in Listing 4-6 puts a window (a Java frame) on your computer screen. To keep Listing 4-6 as simple as possible, I didn't include any code to help you close the window. So, if you run the program in Listing 4-6 and click the window's close button, then nothing will happen. The window won't close. (If you're a Microsoft Windows user, the close button is the little × in the upper right-hand corner of the window.) At that point, you'll do what anyone else would do. You'll click the window's close button again, this time a bit slower and quite a bit harder. Even so, nothing will happen. In Listing 4-6, the extra code (the code that I would need to add to make the close button work) isn't a big deal. But at this point in the discussion, that extra code would just muddy the waters. For now, if you want to close the window, you'll have to get your operating system to close it. (On a Microsoft Windows computer, press Ctrl+Alt+Delete. Alternatively, you can pull your computer's power cord out of the wall outlet. That always works for me.)

The program in Listing 4-6 uses two references types. Both of these types are defined in the Java API. One of the types (the one that you'll use all the time) is called *String*. The other type (the one that you'll use if you create GUIs) is called *Frame*.

A *String* is a bunch of characters. It's like having several char values in a row. So, with the myTitle variable declared to be of type String, assigning "Blank Frame" to the myTitle variable makes sense in Listing 4-6. The String class is declared in the Java API.

In a Java program, double quote marks surround the letters in a String literal.

A Java frame is a lot like a window. (The only difference is that you call it a frame instead of a window.) To keep Listing 4-6 short and sweet, I decided not to put anything in my frame — no buttons, no fields, nothing.

Even with a completely empty frame, Listing 4-6 uses tricks that I don't describe until later in this book. So don't try reading and interpreting every word of Listing 4-6. The big thing you should get from Listing 4-6 is that the program has two variable declarations. In writing the program, I made up two variable names — myTitle and f. According to the declarations, myTitle is of type String, and f is of type Frame.

In the last section of this chapter, I describe some tips and tricks for reading Java's API documentation. You can look up String and Frame in the documentation. But, even before you do, I can tell you what you'll find. You'll find that String and Frame are the names of Java classes. (To review the notion of a Java class, see Chapter 3.) So, that's the big news. Every class is the name of a reference type. Just as you can reserve amountInAccount for double values by writing

```
double amountInAccount;
```

you can also reserve f for a Frame value by writing

```
Frame f;
```

Every Java class is a reference type. If you declare a variable to have some type that's not a primitive type, then (most of the time) the variable's type is the name of a Java class.

Now, when you declare a variable to have type int, you can visualize what that declaration means in a fairly straightforward way. It means that, somewhere inside the computer's memory, a storage location is reserved for that variable's value. In that storage location is a bunch of bits. The arrangement of the bits assures that a certain whole number is represented.

That explanation is fine for primitive types like int or double, but what does it mean when you declare a variable to have a reference type? What does it mean to declare variable f to be of type Frame?

Well, what does it mean to declare *i thank You God* to be an E. E. Cummings poem? What would it mean to write the following declaration?

```
EECummingsPoem ithankYouGod;
```

It means that a class of things is called E. E. Cummings poems, and *i thank You God* refers to an instance of that class. In other words, *i thank You God* is an object belonging to the E. E. Cummings poems class.

Because Frame is a class, you can create objects from that class. (See Chapter 3.) Each such object (each instance of the Frame class) is an actual frame — a window that appears on the screen when you run the code in Listing 4-6. By declaring the variable f to be of type Frame, you're telling the computer that f refers to an actual Frame-type object. In other words, f is a nickname for one of the windows that appears on the computer screen. The situation is illustrated in Figure 4-8.

When you declare `ClassName variableName;` you're saying that the variable refers to an instance of the class.

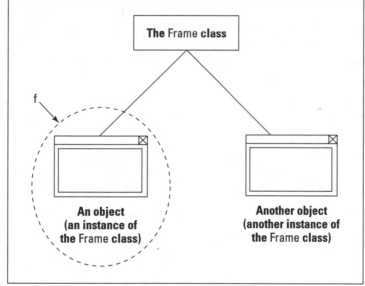

Figure 4-8:
Variable f refers to an instance of the Frame class.

The Frame **class**

f

An object (an instance of the Frame class)

Another object (another instance of the Frame class)

Creating New Values by Applying Operators

What could be more comforting than your old friend, the plus sign? It was the first thing you learned about in elementary-school math. Almost everybody knows how to add two and two. In fact, in English usage, adding two and two is a metaphor for something that's easy to do. Whenever you see a plus sign, a cell in your brain says, "Thank goodness — it could be something much more complicated."

Primitive type stew

While I'm on the subject of frames, what's a frame anyway? A frame is a window that has a certain height and width and a certain location on your computer's screen. So, deep inside the declaration of the Frame class, you can find variable declarations that look something like this:

```
int width;
int height;
int x;
int y;
```

Here's another example — a Time. An instance of the Time class may have an hour (a number from 1 to 12), a number of minutes (from 0 to 59), and a letter (*a* for a.m.; *p* for p.m.).

```
int hour;
int minutes;
char amOrPm;
```

So notice that this high and mighty thing called a Java API class is neither high nor mighty. A class is just a collection of declarations. Some of those declarations are the declarations of variables. Some of those variable declarations use primitive types, and other variable declarations use reference types. These reference types, however, come from other classes, and the declarations of those classes have variables. The chain goes on and on. Ultimately, everything comes, in one way or another, from the primitive types.

So Java has a plus sign. You can use it for several different purposes. You can use the plus sign to add two numbers, like this:

```
int apples, oranges, fruit;
apples = 5;
oranges = 16;
fruit = apples + oranges;
```

You can also use the plus sign to paste String values together:

```
String startOfChapter =
   "It's three in the morning. I'm dreaming about the "+
   "history course that I failed in high school.";
System.out.println(startOfChapter);
```

This can be handy because, in Java, you're not allowed to make a String straddle from one line to another. In other words, the following code wouldn't work at all:

```
String thisIsBadCode =
   "It's three in the morning. I'm dreaming about the
    history course that I failed in high school.";
System.out.println(thisIsBadCode);
```

The correct way to say that you're "pasting String values together" is to say that you're *concatenating* String values.

You can even use the plus sign to paste numbers next to String values.

```
int apples, oranges, fruit;
apples = 5;
oranges = 16;
fruit = apples + oranges;
System.out.println("You have " + fruit +
                     " pieces of fruit.");
```

Of course, the old minus sign is available too (but not for String values).

```
apples = fruit - oranges;
```

Use an asterisk for multiplication and a forward slash for division.

```
double rate, pay;
int hours;

rate = 6.25;
hours = 35;
pay = rate*hours;
System.out.println(pay);
```

(For an example using division, refer to Listing 4-3.)

When you divide an int value by another int value, you get an int value. The computer doesn't round. Instead, the computer chops off any remainder. If you put System.out.println(11/4) in your program, the computer prints 2, not 2.75. To get past this, make either (or both) of the numbers you're dividing double values. If you put System.out.println(11.0/4) in your program, the computer prints 2.75.

Another useful arithmetic operator is called the *remainder* operator. The symbol for the remainder operator is the percent sign (%). When you put System.out.println(11%4) in your program, the computer prints 3. It does this because, 4 goes into 11 who-cares-how-many times, with a remainder of 3. The remainder operator turns out to be fairly useful. Listing 4-7 has an example.

Listing 4-7:   Making change

```
public class MakeChange
{
   public static void main(String args[])
   {
      int quarters, dimes, nickels, cents;
      int whatsLeft, total;

      total = 248;
```

(continued)

Listing 4-7: *(continued)*

```
        quarters = total/25;
        whatsLeft = total%25;

        dimes = whatsLeft/10;
        whatsLeft = total%10;

        nickels = whatsLeft/5;
        whatsLeft = total%5;

        cents = whatsLeft;

        System.out.println("From " + total + " cents get");
        System.out.println(quarters + " quarters");
        System.out.println(dimes + " dimes");
        System.out.println(nickels + " nickels");
        System.out.println(cents + " cents");
    }
}
```

A run of the code in Listing 4-7 is shown in Figure 4-9. You start with a total of 248 cents. The statement

```
quarters = total/25;
```

divides 248 by 25, giving 9. That means you can make 9 quarters from 248 cents. Next, the statement

```
whatsLeft = total%25;
```

divides 248 by 25 again, and puts only the remainder, 23, into whatsLeft. Now you're ready for the next step, which is to take as many dimes as you can out of 23 cents.

Figure 4-9:
Change for
$2.48.

```
C:\JavaPrograms>java MakeChange
From 248 cents get
9 quarters
2 dimes
1 nickels
3 cents

C:\JavaPrograms>
```

The increment and decrement operators

Java has some neat little operators that make life easier (for the computer's processor, for your brain, and for your fingers). Altogether there are four such operators — two increment operators and two decrement operators. The increment operators add one, and the decrement operators subtract one. The increment operators use double plus signs (++), and the decrement operator uses double minus signs (-). To see how they work, you need some examples. The first example is in Figure 4-10.

A run of the program in Figure 4-10 is shown in Figure 4-11. In this horribly uneventful run, the count of bunnies is printed three times.

The double plus signs go by two different names, depending on where you put them. When you put the ++ before a variable, the ++ is called the *preincrement* operator (the *pre* stands for *before*).

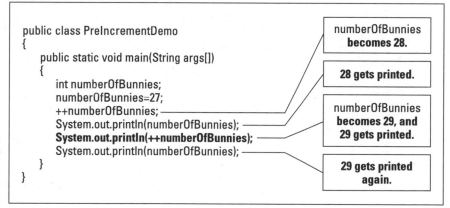

Figure 4-10:
Using pre-
increment.

Figure 4-11:
A run of the
pre-
increment
code
(the code in
Figure 4-10).

- You're putting ++ before the variable.
- The computer adds 1 to the variable's value before the variable is used in any other part of the statement.

To understand this, look at the bold line in Figure 4-10. The computer adds 1 to numberOfBunnies (raising the value of numberOfBunnies to 29), and then the computer prints 29 on the screen.

With `System.out.println(++numberOfBunnies)`, the computer adds 1 to numberOfBunnies before printing the new value of numberOfBunnies on the screen.

An alternative to preincrement is *postincrement* (the *post* stands for *after*). The word *after* has two different meanings:

- ✔ You put ++ after the variable.
- ✔ The computer adds 1 to the variable's value after the variable is used in any other part of the statement.

To see more clearly how postincrement works, look at the bold line in Figure 4-12. The computer prints the old value of numberOfBunnies (which is 28) on the screen, and then the computer adds 1 to numberOfBunnies, which raises the value of numberOfBunnies to 29.

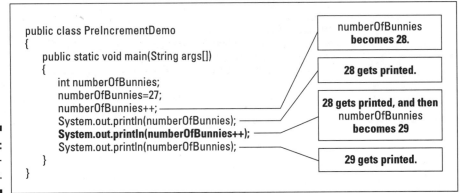

Figure 4-12: Using post-increment.

With `System.out.println(numberOfBunnies++)`, the computer adds 1 to numberOfBunnies after printing the old value that numberOfBunnies already had.

A run of the code in Figure 4-12 is shown in Figure 4-13. Compare Figure 4-13 with the run in Figure 4-11:

- ✔ With preincrement in Figure 4-11, the second number is 29.
- ✔ With postincrement in Figure 4-13, the second number is 28.

  In Figure 4-13, the number 29 doesn't show up on the screen until the end of the run, when the computer executes one last `System.out.println(numberOfBunnies)`.

Figure 4-13:
A run of
the post-
increment
code (the
code in
Figure 4-12).

```
C:\JavaPrograms>java PostIncrementDemo
28
28
29
C:\JavaPrograms>_
```

Are you trying to decide between using preincrement or postincrement? Try no longer. Most programmers use postincrement. In a typical Java program, you'll often see things like `numberOfBunnies++`. You'll seldom see things like `++numberOfBunnies`.

In addition to preincrement and postincrement, Java has two operators that use -. These operators are called *predecrement* and *postdecrement*.

- ✔ With predecrement (`-numberOfBunnies`), the computer subtracts 1 from the variable's value before the variable is used in the rest of the statement.

- ✔ With postdecrement (`numberOfBunnies-`), the computer subtracts 1 from the variable's value after the variable is used in the rest of the statement.

Instead of writing `++numberOfBunnies`, you could achieve the same effect by writing `numberOfBunnies = numberOfBunnies + 1`. So some people conclude that Java's ++ and - operators are for saving keystrokes — to keep those poor fingers from overworking themselves. This is entirely incorrect. The best reason for using ++ is to avoid the inefficient and error-prone practice of writing the same variable name, such as numberOfBunnies, twice in the same statement. If you write numberOfBunnies only once (as you do when you use ++ or -), then the computer has to figure out what numberOfBunnies means only once. On top of that, when you write numberOfBunnies only once, you have only one chance (instead of two chances) to type the variable name incorrectly. With simple expressions like `numberOfBunnies++`, these advantages hardly make a difference. But with more complicated expressions, like `inventoryItems[(quantityReceived@hy*itemsPerBox+17)]++`, the efficiency and accuracy you gain by using ++ and - is significant.

Assignment operators

If you read the preceding section, which is about operators that add 1, you may be wondering if you can manipulate these operators to add 2 or add 5 or add 1000000. Can you write `numberOfBunnies++++`, and still call yourself a Java programmer? Well, you can't. If you try it, then an error message appears when you try to compile your code.

Statements and expressions

You can describe the pre- and postincrement and decrement operators in two ways: the way everyone understands it and the right way. The way I explain it in most of this section (in terms of time, with *before* and *after)* is the way everyone understands the concept. Unfortunately, the way everyone understands the concept isn't really the right way. When you see ++ or -, you can think in terms of time sequence. But occasionally some programmer uses ++ or - in a convoluted way, and the notions of *before* and *after* break down. So, if you're ever in a tight spot, you should think about these operators in terms of statements and expressions.

First, remember that a statement tells the computer to do something, and an expression has a value. (I discuss statements in Chapter 3, and I describe expressions earlier in this chapter.) Which category does `numberOfBunnies++` belong to? The surprising answer is, both. The Java code `numberOfBunnies++` is both a statement and an expression.

Assume that, before the computer executes the code `System.out. println(numberOf Bunnies++)`, the value of numberOfBunnies is 28.

✔ As a statement, `numberOfBunnies++` tells the computer to add 1 to numberOfBunnies.

✔ As an expression, the value of `numberOfBunnies++` is 28, not 29.

So, even though the computer adds 1 to numberOfBunnies, the code `System.out. println(numberOfBunnies++)` really means `System.out.println(28)`.

Now, almost everything you just read about `numberOfBunnies++` is true about `++numberOfBunnies`. The only difference is, as an expression, `++numberOfBunnies` behaves in a more intuitive way.

✔ As a statement, `++numberOfBunnies` tells the computer to add 1 to numberOfBunnies.

✔ As an expression, the value of `++numberOfBunnies` is 29.

So, with `System.out.println(++numberOfBunnies)`, the computer adds one to the variable numberOfBunnies, and the code `System.out.println(++numberOfBunnies)` really means `System.out.println(29)`.

So what can you do? As luck would have it, Java has plenty of assignment operators you can use. With an *assignment operator,* you can add, subtract, multiply, or divide by anything you want. You can do other cool operations, too. Listing 4-8 has a smorgasbord of assignment operators (the things with equal signs). Figure 4-14 shows the output from running Listing 4-8.

Listing 4-8:   Assignment operators

```
public class UseAssignmentOperators
{
    public static void main(String args[])
    {
```

```
      int numberOfBunnies;
      int numberExtra;
      numberOfBunnies=27;
      numberExtra=53;

      numberOfBunnies += 1;
      System.out.println(numberOfBunnies);

      numberOfBunnies += 5;
      System.out.println(numberOfBunnies);

      numberOfBunnies += numberExtra;
      System.out.println(numberOfBunnies);

      numberOfBunnies *= 2;
      System.out.println(numberOfBunnies);

      System.out.println(numberOfBunnies -= 7);

      System.out.println(numberOfBunnies = 100);
   }
}
```

Figure 4-14:
A run of the code in Listing 4-8.

```
C:\JavaPrograms>java UseAssignmentOperators
28
33
66
119
112
100

C:\JavaPrograms>
```

Listing 4-8 shows how versatile Java's assignment operators are. With the assignment operators, you can add, subtract, multiply, or divide a variable by any number. Notice how += 5 adds 5 to numberOfBunnies, and how *= 2 multiplies numberOfBunnies by 2. You can even use another expression's value (in Listing 4-8, numberExtra) as the number to be applied.

The last two lines in Listing 4-8 demonstrate a special feature of Java's assignment operators. You can use an assignment operator as part of a larger Java statement. In the next to last line of Listing 4-8, the operator subtracts 7 from numberOfBunnies, decreasing the value of numberOfBunnies from 119 to 112. But then the whole assignment business is stuffed into a call to System.out.println, so the number 112 is printed on the computer screen.

Lo and behold, the last line of Listing 4-8 shows how you can do the same thing with Java's plain old equal sign. The thing that I called an assignment statement near the start of this chapter is really one of the assignment operators that I've been describing in this section. So, whenever you assign a value to something, you can make that assignment be part of a larger statement.

Each use of an assignment operator does double duty as both a statement and an expression. In all cases, the expression's value equals whatever value you assign. For example, before executing the code `System.out.println(numberOfBunnies -=7)`, the value of **numberOfBunnies** is 119. As a statement, `numberOfBunnies-=7` tells the computer to subtract 7 from numberOfBunnies (so the value of numberOfBunnies goes from 119 down to 112). As an expression, the value of `numberOfBunnies-=7` is 112. So the code `System.out.println(numberOfBunnies-=7)` really means `System.out.println(112)`. The number 112 is displayed on the computer screen. (For a richer explanation of this kind of thing, see the sidebar, "Statements and expressions," in this chapter.)

Reading and Understanding the API Documentation

Not a day goes by when someone doesn't stop me on the street and ask, "How do you make sense of Java's API documentation?" Well, reading the documentation is an art, not a science. Even so, the tips in this section can make your life easier.

You can find things in the API in a number of different ways. (Each way is convenient in one situation or another.) In several of this chapter's listings, I call the System.out.println method. To illustrate the lookup process, I explain how to find println in Java's API docs (the steps explain two ways of looking up stuff).

Here's how to find something by using the index:

1. **Download Sun's Java API documentation.**

   For more help on downloading the documentation, see the first section of Chapter 2.

2. **Open to the front page of the documentation.**

   When you download the documentation, you get several directories. In the top-level directory is a file named `index.html`. Visit this file with your Web browser.

3. **Click the <u>API & Language</u> link, which is near the top of the front page (see Figure 4-15).**

   This takes you farther down on the same Web page.

4. **Click the <u>Java 2 Platform API Specification</u> link (see Figure 4-16).**

   The browser transports you to the start of the API pages, which are shown in Figure 4-17.

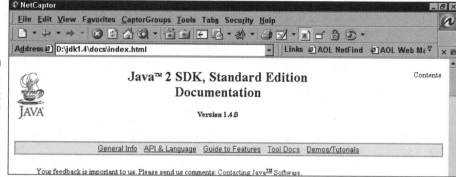

Figure 4-15:
The front
page of
Sun's
documen-
tation.

Figure 4-16:
A link to the
API specifi-
cation.

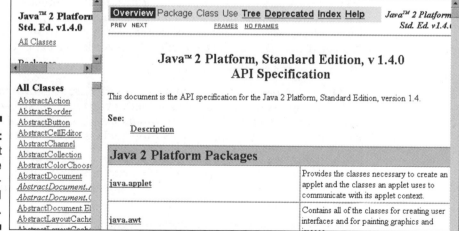

Figure 4-17:
The start
of the
documen-
tation's API
pages.

5. Click the Index link at the top of the page to open the index, as shown in Figure 4-18.

A list of letters is near the top of the index. Click the P to go to the section with println in it.

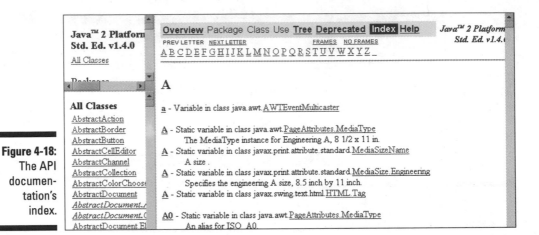

Figure 4-18:
The API
documen-
tation's
index.

6. **In the P section, do a search for *println* to find the println entries.**

   Most Web browsers let you search for something like *println* in the text of a page. First, make sure the browser knows that you want to search the big frame that takes up most of the page (and not the smaller frames on the left side of the screen). To do this, click anywhere inside the big frame. (You don't have to click a link. Clicking the white area does the trick.) Next, open the browser's Find box. On most browsers, pressing Ctrl+F coaxes the Find box out of hiding. When you see the Find box, type **println** in the text box and click the box's Find Next button.

7. **Pick one of the println entries.**

   The P section has a big boatload of println entries, as shown in Figure 4-19. The entries differ from one another in two ways. First, each entry says *println(int), println(String),* or *println(someOtherTypeName).* Next, each entry says that println is a method in class *java.io.blabity-blah-blah.*

   At this point, it pays to poke around. If you're trying to print something like *"Hello world!",* you want one of the println(String) entries. On the other hand, if you're trying to print the value of amountInAccount, you'll probably choose a println(double) entry.

   Now, suppose you've decided on println(String). You can choose from three println(String) entries. One says it's a method in class java.io. PrintStream, the next is a method in class java.io.PrintWriter, and the third is a method in class java.sql.DriverManager. Which of these three entries do you choose? Well, what you're really trying to call is something named *System.out.println.* If you go through the whole lookup rigmarole with System.out, you'll find that System.out has type PrintStream. (See Figure 4-20.) So the entry you decide to choose is *println(String) - Method in class java.io.PrintStream.*

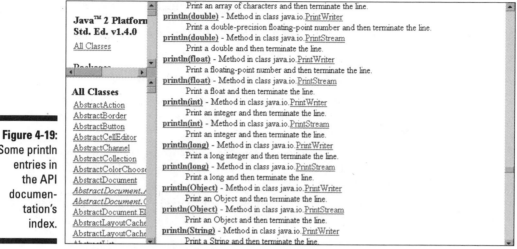

Figure 4-19:
Some println
entries in
the API
documen-
tation's
index.

Figure 4-20:
The out
variable has
type
PrintStream.

8. Click the link for the entry that you've chosen.

When you click the <u>println(String)</u> link, the browser takes you to a page
that explains a println method, as shown in Figure 4-21. The page tells
you what println does ("Print a String and then . . . .") and points to
other useful pages, like the page with the documentation for String.

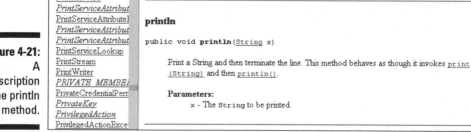

Figure 4-21:
A
description
of the println
method.

Here's how to find an entry in the API by starting in the list of classes:

1. **Navigate to the start of the documentation's API pages.**

   To do this, follow the first three steps listed above.

2. **Find the page that documents the System class.**

   You're looking for documentation that explains System.out.println. You start by looking up *System,* work your way to *out,* and from there work your way to *println.*

   To find a link to System, look in the lower frame on the left side of the page. (See Figure 4-22.) For hints on finding text on the page, see Step 6 in the previous set of steps.

   Clicking the <u>System</u> link makes your browser display the documentation page for the System class. (See Figure 4-23.)

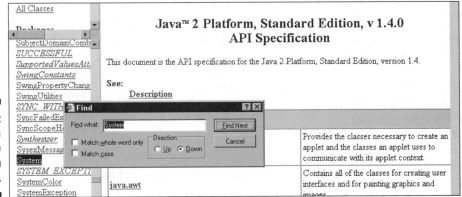

Figure 4-22: Finding a link to the System class.

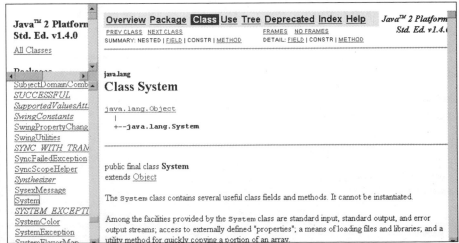

Figure 4-23: The System class's documentation.

3. **On the documentation page for the System class, find the out variable.**

   If you use your Web browser's Find box, you have to click the Find Next button several times. (The word *out* is so common, it appears several times in several different contexts on the System documentation page.) When you've found what you're looking for, you see a table like the one in Figure 4-20.

4. **In the table's out row, click the <u>PrintStream</u> link.**

   According to the documentation, the out variable refers to an object of type PrintStream. This means that println is part of the PrintStream class. That's why you're clicking the <u>PrintStream</u> link.

5. **On the documentation page for PrintStream, find *println(String)*.**

   You see an explanation like the one shown in Figure 4-21.

After following the steps in this section, you may be tempted to say, "Big deal, I can find println in the API docs, but I probably can't find anything else. And if people create documentation for stuff that they program on their own, I'm up a creek." And my response is "Nonsense!" Most of the tricks you need for finding things in the Java documentation are illustrated in this section's step-by-step instructions. (As you learn more about Java and the relationships among classes, methods, and variables, these instructions will feel much more natural.)

As for reading other people's documentation, you can scratch that problem right off your list. The official API docs weren't typed by hand. They were generated automatically from actual Java program code. In the code for `PrintStream.java` are a few extra lines that look something like this:

```
/**
 * Print a String and then terminate the line.
 * This method behaves as though it invokes
 * <code>{@link #print(String)}</code>
 * and then <code>{@link #println()}</code>.
 *
 * @param x  The <code>String</code> to be printed.
 */
```

To create the API documentation, the folks from Sun Microsystems ran a program called *javadoc*. The javadoc program took lines like these right out of the `PrintStream.java` file and used the lines to make the documentation that you see in your Web browser.

Other Java programmers — people who don't work for Sun Microsystems — do the same thing. In fact, everyone who writes Java code uses the javadoc program to generate documentation. So everyone's Java documentation looks like everyone else's Java documentation. When you know how to read the standard API documentation, you know how to read any old Joe's home-grown Java docs.

And yes, you can use the javadoc program. When you download the Java SDK (see Chapter 2 for the details), you get javadoc as part of the deal. Although this book doesn't tell you how to use javadoc, you can experiment and create your own nice-looking documentation.

Chapter 5

Controlling Program Flow with Decision-Making Statements

· ·

In This Chapter

▶ Writing statements that choose between alternatives

▶ Putting statements inside one another

▶ Choosing among many alternatives

· ·

*T*he TV show *Dennis the Menace* aired on CBS from 1959 to 1963. I remember one episode in which Mr. Wilson was having trouble making an important decision. I think it was something about changing jobs or moving to a new town. Anyway, I can still see that shot of Mr. Wilson sitting in his yard, sipping lemonade, and staring into nowhere for the whole afternoon. Of course, the annoying character Dennis was constantly interrupting Mr. Wilson's peace and quiet. That's what made this situation funny.

What impressed me about this episode (the reason why I remember it so clearly even now) was Mr. Wilson's dogged intent in making the decision. This guy wasn't going about his everyday business, roaming around the neighborhood, while thoughts about the decision wandered in and out of his mind. He was sitting quietly in his yard, making marks carefully and logically on his mental balance sheet. How many people actually make decisions this way?

At that time, I was still pretty young. I'd never faced the responsibility of having to make a big decision that affected my family and me. But I wondered what such a decision-making process would be like. Would it help to sit there like a stump for hours on end? Would I make my decisions by the careful weighing and tallying of options? Or would I shoot in the dark, take risks, and act on impulse? Only time would tell.

Making Decisions (Java if Statements)

When you're writing computer programs, you're constantly hitting forks in roads. Did the user correctly type his or her password? If yes, then let the user work; if no, then kick the bum out. So the Java programming language needs a way of making a program branch in one of two directions. Fortunately, the language has a way. It's called an *if statement*.

Guess the number

The use of an if statement is illustrated in Listing 5-1. Two runs of the program in Listing 5-1 are shown in Figure 5-1.

Listing 5-1: A guessing game

```
public class GuessingGame
{

    public static void main(String args[])
    {
        int inputNumber;
        System.out.print("Enter an int from 1 to 10: ");
        inputNumber=DummiesIO.getInt();

        int randomNumber=DummiesRandom.getInt();

        if(inputNumber==randomNumber)
            System.out.println("You win.");
        else
            System.out.println("You lose.");

        System.out.print("The random number was ");
        System.out.println(randomNumber + ".");
    }
}
```

Figure 5-1:
Two runs
of the
guessing
game.

```
C:\JavaPrograms>java GuessingGame
Enter an int from 1 to 10: 2
You win.
The random number was 2.

C:\JavaPrograms>java GuessingGame
Enter an int from 1 to 10: 4
You lose.
The random number was 3.

C:\JavaPrograms>
```

The program in Listing 5-1 plays a guessing game with the user. The program gets a number (a guess) from the user and then generates a random number between 1 and 10. If the number the user entered is the same as the random number, the user wins. Otherwise, the user loses. In either case, the program tells the user what the random number was.

Using the prewritten Dummies methods

The program in Listing 5-1 uses two methods that aren't in the standard Java API. I wrote these two methods, DummiesIO.getInt and DummiesRandom.getInt, just for this book. I won't bother you with the inner details of these two methods, but you can see the details if you want. The files `DummiesIO.java` and `DummiesRandom.java` are on this book's CD-ROM. (Even so, you may want to wait until you've read Chapters 7 and 10 before you take a look at these two files.) One way or another, DummiesIO.getInt gets a number from the user (via the user's keyboard), and the other method, DummiesRandom.getInt, generates a random number between 1 and 10 (inclusive).

Before attempting to run any of the code from this chapter, you should copy `DummiesIO.java` and `DummiesRandom.java` from the book's CD-ROM to your computer's JavaPrograms directory.

Good programmers use prewritten classes and methods without looking at the Java program code. They don't do it this way because they're lazy. They do it because the details inside prewritten code should be hidden from everyone, even from the programmer who uses things defined in the prewritten code. Good programming practice dictates that prewritten code should be treated like a black box.

The if statement

At the core of Listing 5-1 is a Java if statement. This if statement represents a fork in the road. (See Figure 5-2.) The computer follows one of two prongs — the prong that prints You win or the prong that prints You lose. The computer decides which prong to take by testing the truth or falsehood of a *condition*. In Listing 5-1, the condition being tested is

```
inputNumber==randomNumber
```

Does the value of inputNumber equal the value of randomNumber? When the condition is true, the computer does the stuff between the condition and the word *else*. When the condition turns out to be false, the computer does the stuff after the word *else*. Either way, the computer goes on to execute the last two print calls — the statements starting with The random number was.

The condition in an if statement must be enclosed in parentheses. However, a line like `if(inputNumber==randomNumber)` is not a complete statement, so this line should not end with a semicolon.

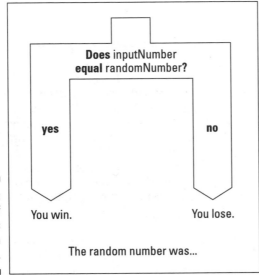

Figure 5-2:
An if
statement is
like a fork in
the road.

Does inputNumber
equal randomNumber?

yes

no

You win.

You lose.

The random number was...

Sometimes, when I'm writing about a condition that's being tested, I slip into using the word *expression* instead of *condition*. That's okay, because every condition is an expression. An expression is something that has a value and, sure enough, every condition has a value. The condition's value is either true or false. (For revealing information about expressions, and values like true and false, see Chapter 4.)

The double equal sign

In Listing 5-1, in the if statement's condition, notice the use of the double equal sign. Comparing two numbers to see if they're the same is not the same as setting something equal to something else. That's why the symbol to compare for equality is not the same as the symbol used in an assignment statement. In an if statement's condition, you can't replace the double equal sign with a single equal sign. If you do, your program just won't work. (You'll almost always get an error message when you try to compile your code.)

On the other hand, if you never make the mistake of using a single equal sign in a condition, then you're not normal. Not long ago, while I was teaching an introductory Java course, I promised that I'd swallow my laser pointer if no one made the single equal sign mistake during any of the lab sessions. This wasn't an idle promise. I knew I'd never have to keep it. As it turned out, even if I had ignored the first ten times anybody made the single equal sign mistake during those lab sessions, I would still be laser-pointer-free. Everybody mistakenly uses the single equal sign several times in his or her programming career. The trick is not to avoid making the mistake; the trick is to catch the mistake whenever you make it.

Indenting if statements in your code

Notice how, in Listing 5-1, the println calls inside the if statement are indented. (This includes both the "You win" and "You lose" statements. The "You lose" that comes after the word *else* is still part of the if statement.) Strictly speaking, you don't have to indent the statements that are inside an if statement. For all the compiler cares, you can write your whole program on a single line or place all your statements in an artful, misshapen zigzag. The problem is that if you don't indent your statements in some logical fashion, then neither you nor anyone else can make sense of your code. In Listing 5-1, the indenting of the "You win" and "You lose" statements helps your eye (and brain) see quickly that these statements are subordinate to the overall if/else flow.

In a small program, unindented or poorly indented code is barely tolerable. But in a complicated program, indentation that doesn't follow a neat, logical pattern is a big, ugly nightmare.

Always indent your code to make the program's flow apparent at a glance.

Elseless in Ifghanistan

Okay, so the title of this section is contrived. Big deal! The idea is that you can create an if statement without the else part. Take, for instance, the code in Listing 5-1. Maybe you'd rather not rub it in whenever the user loses the game. The modified code in Listing 5-2 shows you how to do this (and Figure 5-3 shows you the result).

Listing 5-2:   A kinder, gentler guessing game

```
public class DontTellThemTheyLost
{

    public static void main(String args[])
    {
        int inputNumber;
        System.out.print("Enter an int from 1 to 10: ");
        inputNumber=DummiesIO.getInt();

        int randomNumber=DummiesRandom.getInt();

        if(inputNumber==randomNumber)
            System.out.println("You win.");

        System.out.println("That was a very good guess :-)");
        System.out.print("The random number was ");
        System.out.println(randomNumber + ".");
    }
}
```

Figure 5-3:
Two runs of
the game in
Listing 5-2.

```
C:\JavaPrograms>java DontTellThemTheyLost
Enter an int from 1 to 10: 4
You win.
That was a very good guess :-)
The random number was 4.

C:\JavaPrograms>java DontTellThemTheyLost
Enter an int from 1 to 10: 4
That was a very good guess :-)
The random number was 10.

C:\JavaPrograms>_
```

The if statement in Listing 5-2 has no else part. When inputNumber is the same as randomNumber, the computer prints You win. When inputNumber is different from randomNumber, the computer doesn't print You win.

Packing more stuff into an if statement

Look at the program runs in Figure 5-1. Notice how the program reports its random number no matter what the outcome of the game happens to be. In the second run, the computer informs the user that the random number is 1, not 4. This proves to the user that his or her guess is wrong. But in the first of the two runs, such proof isn't necessary. A user who has already won doesn't need any extra convincing. Also, whenever the user wins, the user knows that the random number is the same as his or her input.

So, I want to slim down the guessing game program. In particular, I want the printing of The random number was . . . . to take place only when the user guesses the wrong number. The 12-step diet for the guessing game program is shown in Listing 5-3. Two runs of the program in Listing 5-3 are shown in Figure 5-4.

Listing 5-3:   An improved guessing game

```
public class BetterGuessingGame
{

    public static void main(String args[])
    {
        int inputNumber;
        System.out.print("Enter an int from 1 to 10: ");
        inputNumber=DummiesIO.getInt();

        int randomNumber=DummiesRandom.getInt();

        if(inputNumber==randomNumber)
            System.out.println("You win.");
        else
        {
            System.out.println("You lose.");
            System.out.print("The random number was ");
            System.out.println(randomNumber + ".");
        }
    }
}
```

Figure 5-4:
Two runs
of the
improved
guessing
game.

```
C:\JavaPrograms>java BetterGuessingGame
Enter an int from 1 to 10: 7
You win.
C:\JavaPrograms>java BetterGuessingGame
Enter an int from 1 to 10: 7
You lose.
The random number was 5.
C:\JavaPrograms>
```

The code in Listing 5-3 is very much like its counterpart in Listing 5-1. The big difference is in the else part of the if statement. In Listing 5-3, the else part seems to have more than one statement in it. You make this happen by enclosing the three statements of the else part in a pair of curly braces. The curly braces turn the forking situation from the one shown in Figure 5-2 to the one shown in Figure 5-5. With the curly braces, the program's last three calls to print and println are tucked away safely inside the if statement's else part. With the curly braces, the words The random number was . . . . are displayed only when the user's guess is wrong.

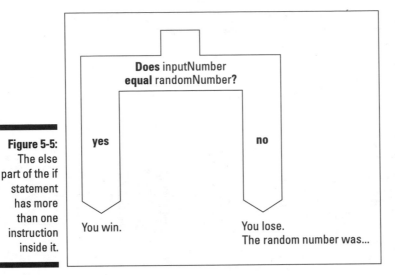

Figure 5-5:
The else
part of the if
statement
has more
than one
instruction
inside it.

The rule for curly braces applies to the top part (as well as the else part) of an if statement. Whenever you have several things to do in response to a true condition, you put those things in curly braces. Listing 5-4 has an example.

In Listing 5-4, whenever inputNumber equals randomNumber, the computer executes three println calls. To convince the computer that all three of these calls are inside the if statement, you enclose these three calls in a pair of curly braces. Two runs of the game in Listing 5-4 are shown in Figure 5-6.

Listing 5-4:   Yet another guessing game

```
public class FancyGuessingGame
{

    public static void main(String args[])
    {
        int inputNumber;
        System.out.print("Enter an int from 1 to 10: ");
        inputNumber=DummiesIO.getInt();

        int randomNumber=DummiesRandom.getInt();

        if(inputNumber==randomNumber)
        {
            System.out.println("**********");
            System.out.println("*You win.*");
            System.out.println("**********");
        }
```

```
        else
        {
            System.out.println("You lose.");
            System.out.print("The random number was ");
            System.out.println(randomNumber + ".");
        }
    }
}
```

Figure 5-6:
Two runs of
the game in
Listing 5-4.

```
C:\JavaPrograms>java FancyGuessingGame
Enter an int from 1 to 10: 8
You lose.
The random number was 3.

C:\JavaPrograms>java FancyGuessingGame
Enter an int from 1 to 10: 8
**********
*You win.*
**********

C:\JavaPrograms>
```

Statements and blocks

There's an elegant way to think about the rule for curly braces in if statements. Just remember that you can put only one statement inside each part of an if statement.

```
if (condition)
    statement
else
    statement
```

On first reading of this one-statement rule, you're probably thinking that a misprint is somewhere. After all, in Listing 5-4, three statements are inside each part of the if statement. Right?

Well, no, three statements aren't really inside each part of that if statement. Technically, Listing 5-4 has only one statement between the if and the else, and only one statement after the else. The trick is, when you surround a bunch of statements inside curly braces, you get what's called a *block*, and a block behaves, in all respects, like a single statement. In fact, the official Java documentation lists blocks as one

of the many kinds of statements. So, in Listing 5-4, the block

```
{
    System.out.println("You
    lose.");
    System.out.print("The random
    number was ");
    System.out.println(randomNu
    mber + ".");
}
```

is a single statement. It's a statement that has, within it, three smaller statements. So this big block, this single statement, is the one statement that's inside the else part of the if statement.

That's how the one-statement rule works. In an if statement, when you want the computer to execute several statements, you combine those statements into one big statement. To do this, you make a block by using curly braces.

More variations on the if statement theme

Are there times, in an if statement, when you can't use curly braces? No, not really. You can use braces even when you have only one statement to execute. Listing 5-5 has an example.

Listing 5-5: I'm tired of playing guessing games

```java
public class SimpleGuessingGame
{

    public static void main(String args[])
    {
        int inputNumber;
        System.out.print("Enter an int from 1 to 10: ");
        inputNumber=DummiesIO.getInt();

        int randomNumber=DummiesRandom.getInt();

        if(inputNumber==randomNumber)
        {
            System.out.println("You win.");
        }
        else
        {
            System.out.println("You lose.");
        }
    }
}
```

The if statement in Listing 5-5 works with or without its curly braces. If you want to write concise code, don't include the braces. On the other hand, nothing is wrong with less-than-concise code. Lots of wide-open spaces can make your code easier to read. By adding extra stuff to the if statement in Listing 5-5, you're bracing yourself for the possibility of adding more statements inside the if statement at a later time.

When you write if statements, you may be tempted to chuck all the rules about curly braces out the window and just rely on indentation. Unfortunately, this seldom works. If you indent five statements after the word *else* and forget to enclose those statements in curly braces, then the computer thinks that the else part includes only the first of the five statements. What's worse, the indentation misleads you into believing that the else part includes all five statements. This makes it more difficult for you to figure out why your code isn't behaving the way you think it should behave. So watch those braces!

Forming Conditions with Comparisons and Logical Operators

The Java programming language has plenty of little squiggles and doodads for all your condition-forming needs. This section tells you all about them.

Comparing numbers; comparing characters

Table 5-1 shows you the operators that you can use to compare things with one another.

Table 5-1	Comparison Operators	
Operator Symbol	*Meaning*	*Example*
==	is equal to	numberOfCows==5
!=	is not equal to	buttonClicked != panicButton
<	is less than	numberOfCows<5
>	is greater than	myInitial>'B'
<=	is less than or equal to	numberOfCows<=5
>=	is greater than or equal to	myInitial>='B'

You can use all of Java's comparison operators to compare numbers and characters. When you compare numbers, things go pretty much the way you think they should go. But, when you compare characters, things are a little strange. Comparing uppercase letters with one another is no problem. Because the letter *B* comes alphabetically before *H,* the condition 'B' < 'H' is true. Comparing lowercase letters with one another is also okay. What's strange is that, when you compare an uppercase letter with a lowercase letter, the uppercase letter is always smaller. So, even though 'Z' < 'A' is false, 'Z' < 'a' is true.

Under the hood, the letters *A* through *Z* are stored with numeric codes 65 through 90. The letters *a* through *z* are stored with codes 97 through 122. That's why each uppercase letter is "smaller than" each lowercase letter.

Be careful when you compare two numbers for equality (with ==) or inequality (with !=). After doing some calculations and obtaining two double values or two float values, the values you have are seldom dead-on equal to one another. (The problem comes from those pesky digits beyond the decimal point.) For instance, the Fahrenheit equivalent of 21 degrees Celsius is 69.8, and when you calculate 9.0/5*21+32 by hand, you get 69.8. But the condition 9.0/5*21+32==69.8 turns out to be false. That's because, when the computer calculates 9.0/5*21+32, it gets 69.80000000000001, not 69.8.

Comparing objects

When you start working with objects, you'll find that you can use == and != to compare objects with one another. For instance, a button that you see on the computer screen is an object. In Bonus Chapter A (on the CD), you ask if the thing that was just mouse-clicked is a particular button on your screen. You do this with Java's equality operator.

```
if (e.getSource() == bCopy) {
    clipboard.setText(which.getText());
```

The big gotcha with Java's comparison scheme comes when you compare two strings. (For a word or two about Java's String type, see the section about reference types in Chapter 4.) When you compare two strings with one another, you don't want to use the double equal sign. Using the double equal sign would ask, "Is this string stored in exactly the same place in memory as that other string?" That's usually not what you want to ask. Instead, you usually want to ask, "Does this string have the same characters in it as that other string?" To ask the second question (the more appropriate question) Java's String type has a method named *equals*. (Like everything else in the known universe, this equals method is defined in the Java API.) The equals method compares two strings to see if they have the same characters in them. For an example using Java's equals method, see Listing 5-6. (A run of the program in Listing 5-6 is shown in Figure 5-7.)

Listing 5-6:   Checking a password

```
public class CheckPassword
{
    public static void main(String args[])
    {

        System.out.print("What's the password? ");
        String password=DummiesIO.getString();
        System.out.println("You typed >>" + password + "<<");
        System.out.println();

        if (password=="swordfish")
        {
```

```
                System.out.println("The word you typed is stored");
                System.out.println("in the same place as the real");
                System.out.println("password. You must be a");
                System.out.println("hacker.");
            }
            else
            {
                System.out.println("The word you typed is not");
                System.out.println("stored in the same place as");
                System.out.println("the real password, but that's");
                System.out.println("no big deal.");
            }
            System.out.println();

            if (password.equals("swordfish"))
            {
                System.out.println("The word you typed has the");
                System.out.println("same characters as the real");
                System.out.println("password. You can use our");
                System.out.println("precious system.");
            }
            else
            {
                System.out.println("The word you typed doesn't");
                System.out.println("have the same characters as");
                System.out.println("the real password. You can't");
                System.out.println("use our precious system.");
            }
        }
    }
```

Figure 5-7:
The result of
using ==
and using
Java's
equals
method.

```
C:\JavaPrograms>java CheckPassword
What's the password? swordfish
You typed >>swordfish<<

The word you typed is not
stored in the same place as
the real password, but that's
no big deal.

The word you typed has the
same characters as the real
password. You can use our
precious system.

C:\JavaPrograms>
```

The equals method looks funny when you call it, because you put a dot after
one string and put the other string in parentheses. But that's the way you
have to do it.

In calling Java's equals method, it doesn't matter which string gets the dot
and which gets the parentheses. For instance, in Listing 5-6, you could have
written

```
if ("swordfish".equals(password))
```

The method would work just as well.

A call to Java's equals method looks imbalanced, but it's not. There's a reason behind the apparent imbalance between the dot and the parentheses. The idea is, you have two objects: the password object and the `"swordfish"` object. Each of these two objects is of type String. (However, password is a variable of type String, `"swordfish"` is a String literal.) When you write `password.equals("swordfish")`, you're calling an equals method that belongs to the password object. As you call that method, you're feeding `"swordfish"` to the method as the method's parameter (pun intended). You can read more about this kind of thing in Chapter 7.

When comparing strings with one another, use the equals method, not the double equal sign.

Java's logical operators

Mr. Spock would be pleased. Java has all the operators you need for mixing and matching logical tests. The operators are shown in Table 5-2.

Table 5-2		Logical Operators
Operator Symbol	*Meaning*	*Example*
&&	and	5 < x && x < 10
||	or	x < 5 || 10 < x
!	not	!password.equals("swordfish")

You can use these operators to form all kinds of elaborate conditions. Listing 5-7 has an example.

Listing 5-7: Checking username and password

```
public class Authenticator
{
    public static void main(String args[])
    {
        System.out.print("Username: ");
        String username=DummiesIO.getString();
        System.out.print("Password: ");
        String password=DummiesIO.getString();

        if (
            (username.equals("bburd") &&
             password.equals("swordfish")) ||
```

```
            (username.equals("hritter") &&
             password.equals("preakston"))
        )
            System.out.println("You're in.");
        else
            System.out.println("You're suspicious.");
    }
}
```

Some runs of the program of Listing 5-7 are shown in Figure 5-8. When the username is *bburd* and the password is *swordfish* or when the username is *hritter* and the password is *preakston,* then the user gets a nice message. Otherwise, the user is a bum who gets the nasty message that he or she deserves.

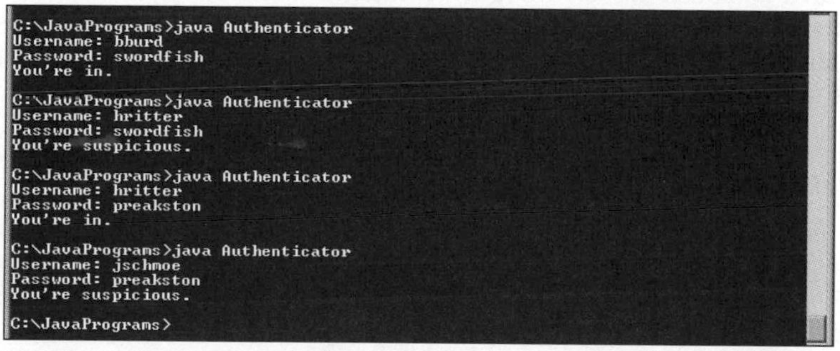

Figure 5-8: Using logical operators.

```
C:\JavaPrograms>java Authenticator
Username: bburd
Password: swordfish
You're in.

C:\JavaPrograms>java Authenticator
Username: hritter
Password: swordfish
You're suspicious.

C:\JavaPrograms>java Authenticator
Username: hritter
Password: preakston
You're in.

C:\JavaPrograms>java Authenticator
Username: jschmoe
Password: preakston
You're suspicious.

C:\JavaPrograms>
```

Keep an eye on those parentheses! When you're combining comparisons with logical operators, it's better to waste typing effort and add unneeded parentheses than to goof up your result by using too few parentheses. Take, for example, the expression

```
2<5 || 100<6 && 27<1
```

By misreading this expression, you may come to the conclusion that the expression is false. That is, you could wrongly read the expression as meaning (something-or-other) && 27<1. Because 27<1 is false, you would conclude that the whole expression is false. The fact is that, in Java, any && operator is evaluated before any || operator. So the expression really asks if 2<5 || (something-or-other). Because 2<5 is true, the whole expression is true.

To change the expression's value from true to false, you can put the expression's first two comparisons in parentheses, like this:

```
(2<5 || 100<6) && 27<1
```

Java's || operator is *inclusive*. This means that you get true whenever the thing on the left side is true, the thing on the right side is true, or both things are true. For instance, the expression 2<10 || 20<30 is true.

In Java, you can't combine comparisons the way you do in ordinary English. In English, you may say, "We'll have between three and ten people at the dinner table." But in Java, you get an error message if you write 3 <= people <= 10. To do this comparison, you need something like 3<=people && people<=10.

Building a Nest

Have you seen those cute Russian Matryoshka nesting dolls? Open up one, and another one is inside. Open up the other, and a third one is inside it. You can do the same thing with Java's if statements. (Talk about fun!) Listing 5-8 shows you how.

Listing 5-8:   Nested if statements

```
public class Authenticator2
{
    public static void main(String args[])
    {
        System.out.print("Username: ");
        String username=DummiesIO.getString();

        if (username.equals("bburd"))
        {
            System.out.print("Password: ");
            String password=DummiesIO.getString();
            if (password.equals("swordfish"))
                System.out.println("You're in.");
            else
                System.out.println("Incorrect password");
        }
        else
            System.out.println("Unknown user");
    }
}
```

Figure 5-9 shows several runs of the code in Listing 5-8. The main idea is that, to log on, you have to pass two tests. (In other words, two conditions must be true.) The first condition tests for a valid username; the second condition tests for the correct password. If you pass the first test (the username test), you march right into another if statement that performs a second test (the password test). If you fail the first test, then you never make it to the second test. The overall plan is shown in Figure 5-10.

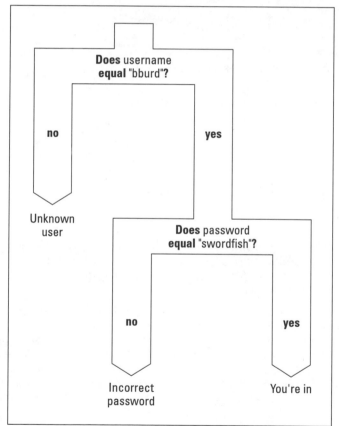

```
C:\JavaPrograms>java Authenticator2
Username: bburd
Password: swordfish
You're in.

C:\JavaPrograms>java Authenticator2
Username: bburd
Password: catfish
Incorrect password

C:\JavaPrograms>java Authenticator2
Username: jschmoe
Unknown user

C:\JavaPrograms>_
```

Figure 5-9:
Authenti-
cating a
user.

Does username
equal "bburd"?

no

yes

Unknown
user

Does password
equal "swordfish"?

no

yes

Figure 5-10:
Don't try
eating with
this fork.

Incorrect
password

You're in

The code in Listing 5-8 does a good job with nested if statements, but it does a terrible job with real-world user authentication. First of all, you should never show a password in plain view (without asterisks to masquerade the password). Second, you don't handle passwords without encrypting them. Third, you don't tell the malicious user which of the two words (the user-name or the password) was entered incorrectly. Fourth . . . well I could go on and on. The code in Listing 5-8 just isn't meant to illustrate good username/password practices.

Excuse me, but your else is dangling

You can play all kinds of games with nested if statements. Most of the time, these games are fun, harmless, and even useful. Once in a while, they get you into trouble. Take, for instance, the rule that you can have an if statement with no else part. If you use that rule in conjunction with nested if statements, you can get the following (very bad) code:

```java
public class ADangleForReflection
{
    public static void main(String args[])
    {
        System.out.print("Username: ");
        String username=DummiesIO.getString();
        System.out.print("Password: ");
        String password=DummiesIO.getString();

        if (username.equals("bburd"))
            if (password.equals("swordfish"))
                System.out.println("You're in.");
        else
            System.out.println("Try again.");
    }
}
```

The trick questions are, what happens when the user types **jschmoe** instead of **bburd**, and what happens when the user types **bburd** with password **catfish**? If you fall into my clever little trap, you'll answer the questions incorrectly. (To answer incorrectly, say, "jschmoe gets `Try again`, and bburd with catfish gets no response.")

The fact is that an else becomes very lonely when it doesn't have an if. The else becomes so lonely that it latches onto the nearest if that doesn't already have a steady elsefriend. (As Becky Huehls, the very perceptive copy editor, says, "No if is an island unto its else.") In the code shown above, the desperate else associates itself with the very nearest if — the if that checks whether the password is equal to `"swordfish"`. So the indentation in the code is misleading. (And remember, the computer completely ignores your indentation.) The more informative indentation would look like this:

```java
if (username.equals("bburd"))
    if (password.equals("swordfish"))
        System.out.println("You're in.");
    else
        System.out.println("Try again.");
```

Now, the code is clearer. Everything is dependent on the username being `"bburd"`. When a user types **jschmoe** instead of **bburd**, the user gets no response. But, when a user types **bburd**, the user is destined to get a response. If the user types **bburd** for the username and **catfish** for the password, the computer displays the message, `Try again`.

This situation, in which an else is forced to roam the streets looking for an available if, is called the *dangling else problem.*

Choosing among Many Alternatives (Java switch Statements)

I'm the first to admit that I hate making decisions. If things go wrong, I would rather have the problem be someone else's fault. Writing the last several sections (on making decisions with Java's if statement) knocked the stuffing right out of me. That's why my mind boggles as I begin this section on choosing among many alternatives. What a relief it is to have that confession out of the way!

Your basic switch statement

Now, it's time to explore situations in which you have a decision with many branches. Take, for instance, the popular campfire song "Al's All Wet." (For a review of the lyrics, see the sidebar.) You're eager to write code that prints this song's lyrics. Fortunately, you don't have to type all the words over and over again. Instead, you can take advantage of the repetition in the lyrics.

"Al's All Wet"

Sung to the tune of "Gentille Alouette":

Al's all wet. Oh, why is Al all wet? Oh,
Al's all wet 'cause he's standing in the rain.
Why is Al out in the rain?
That's because he has no brain.
Has no brain, has no brain,
In the rain, in the rain.
Ohhhhhhhh. . . .

Al's all wet. Oh, why is Al all wet? Oh,
Al's all wet 'cause he's standing in the rain.
Why is Al out in the rain?
That's because he is a pain.
He's a pain, he's a pain,
Has no brain, has no brain,
In the rain, in the rain.
Ohhhhhhhh. . . .

Al's all wet. Oh, why is Al all wet? Oh,
Al's all wet 'cause he's standing in the rain.
Why is Al out in the rain?
'Cause this is the last refrain.
Last refrain, last refrain,
He's a pain, he's a pain,
Has no brain, has no brain,
In the rain, in the rain.
Ohhhhhhhh. . . .

Al's all wet. Oh, why is Al all wet? Oh,
Al's all wet 'cause he's standing in the rain.

–Harriet Ritter and Barry Burd

A complete program to display the "Al's All Wet" lyrics won't come until Chapter 6. In the meantime, assume that you have a variable named *verse*. The value of verse is 1, 2, 3, or 4, depending on which verse of "Al's All Wet" that you're trying to print. You could have a big, clumsy bunch of if statements that checks each possible verse number.

```
if (verse==1)
    System.out.println("That's because he has no brain.");
if (verse==2)
    System.out.println("That's because he is a pain.");
if (verse==3)
    System.out.println("'Cause this is the last refrain.");
```

But that approach seems wasteful. Why not create a statement that checks the value of verse just once and then takes an action based on the value that it finds? Fortunately, there's just such a statement. It's called a *switch* statement. Listing 5-9 has an example of a switch statement.

Listing 5-9: A switch statement

```
public class JustSwitchIt
{
    public static void main(String args[])
    {
        System.out.print("Which verse? ");
        int verse = DummiesIO.getInt();

        switch (verse)
        {
            case 1:  System.out.println
                        ("That's because he has no brain.");
                     break;
            case 2:  System.out.println
                        ("That's because he is a pain.");
                     break;
            case 3:  System.out.println
                        ("'Cause this is the last refrain.");
                     break;
            default: System.out.println("Nothing to print");
                     break;
        }

        System.out.println("This program is finished.");
    }

}
```

Figure 5-11 shows two runs of the program in Listing 5-9. (The overall idea behind the program is illustrated in Figure 5-12.) First, the user types a number, like the number 2. Then, execution of the program reaches the top of the switch statement. The computer checks the value of the verse variable.

When the computer determines that verse's value is 2, the computer checks each case of the switch statement. The value 2 doesn't match the topmost case, so the computer proceeds on to the middle of the three cases. The value posted for the middle case (the number 2) matches the value of the verse variable, so the computer executes the statements that come immediately after case 2. These two statements are

```
System.out.println("That's because he is a pain.");
break;
```

The first of the two statements displays the line That's because he is a pain on the screen. The second statement is called a *break* statement. (What a surprise!) When the computer encounters a break statement, the computer jumps out of whatever switch statement it's in. So, in Listing 5-9, the computer skips right past the case that would display 'Cause this is the last refrain. In fact, the computer jumps out of the entire switch and goes straight to the statement just after the end of the switch. The computer displays This program is finished, because that's what the statement after the switch tells the computer to do.

Figure 5-11:
Running the code of Listing 5-9.

```
C:\JavaPrograms>java JustSwitchIt
Which verse? 2
That's because he is a pain.
This program is finished.

C:\JavaPrograms>java JustSwitchIt
Which verse? 6
Nothing to print
This program is finished.

C:\JavaPrograms>_
```

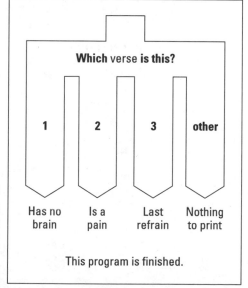

Figure 5-12:
The big fork in the code of Listing 5-9.

Which verse is this?

| 1 | 2 | 3 | other |

Has no brain | Is a pain | Last refrain | Nothing to print

This program is finished.

If the pesky user asks for verse 6, then the computer responds by dropping past cases 1, 2, and 3. Instead, the computer does the default. In the default, the computer displays Nothing to print, and then breaks out of the switch statement. After the computer is out of the switch statement, the computer displays This program is finished.

You don't really need to put a break at the very end of a switch statement. In Listing 5-9, the last break (the break that's part of the default) is just for the sake of overall tidiness.

To break or not to break

In every Java programmer's life, a time comes when he or she forgets to use break statements. At first, the resulting output is confusing, but then the programmer remembers fall-through. The term *fall-through* describes what happens when you end a case without a break statement. What happens is, execution of the code falls right through to the next case in line. Execution keeps falling through until you eventually reach a break statement or the end of the entire switch statement.

Usually, when you're using a switch statement, you don't want fall-through, so you pepper break statements throughout the switch. But, occasionally, fall-through is just the thing you need. Take, for instance, the "Al's All Wet" song. (The classy lyrics are shown in the sidebar bearing the song's name.) Each verse of "Al's All Wet" adds new lines in addition to the lines from previous verses. This situation (accumulating lines from one verse to another) cries out for a switch statement with fall-through. Listing 5-10 demonstrates the idea.

Listing 5-10: A switch statement with fall-through

```
public class FallingForYou
{
    public static void main(String args[])
    {
        System.out.print("Which verse? ");
        int verse = DummiesIO.getInt();

        switch (verse)
        {
            case 3: System.out.print  ("Last refrain, ");
                    System.out.println("last refrain,");
            case 2: System.out.print  ("He's a pain, ");
                    System.out.println("he's a pain,");
            case 1: System.out.print  ("Has no brain, ");
                    System.out.println("has no brain,");
        }
```

```
        System.out.println("In the rain, in the rain.");
        System.out.println("Ohhhhhhhh...");
        System.out.println();
    }

}
```

Figure 5-13 shows several runs of the program in Listing 5-10. Because the switch has no break statements in it, fall-through happens all over the place. For instance, when the user chooses verse 2, the computer executes the two statements in case 2:

```
System.out.print  ("He's a pain, ");
System.out.println("he's a pain,");
```

Then, the computer marches right on to execute the two statements in case 1:

```
System.out.print  ("Has no brain, ");
System.out.println("has no brain,");
```

That's good, because the song's second verse has all these lines in it.

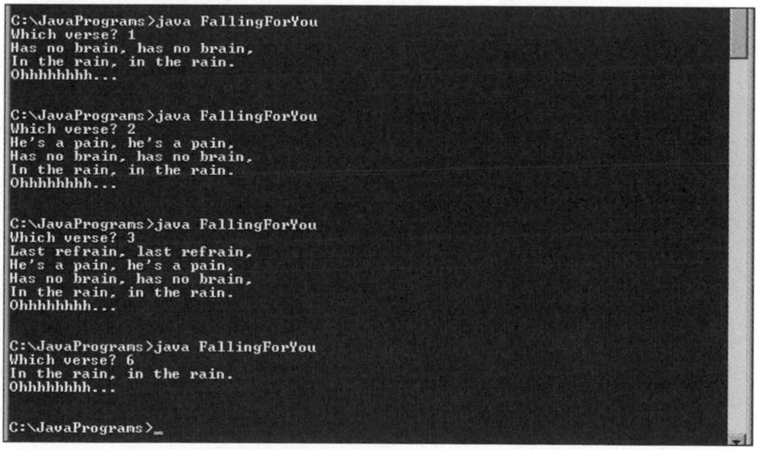

Figure 5-13:
Running the
code of
Listing 5-10.

Notice what happens when the user asks for verse 6. The switch statement in Listing 5-10 has no case 6 and no default, so none of the actions inside the switch statement are executed. Even so, with statements that print In the rain and Ohhhhhhhh right after the switch statement, the computer displays something when the user asks for verse 6.

Chapter 6

Controlling Program Flow
with Loops

● ●

In This Chapter

▶ Basic looping

▶ Counting as you loop

▶ Variations on the basic looping mechanism

● ●

*1*n 1966, the company that brings you Head & Shoulders shampoo made history. On the back of the bottle, the directions for using the shampoo read, "LATHER-RINSE-REPEAT." Never before had a complete set of directions (for doing anything, let alone shampooing your hair) been summarized so succinctly. People in the direction-writing business hailed this as a monumental achievement. Directions like these stood in stark contrast to others of the time. (For instance, the first sentence on a can of bug spray read, "Turn this can so that it points away from your face." Duh!)

Aside from their brevity, the thing that made the Head & Shoulders directions so cool was that, with three simple words, they managed to capture a notion that's at the heart of all instruction giving — the notion of repetition. That last word, *REPEAT,* took an otherwise bland instructional drone and turned it into a sophisticated recipe for action.

The fundamental idea is that when you're following directions, you don't just follow one instruction after another. Instead, you take turns in the road. You make decisions ("If HAIR IS DRY, then USE CONDITIONER,") and you go into loops ("LATHER-RINSE, and then LATHER-RINSE again.") In computer programming you use decision making and looping all the time. This chapter explores looping in Java.

Repeating Instructions Over and Over Again (Java while Statements)

Here's a guessing game for you. The computer generates a random number from 1 to 10. The computer asks you to guess the number. If you guess incorrectly the game continues. As soon as you guess correctly, the game is over. The program to play the game is shown in Listing 6-1, and a round of play is shown in Figure 6-1.

Listing 6-1:   A repeating guessing game

```
public class GuessAgain
{

    public static void main(String args[])
    {
        int inputNumber, randomNumber, numGuesses=0;
        randomNumber=DummiesRandom.getInt();

        System.out.println("        ***********        ");
        System.out.println("Welcome to the Guessing Game");
        System.out.println("        ***********        ");
        System.out.println();

        System.out.print("Enter an int from 1 to 10: ");
        inputNumber=DummiesIO.getInt();
        numGuesses++;

        while (inputNumber!=randomNumber)
        {
            System.out.println();
            System.out.println("Try again...");
            System.out.print("Enter an int from 1 to 10: ");
            inputNumber=DummiesIO.getInt();
            numGuesses++;
        }

        System.out.print("You win after ");
        System.out.println(numGuesses + " guesses.");
    }

}
```

```
C:\JavaPrograms>java GuessAgain
           ***********
Welcome to the Guessing Game
           ***********

Enter an int from 1 to 10: 2

Try again...
Enter an int from 1 to 10: 5

Try again...
Enter an int from 1 to 10: 8

Try again...
Enter an int from 1 to 10: 3
You win after 4 guesses.

C:\JavaPrograms>_
```

Figure 6-1:
Play until
you drop.

In Figure 6-1, the user makes four guesses. Each time around, the computer checks to see if the guess is correct. An incorrect guess generates a request to try again. For a correct guess, the user gets a rousing You win, along with a tally of the number of guesses he or she made. The computer is repeating several statements over and over again, checking each time through to see if the user's guess is the same as a certain randomly generated number. Each time the user makes a guess, the computer adds 1 to its tally of guesses. When the user makes the correct guess, the computer displays that tally. The flow of action is illustrated in Figure 6-2.

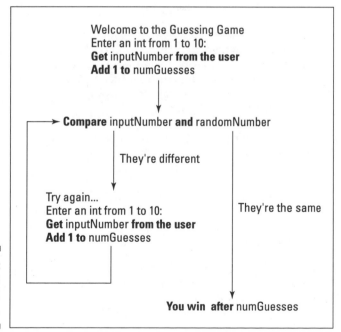

Welcome to the Guessing Game
Enter an int from 1 to 10:
Get inputNumber **from the user**
Add 1 to numGuesses

Compare inputNumber **and** randomNumber

They're different

Try again...
Enter an int from 1 to 10:
Get inputNumber **from the user**
Add 1 to numGuesses

They're the same

You win after numGuesses

Figure 6-2:
Around
and around
you go.

When you look over Listing 6-1, you see the code that does all this work. At the core of the code is a thing called a *while statement* (also known as a *while loop*). Rephrased in English, the while statement would say

```
while the inputNumber is not equal to the randomNumber
keep doing all the stuff in curly braces:
{



}
```

The stuff in curly braces (the stuff that is repeated over and over again) is the code that prints Try again and then Enter an int. . ., gets a value from the keyboard, and adds 1 to the count of the user's guesses.

When you're dealing with counters, like numGuesses in Listing 6-1, you may easily become confused and be off by one in either direction. You can avoid this headache by making sure that the ++ statements stay close to the statements whose events you're counting. For example, in Listing 6-1, the variable numGuesses starts off with value 0. That's because, when the program starts running, the user hasn't made any guesses. Later in the program, right after each call to DummiesIO.getInt is a numGuesses++ statement. That's how you do it — you increment the counter as soon as the user enters another guess.

The statements in curly braces are repeated as long as inputNumber != randomNumber keeps being true. Each repetition of the statements in the loop is called an *iteration* of the loop. In Figure 6-1, the loop undergoes three iterations. (If you don't believe that Figure 6-1 has exactly three iterations, count the number of Try again printings in the program's output. A Try again appears for each incorrect guess.)

When, at long last, the user enters the correct guess, the computer goes back to the top of the while statement, checks the condition in parentheses, and finds itself in double negative land. The not equal (!=) relationship between inputNumber and randomNumber no longer holds. In other words, the while statement's condition, inputNumber != randomNumber, has become false. Because the while statement's condition is false, the computer jumps past the while loop and goes on to the statements just below the while loop. In these two statements, the computer prints You win after 4 guesses.

With code of the kind shown in Listing 6-1, the computer never jumps out in mid-loop. When the computer finds that inputNumber isn't equal to randomNumber, the computer marches on and executes all five statements inside the loop's curly braces. The computer performs the test again (to see if inputNumber is still not equal to randomNumber) only after it fully executes all five statements in the loop.

When I discuss if statements in Chapter 5, I make a big commotion over the use of blocks and curly braces. Almost everything that's true about an if statement's curly braces is also true about a loop's curly braces. In particular, you can bypass the curly braces as long as the loop contains only one statement. Listing 6-2 has an example.

Listing 6-2: The simplest game in town

```
public class SmallLoop
{

    public static void main(String args[])
    {
        int inputNumber, randomNumber;
        randomNumber=DummiesRandom.getInt();

        inputNumber=DummiesIO.getInt();

        while (inputNumber!=randomNumber)
            inputNumber=DummiesIO.getInt();

        System.out.print("ok");
    }
}
```

A run of the code in Listing 6-2 is shown in Figure 6-3. Whoever wrote this code obviously gave no thought to making life pleasant for the user. The code has no print statements to tell the user what kind of values to enter. At the end of the run, when the user guesses the right number, the program doesn't even bother to say You win. Clearly, a thoughtless and callous individual wrote this code. (Hey, wait! I wrote this code.) One way or another, the code illustrates the simple rule. When you have only one statement inside your loop, you don't need to enclose the statement in curly braces.

Figure 6-3:
A minimalist
guessing
game.

```
C:\JavaPrograms>java SmallLoop
2
5
6
1
ok
C:\JavaPrograms>_
```

If your loop has more than one statement in it, don't forget to enclose the statements in curly braces.

Repeating a Certain Number of Times (Java for Statements)

"Write 'I will not talk in class' on the blackboard one hundred times."

What your teacher really meant was,

```
Set the count to 0.
As long as the count is less than 100,
    Write 'I will not talk in class' on the blackboard,
    Add 1 to the count.
```

Fortunately, you didn't know about loops and counters at the time. If you pointed all this stuff out to your teacher, you'd get into a lot more trouble than you were already in.

One way or another, life is filled with examples of counting loops. And computer programming mirrors life (. . . .or is it the other way around?). When you tell a computer what to do, you're often telling the computer to print three lines, process ten accounts, dial a million phone numbers, or whatever. Because counting loops are so common in programming, the people who create programming languages have developed statements just for loops of this kind. In Java, the statement that repeats something a certain number of times is called a *for* statement. The use of the for statement is illustrated in Listings 6-3 and 6-4. Listing 6-3 has a rock-bottom simple example, and Listing 6-4 has a more exotic example. Take your pick.

Listing 6-3:   The world's most boring for loop

```java
public class Yawn
{
    public static void main(String args[])
    {
        for (int count=1; count<=10; count++)
        {
            System.out.print("The value of count is ");
            System.out.print(count);
            System.out.println(".");
        }

        System.out.println("Done!");
    }
}
```

Figure 6-4 shows you what you get when you run the program of Listing 6-3. (You get exactly what you deserve.) The for statement in Listing 6-3 starts by setting the count variable equal to 1. Then the statement tests to make sure that count is less than or equal to 10 (which it certainly is). Then, the for statement dives ahead and executes the printing statements between the curly braces. (At this early stage of the game, the computer prints `The value of count is 1.`) Finally, the for statement does that last thing inside its parentheses — it adds 1 to the value of count.

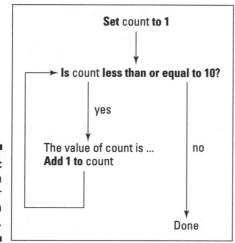

```
C:\JavaPrograms>java Yawn
The value of count is 1.
The value of count is 2.
The value of count is 3.
The value of count is 4.
The value of count is 5.
The value of count is 6.
The value of count is 7.
The value of count is 8.
The value of count is 9.
The value of count is 10.
Done!

C:\JavaPrograms>
```

Figure 6-4:
Counting
to ten.

With count now equal to 2, the for statement checks again to make sure that count is less than or equal to 10. (Yes, two is smaller than ten.) Because the test turns out okay, the for statement marches back into the curly braced statements and prints `The value of count is 2` on the screen. Finally, the for statement does that last thing inside its parentheses — it adds 1 to the value of count, increasing the value of count to 3.

And so on. This whole thing keeps being repeated over and over again until, after ten iterations, the value of count finally reaches 11. When this happens, the check for count being less than or equal to 10 fails, and the loop's execution ends. The computer jumps to whatever statement comes immediately after the for statement. In Listing 6-3, the computer prints `Done!` The whole process is illustrated in Figure 6-5.

Set count to 1

Is count less than or equal to 10?

yes

The value of count is ...
Add 1 to count

no

Figure 6-5:
The action
of the for
loop in
Listing 6-3.

Done

The anatomy of a for statement

After the word *for*, you always put three things in parentheses. The first of these three things is called an *initialization*, the second is an *expression*, and the third thing is called an *update*.

```
for ( initialization ; expression ; update )
```

Each of the three items in parentheses plays its own distinct role:

- ✔ The initialization is executed once, when the run of your program first reaches the for statement.
- ✔ The expression is evaluated several times (before each iteration).
- ✔ The update is also evaluated several times (at the end of each iteration).

If it helps, think of the loop as if its text is shifted all around:

```
int count=1
for count<=10
{
    System.out.print("The value of count is ");
    System.out.print(count);
    System.out.println(".");
    count++
}
```

You can't write a real for statement this way. (The javac program would throw code like this right into the garbage can.) Even so, this is the order in which the parts of the statement are executed.

When I talk about a for statement, I'm including, as part of the statement, all the actions that are repeated over and over again. Without these actions, all you have is the word *for*, followed only by stuff in parentheses. This line alone (the word *for* followed by stuff in parentheses) is not a complete statement. You almost never put a semicolon at the end of this line. If you make a mistake and end this line with a semicolon, you usually put the computer into an endless, do-nothing loop.

If you declare a variable in the initialization of a for loop, you can't use that variable outside the loop. For instance, in Listing 6-3, you get an error message if you try putting `System.out.println(count)` after the end of the loop.

Anything that can be done with a for loop can also be done with a while loop. Choosing to use a for loop is a matter of style and convenience, not necessity.

The world premiere of "Al's All Wet"

Listing 6-3 is very nice, but the program in that listing doesn't do anything interesting. For a more eye-catching example, see Listing 6-4. In Listing 6-4, I make good on a promise I made in Chapter 5. The program in Listing 6-4 prints all the lyrics of the hit single, "Al's All Wet." (You can find the lyrics in Chapter 5.)

Listing 6-4:   The unabridged "Al's All Wet" song

```
public class AlsAllWet
{
    public static void main(String args[])
    {
        for (int verse=1; verse<=3; verse++)
        {
            System.out.print  ("Al's all wet. ");
            System.out.println("Oh, why is Al all wet? Oh,");
            System.out.print  ("Al's all wet 'cause ");
            System.out.println("he's standing in the rain.");
            System.out.println("Why is Al out in the rain?");

            switch (verse)
            {
                case 1: System.out.println
                        ("That's because he has no brain.");
                    break;
                case 2: System.out.println
                        ("That's because he is a pain.");
                    break;
                case 3: System.out.println
                        ("'Cause this is the last refrain.");
                    break;
            }

            switch (verse)
            {
                case 3: System.out.println
                        ("Last refrain, last refrain,");
                case 2: System.out.println
                        ("He's a pain, he's a pain,");
                case 1: System.out.println
                        ("Has no brain, has no brain,");
            }
```

(continued)

Listing 6-4 *(continued)*

```
            System.out.println("In the rain, in the rain.");
            System.out.println("Ohhhhhhhh...");
            System.out.println();
        }

        System.out.print  ("Al's all wet. ");
        System.out.println("Oh, why is Al all wet? Oh,");
        System.out.print  ("Al's all wet 'cause ");
        System.out.println("he's standing in the rain.");
    }

}
```

Listing 6-4 is nice because it combines many of the ideas from Chapters 5 and 6. In Listing 6-4, two switch statements are nested inside a for loop. One of the switch statements uses break statements; the other switch statement uses fall-through. As the value of the for loop's counter variable (verse) goes from 1 to 2, and then to 3, all the cases in the switch statements are executed. When the program is near the end of its run and execution has dropped out of the for loop, the program's last four statements print the song's final verse.

When I boldly declare that a for statement is for counting, I'm stretching the truth just a bit. Java's for statement is very versatile. You can use a for statement in situations that have nothing to do with counting. For instance, a statement with no update part, such as for(i=0; i<10;), just keeps on going. The looping ends when some action inside the loop assigns a big number to the variable i. You can even create a for statement with nothing inside the parentheses. The loop for(; ;) runs forever, which is good if the loop controls a serious piece of machinery. Usually, when you write a for statement, you're counting how many times to repeat something. But, in truth, you can do just about any kind of repetition with a for statement.

Repeating Until You Get What You Want (Java do Statements)

"Fools rush in where angels fear to tread."

–Alexander Pope

Let's be young and foolish (or, at the very least, foolish). Look back at Figure 6-2, and notice how Java's while loop works. As execution enters a while loop, the computer checks to make sure that the loop's condition is true. If the condition isn't true, the statements inside the loop are never executed — not even once. In fact, you can easily cook up a while loop whose statements are never executed (although I can't think of a reason why you would ever want to do it).

```
int twoPlusTwo=2+2;
while (twoPlusTwo==5)
{
    System.out.println("Are you kidding?");
    System.out.println("2+2 doesn't equal 5");
    System.out.print  ("Everyone knows that");
    System.out.println(" 2+2 equals 3");
}
```

In spite of this silly twoPlusTwo example, the while statement turns out to be the most versatile of Java's looping constructs. In particular, the while loop is good for situations in which you must look before you leap. For example: "While money is in my account, write a mortgage check every month." When you first encounter this statement, if your account has a zero balance, you don't want to write a mortgage check — not even one check.

But at times (not many), you want to leap before you look. Take, for instance, the situation in which you're asking the user for a response. Maybe the user's response makes sense, but maybe it doesn't. If it doesn't, you want to ask again. Maybe the user's finger slipped, or perhaps the user didn't understand the question.

Figure 6-6 shows some runs of a program to delete a file. Before deleting the file, the program asks the user if making the deletion is okay. If the user gives a sensible answer (y, Y, n, or N) then the program proceeds according to the user's wishes. But, if the user enters any other letter (or any digit, punctuation symbol, or whatever), then the program asks the user for another response.

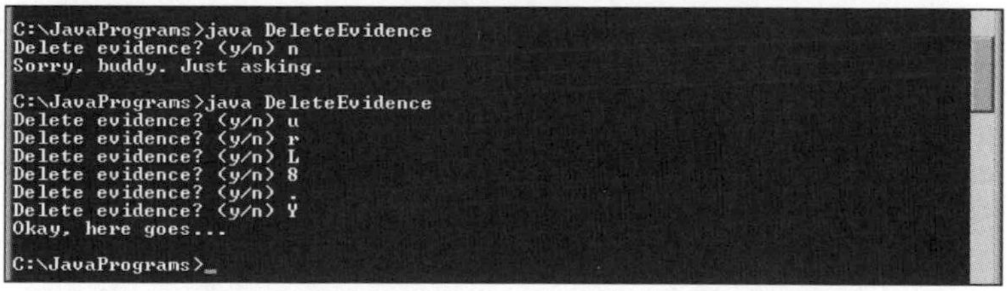

Figure 6-6:
Checking
before you
delete a file.

```
C:\JavaPrograms>java DeleteEvidence
Delete evidence? (y/n) n
Sorry, buddy. Just asking.

C:\JavaPrograms>java DeleteEvidence
Delete evidence? (y/n) u
Delete evidence? (y/n) r
Delete evidence? (y/n) L
Delete evidence? (y/n) 8
Delete evidence? (y/n) ;
Delete evidence? (y/n) Y
Okay, here goes...

C:\JavaPrograms>_
```

To write this program, you need a loop — a loop that repeatedly asks the user if the file should be deleted. The loop keeps asking until the user gives a meaningful response. Now, the thing to notice is that the loop doesn't need to check anything before asking the user the first time. Indeed, before the user gives the first response, the loop has nothing to check. The loop doesn't start with "as long as such-and-such is true, then get a response from the user." Instead, the loop just leaps ahead, gets a response from the user, and then checks the response to see if it made sense.

That's why the program in Listing 6-5 has a *do* loop (also known as a *do . . . while* loop). With a do loop, the program jumps right in, takes action, and then checks a condition to see if the result of the action makes sense. If the result makes sense, then execution of the loop is done. If not, then the program goes back to the top of the loop for another go-around.

Listing 6-5:   To delete, or not to delete

```
public class DeleteEvidence
{
    public static void main(String args[])
    {
        java.io.File evidence =
            new java.io.File("c:\\JavaPrograms\\evidence");
        char reply;

        do
        {
            System.out.print ("Delete evidence? (y/n) ");
            reply = DummiesIO.getChar();
        }
        while(reply!='y'&&reply!='Y'&&reply!='n'&&reply!='N');

        if (reply=='y' || reply=='Y')
        {
            System.out.println("Okay, here goes...");
            evidence.delete();
        }
        else
            System.out.println("Sorry, buddy. Just asking.");
    }
}
```

Figure 6-7 shows the flow of control in the loop of Listing 6-5. With a do loop, the situation in the twoPlusTwo program (shown earlier) can never happen. Because the do loop carries out its first action without testing a condition, every do loop is guaranteed to perform at least one iteration.

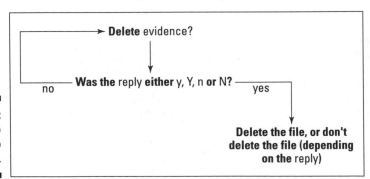

Figure 6-7:
Here we go
loop, do
loop.

In Listing 6-5, the actual file-handling statements deserve some attention. These statements involve the use of classes, objects, and methods. Many of the meaty details about these things are in other chapters, like Chapters 7 and 9. Even so, I can't do any harm by touching on some highlights right here.

So, you can find a class in the Java language API named *java.io.File*. The statement

```
java.io.File evidence =
          new java.io.File("c:\\JavaPrograms\\evidence");
```

creates a new object in the computer's memory. This object, formed from the java.io.File class, describes everything that the program needs to know about the disk file named `c:\JavaPrograms\evidence`. (In Java, when you want to indicate a backslash inside a double-quoted string literal, you use a double-backslash instead.) From this point on in Listing 6-5, the variable evidence refers to the disk file named `c:\JavaPrograms\evidence`.

After you've got all this java.io.File stuff in your head, the only thing left to know is that the evidence object, being an instance of the java.io.File class, has a delete method. (What can I say? It's in the API documentation.) When you call evidence.delete, the computer gets rid of the file for you.

Busting Out of a Loop

Take a gander at the program in Listing 6-1. What's awkward about this program? Well, a few statements appear more than once in the program. Normally, a statement that's copied from one part of a program to another is no cause for concern. But in Listing 6-1, the overall strategy seems suspicious. You get a number from the user before the loop and (again) inside the loop.

```
System.out.print("Enter an int from 1 to 10: ");
inputNumber=DummiesIO.getInt();
numGuesses++;

while (inputNumber!=randomNumber)
{
    System.out.println();
    System.out.println("Try again...");
    System.out.print("Enter an int from 1 to 10: ");
    inputNumber=DummiesIO.getInt();
    numGuesses++;
}
```

To be fair, I shouldn't badmouth this code. The code uses a standard trick for making loops work. It's called *priming* a loop. The pattern is

```
Get input
while the input you have isn't the last input
{
    Get more input
}
```

At the very start of the while loop, the computer checks a condition having to do with the user's input. So the computer doesn't enter the loop until the user gives some input. Then when the computer is inside the loop, the computer asks for more input to feed the loop's next iteration. The trick seems strange, but it works.

Professional programmers use this technique, priming a loop, all the time, so it can't be that bad. But there is another way, and that other way is illustrated in Listing 6-6.

Listing 6-6: A break statement in a loop

```java
public class BustingLoops
{

    public static void main(String args[])
    {
        int inputNumber, randomNumber, numGuesses=0;
        randomNumber=DummiesRandom.getInt();

        System.out.println("      ***********         ");
        System.out.println("Welcome to the Guessing Game");
        System.out.println("      ***********         ");
        System.out.println();

        while (true)
        {
            System.out.print("Enter an int from 1 to 10: ");
            inputNumber=DummiesIO.getInt();
            numGuesses++;
            if (inputNumber==randomNumber)
                break;
            System.out.println();
            System.out.println("Try again...");
        }

        System.out.print("You win after ");
        System.out.println(numGuesses + " guesses.");
    }
}
```

From the user's point of view, the code in Listing 6-6 does exactly the same thing as the code in Listing 6-1. (To see the output of either program, refer to Figure 6-1.) The difference is, Listing 6-6 has only one call to DummiesIO.getInt. That call is inside the loop, so the computer must enter the loop without testing any input.

If you look at the loop's condition, you can see how this works. The loop's condition is always true. (In Java, *true* is a keyword. It stands for a boolean value, which I cover in Chapter 4.) No matter what's going on, the loop's condition always passes its test. So the loop's condition is a big fraud. You never jump out of the loop by failing the test in the loop's condition. Instead, you jump out when you hit the break statement that's inside the loop (. . . .and you hit that break statement when you get past the if (inputNumber == randomNumber) roadblock). The whole thing works very nicely.

When the computer executes a break statement that's in a loop, the computer jumps out of the loop (to the first statement that comes after the loop).

So why do programmers bother to prime their loops? Do break statements have any hidden drawbacks? Well, the answer depends on your point of view. Some programmers think that break statements in loops are confusing. All that jumping around makes them dizzy and reminds them of something from the 1960s called *spaghetti code*. (Spaghetti code uses *goto* statements to jump from one statement to another. In *Pascal by Example*, author B. Burd says, "Programming with goto is like traveling around Paris by swimming through its sewer system. There are plenty of short cuts, but none of them are worth taking.") One way or another, break statements in loops are the exception, not the rule. Use them if you want, but don't expect to find many of them in other people's Java code.

Part III

Working with the Big Picture: Object-Oriented Programming

The 5th Wave — By Rich Tennant

"We're here to clean the code."

In this part . . .

Have you read or heard anything about object-oriented programming? Sometimes, all the object-oriented programmers seem to belong to a little club. There's a secret handshake, a secret sign, and a promise not to reveal object-oriented programming concepts to any outsiders. Well, the secrecy is ending. In this part, I take all the mystery out of object-oriented programming. I take the concepts step by step, and illustrate each concept with a Java program or two.

Chapter 7

Thinking in Terms of Classes and Objects

As a computer book author, I've been told this over and over again — I shouldn't expect people to read sections and chapters in their logical order. People jump around, picking what they need and skipping what they don't feel like reading. With that in mind, I realize that you may have skipped Chapter 3. If that's the case, please don't feel guilty. You can compensate in just sixty seconds by reading the following paragraph from Chapter 3:

> *Java is an object-oriented programming language so, in Java, your primary goal is to describe classes and objects. A class is the idea behind a certain kind of thing. An object is a concrete instance of a class. The programmer defines a class, and from the class definition, the computer makes individual objects.*

Of course, you can certainly choose to skip over the sixty-second summary paragraph. If that's the case, you may want to recoup some of your losses. You can do that by reading the following two-word summary of Chapter 3:

> *Classes; objects.*

Defining a Class (What It Means to Be an Account)

What distinguishes one bank account from another? If you ask a banker this question, you hear a long sales pitch. The banker describes interest rates, fees, penalties — the whole routine. Fortunately for you, I'm not interested in all that. Instead, I want to know how my account is different from your account. After all, my account is named "Barry Burd, trading as Burd Brain Consulting," and your account is named "Jane Q. Reader, trading as Budding Java Expert." My account has $24.02 in it. How about yours?

When you come right down to it, the differences between one account and another can be summarized as values of variables. Maybe there's a variable named *balance*. For me the value of balance is 24.02. For you, the value of balance is 55.63. The question is, in writing a computer program to deal with accounts, how do I separate my balance variable from your balance variable?

The answer is, create two separate objects. Let one balance variable live inside one of the objects, and let the other balance variable live inside the other object. While you're at it, put a name variable and an address variable in each of the objects. And there you have it. You've got two objects, and each object represents an account. More precisely, each object is an instance of the Account class. (See Figure 7-1.)

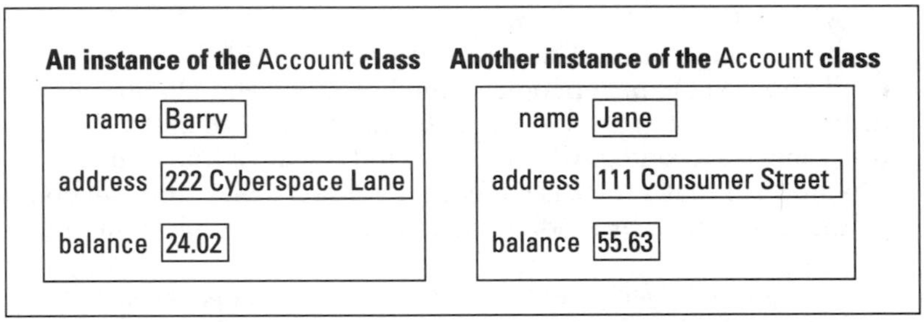

Figure 7-1:
Two objects.

So far, so good. But you still haven't solved the original problem. In your computer program, how do you refer to my balance variable, as opposed to your balance variable? Well, you have two objects sitting around, so maybe you have variables to refer to these two objects. Let's create one variable named myAccount, and another variable named yourAccount. The myAccount variable refers to my object (my instance of the Account class) with all the stuff that's inside it. To refer to my balance, write

```
myAccount.balance
```

To refer to my name, write

```
myAccount.name
```

Then `yourAccount.balance` refers to the value in your object's balance variable, and `yourAccount.name` refers to the value of your object's name variable. To tell the computer how much I have in my account, you can write

```
myAccount.balance = 24.02;
```

To display your name on the screen, you can write

```
System.out.println(yourAccount.name);
```

These ideas come together in Listing 7-1.

Listing 7-1:   Dealing with Account objects

```
public class Account
{
    String name;
    String address;
    double balance;
}


class UseAccount
{

    public static void main(String args[])
    {
        Account myAccount;
        Account yourAccount;

        myAccount = new Account();
        yourAccount = new Account();

        myAccount.name="Barry Burd";
        myAccount.address="222 Cyberspace Lane";
        myAccount.balance=24.02;

        yourAccount.name="Jane Q. Public";
        yourAccount.address="111 Consumer Street";
        yourAccount.balance=55.63;

        System.out.print(yourAccount.name);
        System.out.print(" has $");
        System.out.print(yourAccount.balance);
        System.out.println(" in his or her account.");
    }

}
```

Listing 7-1 has two classes in it: the Account class and the UseAccount class. The Account class defines what it means to be an Account and, conceptually, is easier to understand. The code for the Account class tells you that each of the Account class's instances has three variables — variables called *name, address,* and *balance.* This is consistent with the information in Figure 7-1.

If you've been grappling with the material in Chapters 4 through 6, the code for class Account (Listing 7-1) may come as a big shock to you. Can you really define a complete Java class with only four lines of code (give or take a few curly braces)? You certainly can. In fact, the Account class in Listing 7-1 is quite representative of what Java programmers think of when they think "class." A class is a grouping together of existing things. In the Account class of Listing 7-1, those existing things are two String values and a double value.

In Listing 7-1, the definition of the UseAccount class consumes the rest of the program. The only purpose for having a UseAccount class is because the program needs a main method, and every method has to be in one class or another. This main method has variables of its own — variables named *yourAccount* and *myAccount*.

Declaring variables and creating objects

In a way, the first two lines inside the main method are misleading. Some people read `Account yourAccount` as if it's supposed to mean, "yourAccount is an Account," or "The variable yourAccount refers to an instance of the Account class." That's not really what this first line means. Instead the line `Account yourAccount` means, "If and when I make the variable yourAccount refer to something, then that something will be an instance of the Account class." So, what's the difference?

The difference is, simply declaring `Account yourAccount` doesn't make the yourAccount variable refer to an object. All the declaration does is reserve the variable name *yourAccount,* so that the name can eventually refer to an instance of the Account class. The creation of an actual object doesn't come until later in the code, when the computer executes `new Account()`. (Technically, when the computer executes `new Account()`, you're creating an object by calling the Account class's *constructor.* I have more to say about that in Chapter 9.)

When the computer executes `yourAccount = new Account()`, the computer creates a new object (a new instance of the Account class) and makes the variable yourAccount refer to that new object. (It's the equal sign, the assignment, that makes the variable refer to the new object.) The situation is illustrated in Figure 7-2.

To test the claim I made in the last few paragraphs, I added an extra line to the code of Listing 7-1. I tried to print yourAccount.name after declaring yourAccount, but before calling `new Account()`.

```
        Account myAccount;
        Account yourAccount;

        System.out.println(yourAccount.name);

        myAccount = new Account();
        yourAccount = new Account();
```

After executing
Account yourAccount;

After executing
yourAccount =
        new Account ();

yourAccount [   ]

yourAccount [   ]

name [   ]

address [   ]

balance [   ]

Figure 7-2:
Before and
after a
constructor
is called.

When I tried to javac the new code, I got this error message:

```
D:\book\Listings\Chapter07\UseAccountJunk.java:9: variable
        yourAccount might not have been initialized
    System.out.println(yourAccount.name);
                       ^
1 error
```

So that settles it. Before you do `new Account()`, you can't print the name
variable of an object, because an object doesn't exist.

When a variable has a reference type, simply declaring the variable isn't
enough. You don't get an object until you call a constructor and use the keyword *new*. (For information about reference types, see Chapter 4.)

Initializing a variable

In Chapter 4, I announce that you can initialize a primitive type variable as
part of the variable's declaration.

```
int weightOfAPerson=150;
```

You can do the same thing with reference type variables, such as myAccount and yourAccount in Listing 7-1. You can combine the first four lines in the listing's main method into just two lines, like this:

```
Account myAccount = new Account();
Account yourAccount = new Account();
```

When you combine lines this way, your code is more concise. Of course, concise code isn't always the most readable code. For examples of code with and without variable initializations, see Chapter 10.

Using variables

After you've bit off and chewed the main method's first four lines, the rest of the code in Listing 7-1 is sensible and straightforward. You have three lines that put values in the myAccount object's variables, three lines that put values in the yourAccount object's variables, and four lines that do some printing. The program's output is shown in Figure 7-3.

Figure 7-3:
Running the
code in
Listing 7-1.

```
C:\JavaPrograms>java UseAccount
Jane Q. Public has $55.63 in his or her account.
C:\JavaPrograms>
```

Compiling and Running More Than One Class

All the code in Listing 7-1 can go in either one big file or in two smaller files. You make the decision. Because Listing 7-1 has two classes in it, you can create two separate files. Call one file `Account.java`, and call the other file `UseAccount.java`. Or, if you want, you can keep both classes together in one file. You can take the one-file route because, in Listing 7-1, the UseAccount class isn't declared to be public.

A file with Java code in it can contain at most one public class. If the file has a public class in it, the file's name must be the same as the class's name. Even the filename's capitalization should be same as the class name's capitalization. For instance, a file containing all the code in Listing 7-1 must be named `Account.java`.

Whether or not you put all the code from Listing 7-1 into a single file, when you javac your code, the javac program will create two separate bytecode files. Before you run javac, you may have one file, `Account.java`. After you run javac, you have three files: `Account.java`, `Account.class`, and `UseAccount.class`.

Whether you create one file or two files, you never have to run javac more than once. Just javac the file with the main method in it. When you do, the computer looks for all the other classes it needs. If any of those classes still need to be compiled, then javac automatically compiles them for you.

After applying javac, your next step is to run the code. (See Chapter 2.) If you type

```
java Account
```

you get the following error message.

```
Exception in thread "main" java.lang.NoSuchMethodError: main
```

That's because the Account class has no main method in it. Instead, to get things going, just type

```
java UseAccount
```

Typing this line gets the main method in the UseAccount class running. In turn, the main method fires up the variables declared in the Account class.

Now, here's one of the most common mistakes people make when they're trying to run Java programs: They don't put all the .class files in places where the computer can find them. The code in Listing 7-1 involves two .class files: `Account.class` and `UseAccount.class`. When you type **java UseAccount**, the computer has to hunt around for the other `Account.class` file. You have many options here, but by far the simplest is to do the following:

✔ **Make sure that the file** `Account.class` **is in the same directory as the file** `UseAccount.class`. If you apply javac to a file containing all the code in Listing 7-1, then you don't have to worry about this. Running javac puts the two .class files in the same directory for you.

What if you're not starting with the code in Listing 7-1, and you're not running javac? Instead, you're starting with .class files (Account.class and UseAccount.class) that someone else has already compiled. You're copying these .class files to your own hard drive. In that case, you must make sure to copy both files. Just copying `UseAccount.class` isn't enough.

✔ **Make sure your computer knows to look in the directory containing the** `Account.class` **file.** Believe it or not, you can be working in your JavaPrograms directory, have both `UseAccount.class` and `Account.class` in that directory, type **java UseAccount**, and the computer still may not be able to find the `Account.class` file.

To make sure that the computer can find the Account.class file, look back in Chapter 2, and review that chapter's advice about the CLASS-PATH variable. The value of CLASSPATH tells the computer where to look for .class files. In Chapter 2, you add a single dot to the CLASSPATH variable. The dot tells the computer to look for .class files in your working directory. (That's whatever directory you're using when you type the java command — for instance, your JavaPrograms directory.)

If the computer can't find your classes, you may be having trouble setting your system's CLASSPATH variable. Try modifying the CLASSPATH on the fly as you issue the java command. To do this with the UseAccount class, type **java -classpath . UseAccount**.

Defining a Method within a Class (Displaying an Account)

Imagine a table containing the information about two accounts. (If you have trouble imagining such a thing, just look at Table 7-1.)

Table 7-1	Without Object-Oriented Programming	
Name	*Address*	*Balance*
Barry Burd	222 Cyberspace Lane	24.02
Jane Q. Public	111 Consumer Street	55.63

In Table 7-1, each account has three things — a name, an address, and a balance. That's the way things were done before object-oriented programming came along. But object-oriented programming involved a big shift in thinking. With object-oriented programming, each account can have a name, an address, a balance, and a way of being displayed.

In object-oriented programming, each object has its own built-in functionality. An account knows how to display itself. A string can tell you if it has the same characters inside it as another string. A PrintStream instance, such as System.out, knows how to do println. In object-oriented programming, each object has its own methods. These methods are little subprograms that you can call to have an object do things to (or for) itself.

And why is this a good idea? It's good because you're making pieces of data take responsibility for themselves. With object-oriented programming, all the functionality associated with an account is collected inside the code for Account class. Everything you have to know about a string is located in the file `String.java`. Anything having to do with year numbers (whether they have two or four digits, for instance) is handled right inside the Year class. So, if anybody has problems with your Account class or your Year class, he or she knows just where to look for all the code. That's great!

So imagine an enhanced account table. In this new table, each object has built-in functionality. Each account knows how to display itself on the screen. Each row of the table has its own copy of a display method. Of course, you don't need much imagination to picture this table. I just happen to have a table you can look at. It's Table 7-2.

Table 7-2			The Object-Oriented Way
Name	*Address*	*Balance*	*Display*
Barry Burd	222 Cyberspace Lane	24.02	System.out.print....
Jane Q. Public	111 Consumer Street	55.63	System.out.print....

An account that displays itself

In Table 7-2, each account object has four things — a name, an address, a balance, and a way of displaying itself on the screen. After you make the jump to object-oriented thinking, you'll never turn back. A program that implements the ideas in Table 7-2 is shown in Listing 7-2.

Listing 7-2: **An Account displays itself**

```
public class Account
{
    String name;
    String address;
    double balance;

    public void display()
    {
        System.out.print("Name:    ");
        System.out.println(name);
        System.out.print("Address: ");
        System.out.println(address);
        System.out.print("Balance: ");
        System.out.println(balance);
    }
}
```

(continued)

Listing 7-2 (continued)

```
class UseAccount
{

    public static void main(String args[])
    {
        Account myAccount;
        Account yourAccount;

        myAccount = new Account();
        yourAccount = new Account();

        myAccount.name="Barry Burd";
        myAccount.address="222 Cyberspace Lane";
        myAccount.balance=24.02;

        yourAccount.name="Jane Q. Public";
        yourAccount.address="111 Consumer Street";
        yourAccount.balance=55.63;

        myAccount.display();
        System.out.println();
        yourAccount.display();
    }

}
```

A run of the code in Listing 7-2 is shown in Figure 7-4. In Listing 7-2, the Account class has four things in it — a name, an address, a balance and a display method. These things match up with the four columns in Table 7-2. So each instance of Account class has a name, an address, a balance, and a way of displaying itself. The way you call these things is nice and uniform. To refer to the name stored in myAccount, you write

```
myAccount.name
```

To get myAccount to display itself on the screen, you write

```
myAccount.display()
```

The only difference is the parentheses.

Figure 7-4:
Running the
code in
Listing 7-2.

```
C:\JavaPrograms>java UseAccount
Name:      Barry Burd
Address: 222 Cyberspace Lane
Balance: 24.02

Name:      Jane Q. Public
Address: 111 Consumer Street
Balance: 55.63

C:\JavaPrograms>_
```

When you call a method, you put parentheses after the method's name.

The display method's header

Look again at Listing 7-2. A call to the display method is inside the UseAccount class's main method. But the declaration of the display method is up in the Account class. The declaration has a header and a body. (See Chapter 3.) The header has three words and some parentheses:

- ✔ **The word *public* tells the computer that any other Java code can call this method.** Words like *public* are called *access modifiers*. In Listing 7-2, the word *public* modifies access to the display method. If you want to read more about access modifiers, read Chapter 13.

- ✔ **The word *void* tells the computer that, when the display method is called, the display method doesn't return anything to the place that called it.** To see a method that does return something to the place that called it, see the next section.

- ✔ **The word *display* is the method's name.** Every method must have a name. Otherwise, you don't have a way to call the method.

- ✔ **The parentheses contain all the things you're going to pass to the method when you call it.** When you call a method, you can pass information to that method on the fly. This display example, with its empty parentheses, looks strange. That's because no information is passed to the display method when you call it. For a meatier example, see the next section.

Sending Values to and from Methods (Calculating Interest)

Think about sending someone to the supermarket to buy bread. When you do this, you say, "Go to the supermarket and buy some bread." (Try it at home. You'll have a fresh loaf of bread in no time at all!) Of course, some other time you send that same person to the supermarket to buy bananas. You say, "Go to the supermarket and buy some bananas." And what's the point of all this? Well, you have a method, and you have some on-the-fly information that you pass to the method when you call it. The method is named "Go to the supermarket and buy some. . . ." The on-the-fly information is either "bread" or "bananas," depending on your culinary needs. In Java, the method calls would look like this:

```
goToTheSupermarketAndBuySome(bread);
goToTheSupermarketAndBuySome(bananas);
```

The things in parentheses are called *parameters* or *parameter lists*. With parameters, your methods become much more versatile. Instead of getting the same thing each time, you can send somebody to the supermarket to buy bread one time, bananas another time, and birdseed the third time. When you call your goToTheSupermarketAndBuySome method, you decide right there and then what you're going to ask your pal to buy.

And what happens when your friend returns from the supermarket? "Here's the bread you asked me to buy," says your friend. As a result of carrying out your wishes, your friend returns something to you. You made a method call, and the method returns information (or a loaf of bread).

The thing returned to you is called the method's *return value*. The general type of thing that was returned to you is called the method's *return type*. These concepts are made more concrete in Listing 7-3.

Listing 7-3: Calculating interest

```java
public class Account
{
    String name;
    String address;
    double balance;

    public void display()
    {
        System.out.print("Name:    ");
        System.out.println(name);
        System.out.print("Address: ");
        System.out.println(address);
        System.out.print("Balance: ");
        System.out.println(balance);
    }

    public double getInterest(double percentageRate)
    {
        return balance*percentageRate/100.00;
    }
}


class UseAccount
{

    public static void main(String args[])
    {
        Account myAccount;
        Account yourAccount;

        myAccount = new Account();
        yourAccount = new Account();
```

```
        myAccount.name="Barry Burd";
        myAccount.address="222 Cyberspace Lane";
        myAccount.balance=24.02;

        yourAccount.name="Jane Q. Public";
        yourAccount.address="111 Consumer Street";
        yourAccount.balance=55.63;

        System.out.print("The interest on ");
        System.out.print(myAccount.name);
        System.out.print("'s account is $");
        System.out.println(myAccount.getInterest(5.00));
        System.out.println();

        double yourInterestRate=7.00;
        double yourInterestAmount;
        System.out.print("The interest on ");
        System.out.print(yourAccount.name);
        System.out.print("'s account is $");
        yourInterestAmount =
            yourAccount.getInterest(yourInterestRate);
        System.out.println(yourInterestAmount);
    }

}
```

The output of the code in Listing 7-3 is shown in Figure 7-5. In Listing 7-3, the Account class has a getInterest method. This getInterest method is called twice from the UseAccount class's main method. The actual account balances and interest rates are different each time.

Figure 7-5:
Running the
code in
Listing 7-3.

```
C:\JavaPrograms>java UseAccount
The interest on Barry Burd's account is $1.2009999999999998

The interest on Jane Q. Public's account is $3.8941000000000003

C:\JavaPrograms>
```

✔ **In the first call, the balance is 24.02, and the interest rate is 5.00.** The first call, `myAccount.getInterest(5.00)`, refers to the myAccount object and all the variables inside it. (See Figure 7-6.) When this call is made, the expression `balance*percentageRate/100.00` stands for 24.02*5.00/100.00.

✔ **In the second call, the balance is 55.63, and the interest rate is 7.00.** In the main method, just before this second call is made, the variable yourInterestRate is assigned the value 7.00. The call itself, `yourAccount.getInterest(yourInterestRate)`, refers to the yourAccount object and all the variables inside it. (Again, see Figure 7-6.) So, when the call is made, the expression `balance*percentageRate/100.00` stands for 55.63*7.00/100.00.

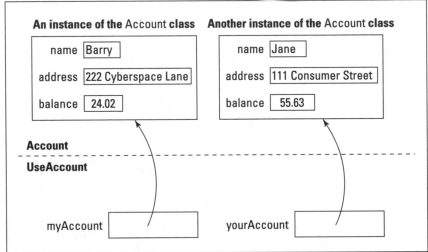

An instance of the Account **class**

name Barry

address 222 Cyberspace Lane

balance 24.02

Another instance of the Account **class**

name Jane

address 111 Consumer Street

balance 55.63

Account
- -
UseAccount

myAccount

yourAccount

Figure 7-6:
My account
and your
account.

By the way, the main method in Listing 7-3 contains two calls to getInterest. One call has the literal 5.00 in its parameter list; the other call has the variable yourInterestRate in its parameter list. Why does one call use a literal and the other call use a variable? No reason. I just wanted to show you that you can do it either way.

Passing a value to a method

Take a look at the getInterest method's header. (As you read the explanation in the next few bullets, you can follow some of the ideas visually with the diagram in Figure 7-7.)

- ✔ **The word *public* tells the computer that any other Java code can call this method.** Access modifiers, like the word *public*, are described in detail in Chapter 13.

- ✔ **The word *double* tells the computer that, when the getInterest method is called, the getInterest method returns a double value back to the place that called it.** The statement in the getInterest method's body confirms this. The statement says `return balance*percentageRate/100.00`, and the expression `balance*percentageRate/ 100.00` has type double. (That's because all the things in the expression — balance, percentageRate, and 100.00 — have type double.)

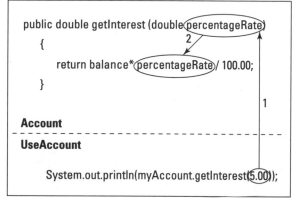

Figure 7-7:
Passing a
value to a
method.

When the getInterest method is called, the return statement calculates `balance*percentageRate/100.00` and hands the calculation's result back to the code that called the method.

- **The word *getInterest* is the method's name.** That's the name you use to call the method when you're writing the code for the UseAccount class.

- **The parentheses contain all the things you're going to pass to the method when you call it.** When you call a method, you can pass information to that method on the fly. This information is the method's parameter list. The getInterest method's header says that the getInterest method takes one piece of information and that piece of information must be of type double.

```
public double getInterest(double percentageRate)
```

Sure enough, if you look at the first call to getInterest (down in the useAccount class's main method), that call has the number 5.00 in it. And 5.00 is a double literal. (See Chapter 4.) When I call getInterest, I'm giving the method a value of type double.

The same story holds true for the second call to getInterest. Down near the bottom of Listing 7-3, I call getInterest and feed the variable yourInterestRate to the method in its parameter list. Luckily for me, I declared yourInterestRate to be of type double just a few lines before that.

When you run the code in Listing 7-3, the flow of action isn't from top to bottom. The action goes from main to getInterest, then back to main, then back to getInterest, and finally back to main again. The whole business is pictured in Figure 7-8.

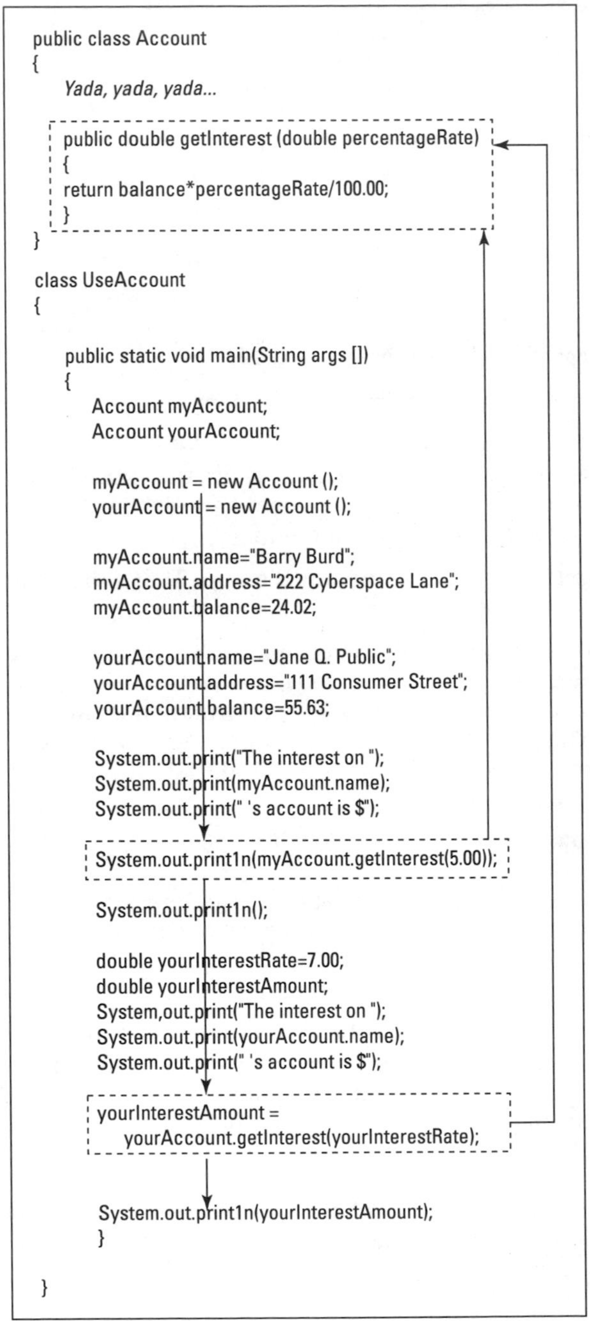

```
public class Account
{
    Yada, yada, yada...

    public double getInterest (double percentageRate)
    {
    return balance*percentageRate/100.00;
    }
}

class UseAccount
{

    public static void main(String args [])
    {
        Account myAccount;
        Account yourAccount;

        myAccount = new Account ();
        yourAccount = new Account ();

        myAccount.name="Barry Burd";
        myAccount.address="222 Cyberspace Lane";
        myAccount.balance=24.02;

        yourAccount.name="Jane Q. Public";
        yourAccount.address="111 Consumer Street";
        yourAccount.balance=55.63;

        System.out.print("The interest on ");
        System.out.print(myAccount.name);
        System.out.print(" 's account is $");

        System.out.print1n(myAccount.getInterest(5.00));

        System.out.print1n();

        double yourInterestRate=7.00;
        double yourInterestAmount;
        System.out.print("The interest on ");
        System.out.print(yourAccount.name);
        System.out.print(" 's account is $");

        yourInterestAmount =
            yourAccount.getInterest(yourInterestRate);

        System.out.print1n(yourInterestAmount);
    }

}
```

Figure 7-8:
The flow of
control in
Listing 7-3.

Returning a value from the getInterest method

When method getInterest is called, the method executes the one statement that's in the method's body: a return statement. The return statement computes the value of `balance*percentageRate/100.00`. If balance happens to be 24.02, and percentageRate is 5.00, then the value of the expression is 1.201 — around $1.20. (Because the computer works exclusively with zeros and ones, the computer gets this number wrong by an ever so tiny amount. The computer gets 1.2009999999999998. That's just something humans have to live with.)

Anyway, after this value is calculated, the computer executes the return, which sends the value back to the place in main where getInterest was called. At that point in the process, the entire method call — `myAccount.getInterest (5.00)` — takes on the value 1.2009999999999998. The call itself is inside a println:

```
System.out.println(myAccount.getInterest(5.00));
```

So the println ends up with the following meaning:

```
System.out.println(1.2009999999999998);
```

The whole process, in which a value is passed back to the method call, is illustrated in Figure 7-9.

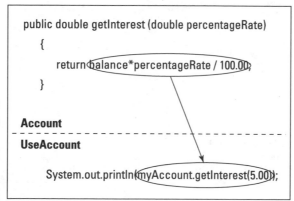

Figure 7-9:
A method
call is an
expression
with a value.

If a method returns anything, then a call to the method is an expression with a value. That value can be printed, assigned to a variable, added to something else, or whatever. Anything you can do with any other kind of value, you can do with a method call.

Making numbers look good

Looking again at Figure 7-5, you may be concerned that the interest on my account is only $1.2009999999999998. Seemingly, the bank is cheating me out of two hundred-trillionths of a cent. I should go straight there and demand my fair interest. Maybe you and I should go together. We'll kick up some fur at that old bank and bust this scam right open. If my guess is correct, this is part of a big *salami scam*. In a salami scam, someone shaves little slices off millions of accounts. People don't notice their tiny little losses, but the person doing the shaving collects enough for a quick escape to Barbados (or for a whole truckload of salami).

But, wait a minute! Nothing is motivating you to come with me to the bank. Checking back at Figure 7-5, I see that you're way ahead of the game. According to my calculations, the program overpays you by three hundred-trillionths of a cent. Between the two of us, we are ahead by a hundred-trillionth of a cent. What gives?

Well, because computers use zeros and ones and don't have an infinite amount of space to do calculations, inaccuracies like the ones shown in Figure 7-5 are inevitable. The best you can do is to display numbers in a more sensible fashion. You can round the numbers and display only two digits beyond the decimal point, and some handy tools from Java's API can help. The code is shown in Listing 7-4, and the pleasant result is displayed in Figure 7-10.

Listing 7-4: Making your numbers look right

```
java.text.NumberFormat currency =
    java.text.NumberFormat.getCurrencyInstance();

System.out.print("The interest on ");
System.out.print(myAccount.name);
System.out.print("'s account is ");
System.out.println
    (currency.format(myAccount.getInterest(5.00)));
System.out.println();

double yourInterestRate=7.00;
double yourInterestAmount;
System.out.print("The interest on ");
System.out.print(yourAccount.name);
System.out.print("'s account is ");
yourInterestAmount =
    yourAccount.getInterest(yourInterestRate);
System.out.println
    (currency.format(yourInterestAmount));
```

Figure 7-10:
Numbers
that look
like dollar
amounts.

```
C:\JavaPrograms>java UseAccount
The interest on Barry Burd's account is $1.20

The interest on Jane Q. Public's account is $3.89

C:\JavaPrograms>_
```

To test the code in Listing 7-4, just replace lines from Listing 7-3 with the corresponding lines in Listing 7-4.

The details of the code in Listing 7-4 aren't terribly important. Whenever you need to display a cash amount, you can just copy and paste lines from Listing 7-4 without thinking much at all. But, if you must know, Listing 7-4 uses a class named `java.text.NumberFormat` (another one of those Java API thingies). Using that class, you create an object called *currency*. (You can call the object anything you want. The name *rustedMetalSpittoon* would work, but a name like currency makes much more sense.)

Then, instead of printing what you get from the getInterest method, you apply what you get to another method named *currency.format*. The call to currency.format returns a nicely formatted string of digit characters. You feed these characters to your println method. The whole thing works very nicely.

The format method doesn't change the way a number is stored internally for calculations. All the format method does is create a nice-looking string of digit characters that can be displayed on your screen.

Hiding Details with Accessor Methods (Why You Shouldn't Micromanage a Bank Teller)

Put down this book and put on your hat. You've been such a loyal reader that I'm taking you out to lunch!

There's just one problem. I'm a bit short on cash. Would you mind if, on the way to lunch, we stopped at an automatic teller machine and picked up a few bucks? And, we have to use your account. My account is a little low.

Fortunately, the teller machine is easy to use. Just step right up and enter your PIN number. After entering your PIN, the machine asks which of several variable names you want to use for your current balance. You have a choice of balance324, myBal, currentBalance, b$, BALANCE, asj999, or conStanTinople. Having selected a variable name, you're ready to choose a memory location for the variable's value. You can choose any number between 022FFF and 0555AA. (Those numbers are in hexadecimal format.) After you've configured the teller machine's software, you can easily get your cash. You did bring a screwdriver, didn't you?

Good programming

When it comes to good computer programming practice, one word stands out above all others — *simplicity.* When you're writing complicated code, the last thing you want is to deal with somebody else's misnamed variables; convoluted solutions to problems; or clever, last-minute kludges. You want a clean interface that makes you solve your own problems and no one else's.

In the automatic teller machine scenario that I describe earlier, the big problem is that the machine's design forces you to worry about other people's concerns. When you should be thinking about getting money for lunch, you're thinking instead about variables and storage locations. Sure, someone has to work out the teller machine's engineering problems. But the banking customer is not the person to solve these problems.

This section is about safety, not security. Safe code keeps you from making accidental programming errors. Secure code (a completely different story) keeps malicious hackers from doing intentional damage.

So this means that everything connected with every aspect of a computer program has to be simple. Right? Well, no. That's not right. Sometimes, to make things simple in the long run, you have to do lots of preparatory work up front. The people who built the automated teller machine worked hard to make sure that the machine is consumer-proof. The machine's interface, with its screen messages and buttons, makes the machine a very complicated, but carefully designed device.

The point is, making things look simple takes some planning. In the case of object-oriented programming, one of the ways to make things look simple is to keep code outside a class from directly using variables defined inside the class. Take a peek at the code in Listing 7-1. You're working at a company that has just spent $10 million for the code in the Account class. (That's more than a million and a half per line!) Now your job is to write the UseAccount class. You would like to write

```
myAccount.name="Barry Burd";
```

but doing so would be getting you too far inside the guts of the Account class. After all, people who use an automatic teller machine aren't allowed to program the machine's variables. They can't use the machine's keypad to type the statement

```
balanceOnAccount29872865457 =
    balanceOnAccount29872865457 + 1000000.00;
```

Instead, they push buttons that do the job in an orderly manner. That's how a programmer achieves safety and simplicity.

So, to keep things nice and orderly, you need to change the Account class from Listing 7-1 by making statements such as the following illegal:

```
myAccount.name="Barry Burd";
```

and

```
System.out.print(yourAccount.balance);
```

But, of course, this poses a problem. You're the person who's writing the code for the UseAccount class. If you can't write `myAccount.name` or `yourAccount.balance`, how are you going to accomplish anything at all? The answer lies in things called *accessor methods*. These methods are demonstrated in Listing 7-5.

Listing 7-5:   Hide those variables

```
public class Account
{
    private String name;
    private String address;
    private double balance;

    public void setName(String n)
    {
        name=n;
    }

    public String getName()
    {
        return name;
    }

    public void setAddress(String a)
    {
        address=a;
    }

    public String getAddress()
    {
```

(continued)

Listing 7-5 *(continued)*

```
        return address;
    }

    public void setBalance(double b)
    {
        balance=b;
    }

    public double getBalance()
    {
        return balance;
    }
}


class UseAccount
{

    public static void main(String args[])
    {
        Account myAccount;
        Account yourAccount;

        myAccount = new Account();
        yourAccount = new Account();

        myAccount.setName("Barry Burd");
        myAccount.setAddress("222 Cyberspace Lane");
        myAccount.setBalance(24.02);

        yourAccount.setName("Jane Q. Public");
        yourAccount.setAddress("111 Consumer Street");
        yourAccount.setBalance(55.63);

        System.out.print(yourAccount.getName());
        System.out.print(" has $");
        System.out.print(yourAccount.getBalance());
        System.out.println(" in his or her account.");
    }

}
```

A run of the code in Listing 7-5 looks no different from a run of Listing 7-1. Either program's run is shown in Figure 7-3. The big difference is, in Listing 7-5, the Account class enforces the carefully controlled use of its internal variables.

Public lives and private dreams: Making a variable name inaccessible

Notice the addition of the word *private* in front of each of the Account class's variable declarations. The word *private* is a Java keyword. When a variable is declared to be private, then no code outside of the class can make direct reference to that variable. So, if you put `myAccount.name="Barry Burd"` in the UseAccount class of Listing 7-5, you get the following error message:

```
name has private access in Account
      myAccount.name="Barry Burd";
              ^
```

Instead of referencing myAccount.name, the UseAccount programmer must call method `myAccount.setName` or method `myAccount.getName`. These methods, setName and getName are called *accessor* methods, because they provide access to the Account class's name variable. (Actually, the term *accessor method* isn't formally a part of the Java programming language. It's just the term people use for methods that do this sort of thing.) To zoom in even more, setName is called a *setter* method, and getName is called a *getter* method. (I bet you won't forget that terminology!)

Notice how, in Listing 7-5, all the setter and getter methods are declared to be public. This ensures that anyone from anywhere can call these two methods. The idea here is that manipulating the actual variables from outside the Account code is impossible, but you can easily reach the approved setter and getter methods for using those variables.

Think again about the automatic teller machine. Someone using the ATM can't type a command that directly changes the value in his or her account's balance variable, but the procedure for depositing a million-dollar check is easy to follow. The people who build the teller machines know that, if the check depositing procedure is complicated, then plenty of customers will mess it up royally. So that's the story — make impossible anything that people shouldn't do, and make sure that the tasks people should be doing are easy.

Nothing about having setter and getter methods is sacred. You don't have to write any setter and getter methods that you're not going to use. For instance, in Listing 7-5, I can omit the declaration of method getAddress, and everything will still work. The only problem if I do this is that anyone else who wants to use my Account class and retrieve the address of an existing account is up a creek.

When you create a method to set the value in a balance variable, you don't have to name your method setBalance. You can name it tunaFish, or whatever you like. The trouble is, the *setVariablename* convention (with lowercase letters in *set*, and an uppercase letter to start the *Variablename* part) is an established stylistic convention in the world of Java programming. If you don't follow the convention, you'll confuse the kumquats out of other Java programmers. You'll also lose the capacity to have a Java development environment interpret your code. (For a word about Java development environments, see Chapter 2.)

When you call a setter method, you feed it a value of the type that's being set. That's why, in Listing 7-5, you call `yourAccount.setBalance(55.63)` with a parameter of type double. In contrast, when you call a getter method, you usually don't feed any values to the method. That's why, in Listing 7-5, you call `yourAccount.getBalance()` with an empty parameter list. Occasionally, you may want to get and set a value with a single statement. To add a dollar to your account's existing balance, you write `yourAccount.setBalance (yourAccount.getBalance() + 1.00)`.

Enforcing rules with accessor methods

Go back to Listing 7-5, and take a quick look at the setName method. Imagine putting the method's assignment statement inside an if statement.

```
if (!n.equals(""))
    name=n;
```

Now, if the programmer in charge of the UseAccount class writes `myAccount.setName("")`, then the call to setName won't have any effect. Furthermore, since the name variable is private, the following statement is illegal in class UseAccount:

```
myAccount.name="";
```

Of course, a call such as `myAccount.setName("Joe Schmoe")` still works, because `"Joe Schmoe"` doesn't equal the empty string `""`.

That's cool. With a private variable and an accessor method, you can prevent someone from assigning the empty string to an account's name variable. With more elaborate if statements, you can enforce any rules you want.

Chapter 8

Saving Time and Money: Reusing Existing Code

• •

In This Chapter

▶ Adding new life to old code

▶ Tweaking your code

▶ Making changes without spending a fortune

• •

*O*nce upon a time, there was a beautiful princess. When the princess turned 25 (the optimal age for strength, good looks, and fine moral character), her kind father brought her a gift in a lovely golden box. Anxious to know what was in the box, the princess ripped off the golden wrapping paper.

When the box was finally opened, the princess was thrilled. To her surprise, her father had given her what she had always wanted — a computer program that always ran correctly. The program did everything the princess wanted, and did it all exactly the way she wanted it to be done. The princess was happy, and so was her kind, old father.

As time went on, the computer program never failed. For years on end, the princess changed her needs, expected more out of life, made increasing demands, expanded her career, reached for more and more fulfillment, juggled the desires of her husband and her kids, stretched the budget, and sought peace within her soul. Through all this, the program remained her steady, faithful companion.

As the princess grew old, the program became old along with her. One evening, as she sat by the fireside, she posed a daunting question to the program. "How do you do it?" she asked. "How do you manage to keep giving the right answers, time after time, year after year?"

"Clean living," replied the program. "I swim twenty apps each day, I take C++ to Word off viruses, I avoid hogarithmic algorithms, I link Java in moderation, I say GNU to bugs, I don't smoke to backup, and I never byte off more than I can queue."

Needless to say, the princess was stunned.

Defining a Class (What It Means to be an Employee)

Wouldn't it be nice if every piece of software did just what you wanted it to do? In an ideal world you could just buy a program, make it work right away, plug it seamlessly into new situations, and update it easily whenever your needs changed. Unfortunately, software of this kind doesn't exist. (Nothing of this kind exists.) The truth is, no matter what you want to do, you can find software that does some of it, but not all of it.

This is one of the reasons why object-oriented programming has been so successful. For years, companies were buying prewritten code, only to learn that the code didn't do what they wanted it to do. So what did these companies do about it? They started messing with the code. Their programmers dug deep into the program files, changed variable names, moved subprograms around, reworked formulas, and generally made the code worse. The reality was, if a program didn't already do what you wanted it to do (even if it did something ever so close to what you wanted), you could never improve the situation by mucking around inside the code. The best option was always to chuck the whole program (expensive as that was) and start all over again. What a sad state of affairs!

With object-oriented programming, there's been a big change. At its heart, an object-oriented program is made to be modified. With correctly written software, you can take advantage of features that are already built-in, add new features of your own, and override features that don't suit your needs. And the best part is that the changes you make are clean. No clawing and digging into other people's brittle program code. Instead, you make nice orderly additions and modifications without touching the existing code's internal logic. It's the ideal solution.

The last word on employees

When you write an object-oriented program, you start by thinking about the data. You're writing about accounts. So what's an account? You're writing code to handle button clicks. So what's a button? You're writing a program to send payroll checks to employees. What's an employee?

In this chapter's first example, an employee is someone with a name and a job title. Sure, employees have other characteristics, but for now I stick to the basics. The code in Listing 8-1 defines what it means to be an employee.

Listing 8-1:   What is an Employee?

```
public class Employee
{
   private String name;
   private String jobTitle;

   public void setName(String nameIn)
   {
      name=nameIn;
   }

   public String getName()
   {
      return name;
   }

   public void setJobTitle(String jobTitleIn)
   {
      jobTitle=jobTitleIn;
   }

   public String getJobTitle()
   {
      return jobTitle;
   }

   public void cutCheck(double amountPaid)
   {
      java.text.NumberFormat currency =
         java.text.NumberFormat.getCurrencyInstance();

      System.out.print("Pay to the order of " + name);
      System.out.print(" (" + jobTitle +")  ***");
      System.out.println(currency.format(amountPaid));
   }
}
```

According to Listing 8-1, each employee has seven features. Two of these features are fairly simple. Each employee has a name and a job title.

And what else does an employee have? Each employee has four methods to handle the values of the employee's name and job title. These methods are called *setName, getName, setJobTitle,* and *getJobTitle.* Methods like these (*accessor* methods) are explained in Chapter 7.

On top of all that, each employee has a cutCheck method. The idea is, the method that writes payroll checks has to belong to one class or another. Because most of the information in the payroll check is customized for a particular employee, you might as well put the cutCheck method inside the Employee class.

Putting your class to good use

You may be wondering what the code in Listing 8-1 is good for. After all, the class in Listing 8-1 has no main method, so there's no starting point for executing. If you try to run the code in Listing 8-1, then the computer gives you this error message: `Exception in thread "main" java.lang.NoSuchMethodError: main`.

Well, you can write a separate program with a main method and use that program to create Employee instances. (To find out how to compile two programs separately, see Chapter 7.) Listing 8-2 shows a class with a main method — one that puts the code in Listing 8-1 to the test.

Listing 8-2:   Writing payroll checks

```
import java.io.BufferedReader;


class DoPayroll
{

    public static void main(String args[])
    {
      BufferedReader empInfo =
          DummiesIO.open("c:\\JavaPrograms\\EmployeeInfo");
      for (int emplNum=1; emplNum<=3; emplNum++)
          payOneEmployee(empInfo);
    }

    public static void payOneEmployee(BufferedReader empInfo)
    {
      Employee anEmployee = new Employee();

      anEmployee.setName(DummiesIO.getString(empInfo));
      anEmployee.setJobTitle(DummiesIO.getString(empInfo));
      anEmployee.cutCheck(DummiesIO.getDouble(empInfo));
    }

}
```

The DoPayroll class in Listing 8-2 has two methods. One of the methods, main, calls the other method, payOneEmployee, three times. Each time around, the payOneEmployee method gets stuff from the EmployeeInfo file and feeds this stuff to the Employee class's methods.

Here's how the variable name *anEmployee* is reused and recycled.

 ✔ The first time payOneEmployee is called, the statement `anEmployee = new Employee()` makes anEmployee refer to a new object.

> ✔ The second time payOneEmployee is called, the computer executes the same statement again. This creates a new incarnation of the anEmployee variable that refers to a brand-new object.
>
> ✔ The third time around, all the same stuff happens again. A new anEmployee variable ends up referring to a third object.

The whole story is pictured in Figure 8-1.

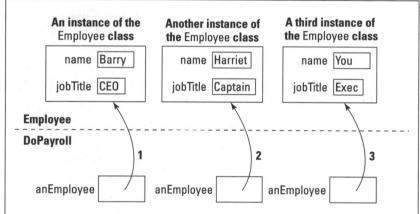

Figure 8-1: Three calls to the payOne Employee method.

An import declaration

Listing 8-2 begins with something called an *import declaration*. The reason for this takes a little explanation. You see, Java has a feature that lets you lump classes into groups of classes. Each lump of classes is called a *package*. In the Java world, programmers customarily give these packages long, dot-filled names. For instance, because I've registered the domain name *BurdBrain.com,* I may name a package `com.burdbrain.utils.textUtils`.

The Java API is actually a big collection of packages. The API has packages with names like *java.lang, java.awt, java.awt.event, java.applet,* and so on. Imagine you write a Java program that reads data from a disk file. You know that your program will work best if it uses a class named *BufferedReader.* This BufferedReader class happens to be part of an API package named *java.io.* (In the name *java.io,* the *io* part stands for "input/output.") The BufferedReader class is public, so you don't need any special dispensation to use this class. To use it, all you do is refer to the class by its fully qualified name, which is `java.io.BufferedReader`. (A class's *fully qualified name* includes the name of the package in which the class is defined.)

Returning to Listing 8-2, the main method in Listing 8-2 could have started with the following statement:

```
java.io.BufferedReader empInfo =
        DummiesIO.open("c:\\JavaPrograms\\EmployeeInfo");
```

This statement uses the fully qualified name `java.io.BufferedReader`. With this change, and no others, the code in Listing 8-2 would still work. But, in the main method in Listing 8-2, I get away with not using the fully qualified name of the `java.io.BufferedReader` class. Why? Because at the top of the file containing the code, I put the line `import java.io.BufferedReader`. This line is called an *import declaration*.

An import declaration allows you to abbreviate the name of a class. At the top of a Java program file, you can put any number of import declarations. For instance, a file containing a Java applet may start with the following lines:

```
import java.applet.Applet;
import java.awt.Graphics;
import java.awt.TextField;
```

An import declaration doesn't give you permission to use a particular class from a package, but this declaration does give you the ability to abbreviate the class's name. You put an import declaration at the top of a Java program file. Then, when you make reference to that class elsewhere in that file, you don't have to use the class's fully qualified name.

If you're lazy, you can import all the classes from the java.io package in one fell swoop. Just put `import java.io.*;` at the top of your Java program file. This trick works for other packages as well.

Reading from a file

The code in Listing 8-2 won't run unless you have some employee data sitting in a file. Listing 8-2 says that this file is named EmployeeInfo, but you can tinker with the name if you like. Anyway, before running the code of Listing 8-2, I created a small EmployeeInfo file of my own. The file is shown in Listing 8-3, and Figure 8-2 shows the resulting output.

Listing 8-3:   An EmployeeInfo file

```
Barry Burd
CEO
5000.00
Harriet Ritter
Captain
7000.00
Your Name Here
Honorary Exec of the Day
10000.00
```

Figure 8-2:
Everybody
gets paid.

```
C:\JavaPrograms>java DoPayroll
Pay to the order of Barry Burd (CEO)   ***$5,000.00
Pay to the order of Harriet Ritter (Captain)   ***$7,000.00
Pay to the order of Your Name Here (Honorary Exec of the Day)   ***$10,000.00

C:\JavaPrograms>_
```

You can copy the EmployeeInfo file from this book's CD-ROM, but you can also create files like EmployeeInfo on your own. Like almost all the listings in this book, the EmployeeInfo file is just another ordinary text file. Open the same editor you use to create Java code, type the text shown in Listing 8-3, and then save the file.

If you use Windows Notepad, be sure to put double quotes around the name ("EmployeeInfo" or `"c:\JavaPrograms\EmployeeInfo"`) in the Windows Save As dialog box. If you forget to do this, you get a file named `EmployeeInfo.txt`.

A successful run of the program in Listing 8-2 depends on code in my DummiesIO class. (For an introduction to the DummiesIO class, see Chapter 5.) In particular, Listing 8-2 uses a DummiesIO method named *open*. You can use the open method in programs that you write yourself. Just copy the statement in Listing 8-2 that calls the open method. Change `c:\\JavaPrograms\\ EmployeeInfo` to whatever name you're using for your data file. (Hey, what's up with those double backslashes? For a reminder, see Listing 6-5.) You can also change the variable name *empInfo* to something that reminds you of the kind of information in the file. (Just be sure to use your new variable name consistently throughout your program.) Don't change the method name *DummiesIO.open,* because that name is defined in DummiesIO's corresponding .java and .class files. And definitely don't change the name *java.io. BufferedReader,* because that name is defined in the Java API.

The call to DummiesIO.open establishes a connection between your Java program and the EmployeeInfo file. Notice how, in Listing 8-2, the call to open is executed only once. This is important. Every time the computer executes a call to my DummiesIO.open method, the computer resets its connection to the EmployeeInfo file. Resetting the connection means starting at the top of the EmployeeInfo file all over again, which is not what you want at all. If you make a mistake and call DummiesIO.open for each employee, the output you get looks like this:

```
Pay to the order of Barry Burd (CEO)   ***$5,000.00
Pay to the order of Barry Burd (CEO)   ***$5,000.00
Pay to the order of Barry Burd (CEO)   ***$5,000.00
```

Sure, I'd like to be paid in triplicate. But that output just isn't right. This problem (the danger of starting over at the beginning of a data file) isn't unique to my own DummiesIO.open method. It's an issue that you'll face with other people's input/output methods as well.

Avoid opening a file more than once per run of a program.

What? You say you still don't believe what I say about calling DummiesIO.open just once? Then try repositioning the call to DummiesIO.open so that the call is made three times, instead of just once. To do this, just move the call so that it's inside the payOneEmployee method, as shown in the following code:

```
public static void payOneEmployee()
{
   Employee anEmployee = new Employee();
   BufferedReader empInfo =
      DummiesIO.open("c:\\JavaPrograms\\EmployeeInfo");

   anEmployee.setName(DummiesIO.getString(empInfo));
   anEmployee.setJobTitle(DummiesIO.getString(empInfo));
   anEmployee.cutCheck(DummiesIO.getDouble(empInfo));
}
```

The output you get from reading the EmployeeInfo file pays Barry, then Barry, and finally Barry.

If you get a `java.io.FileNotFoundException` message when you try to run the code in Listing 8-2, then the EmployeeInfo file isn't available to your program. This is an easy mistake to make and can be frustrating, because to you, the EmployeeInfo file may look like it's available to your program. But remember — computers are stupid. A computer can't read between the lines if you cross every *i* and dot every *t*. So, if your EmployeeInfo file isn't in the right directory on your hard drive or the file's name is spelled incorrectly, the computer chokes when it tries to run the code in Listing 8-2. Just stare carefully at the listing of files in your JavaPrograms directory until you figure out what's wrong.

Defining Subclasses (What It Means to be a Full-Time Employee or a Part-Time Employee)

This time last year, your company paid $10 million for a piece of software. That software comes in a file named `Employee.class`. People at Burd Brain Consulting (the company that created the software) don't want you to know about the innards of the software (otherwise, you may steal their ideas). So you don't have the Java program file that the software came from. (In other words, you don't have `Employee.java`.) You do have a Web document named `Employee.html`. The core content of the `Employee.html` page is shown in Figure 8-3.

Field Summary	
String	**name**
	The legal name of your employee.
String	**jobTitle**
	The job the employee performs in your company.

Method Summary	
void	**cutCheck**(double amountPaid)
	Writes a check to be sent to the employee.
String	**getJobTitle**()
	Returns the employee's job title.
String	**getName**()
	Returns the employee's name.
void	**setJobTitle**(String jobTitleIn)
	Sets the employee's job title to jobTitleIn.
void	**setName**(String nameIn)
	Sets the employee's name to nameIn.

Figure 8-3:
The mythical Employee class documentation.

By creating instances of the Employee class, you can send payroll checks to all your employees. (In fact, you paid your employees when you ran the code in Listing 8-2.)

Since this time last year, your company has grown. Unlike the old days, your company now has two kinds of employees: full-time and part-time. Each full-time employee is on a fixed, weekly salary. (If the employee works nights and weekends, then, in return for this monumental effort, the employee receives a hearty handshake.) In contrast, each part-time employee works for an hourly wage. Your company deducts an amount from each full-time employee's paycheck to pay for the company's benefits package. Part-time employees, however, don't get benefits.

The question is, how can the software you bought last year keep up with the company's growth? You've invested in a great program to handle employees and their payroll, but the program doesn't differentiate between your full-time and part-time employees. You have several options:

✔ Call your next-door neighbor, whose 12-year-old child knows more about computer programming than anyone in your company. Get this uppity little brat to take the employee software apart, rewrite it, and hand it back to you with all the changes and additions your company requires.

On second thought, you can't do that. No matter how smart that kid is, the complexities of the employee software will probably confuse the kid. By the time you get the software back, it'll be filled with bugs and inconsistencies. Besides, you don't even have the Employee.java file to hand to the kid. All you have is the Employee.class file. And the Employee.class file cannot be read or modified with a text editor. (See Chapter 2.) Besides, your kid just beat up the neighbor's kid. You don't want to give your neighbor the satisfaction of seeing you beg for the whiz kid's help.

✔ Scrap the $10 million employee software. Get someone in your company to rewrite the software from scratch.

In other words, say goodbye to your time and your money.

✔ Write a new front end for the employee software. That is, build a piece of code that does some preliminary processing on full-time employees and then hands the preliminary results to your $10 million software. Do the same for part-time employees.

This idea could be decent or spell disaster. Are you sure that the existing employee software has convenient "hooks" in it? (That is, does the employee software contain entry points that allow your front-end software to easily send preliminary data to the expensive employee software?) Remember, this plan treats the existing software as one big, monolithic lump, which can become cumbersome. Dividing the labor between your front-end code and the existing employee program is difficult. And if you add layer upon layer to existing black box code, you'll probably end up with a fairly inefficient system.

✔ Call Burd Brain Consulting, the company that sold you the employee software. Tell Dr. Burd that you want the next version of his software to differentiate between full-time and part-time employees.

"No problem," says Dr. Burd. "It'll be ready by the start of the next fiscal quarter." That evening, Dr. Burd makes a discrete phone call to his next-door neighbor's house. . . .

✔ Create two new Java classes named *FullTimeEmployee* and *PartTimeEmployee*. Have each new class extend the existing functionality of the expensive Employee class. But have each new class define its own specialized functionality for certain kinds of employees.

Way to go! Figure 8-4 shows the structure you want to create.

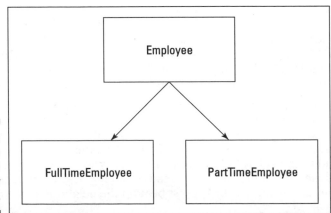

Figure 8-4:
The
Employee
class family
tree.

Creating a subclass

In Listing 8-1, I define an Employee class. I can use what I define in Listing 8-1 and extend the definition to create new, more specialized classes. So in Listing 8-4, I define a new class — a FullTimeEmployee class.

Listing 8-4:   What is a FullTimeEmployee?

```
public class FullTimeEmployee extends Employee
{

    private double weeklySalary;
    private double benefitDeduction;

    public void setWeeklySalary(double weeklySalaryIn)
    {
        weeklySalary=weeklySalaryIn;
    }

    public double getWeeklySalary()
    {
        return weeklySalary;
    }

    public void setBenefitDeduction(double benefitDedIn)
    {
        benefitDeduction=benefitDedIn;
    }

    public double getBenefitDeduction()
    {
        return benefitDeduction;
    }

    public double findPaymentAmount()
    {
        return weeklySalary-benefitDeduction;
    }

}
```

Looking at Listing 8-4, you can see that each instance of the FullTimeEmployee class has two variables: weeklySalary and benefitDeduction. But are those the only variables that each FullTimeEmployee instance has? No, they're not. The first line of Listing 8-4 says that the FullTimeEmployee class extends the existing Employee class. This means that, in addition to having a weeklySalary and a benefitDeduction, each FullTimeEmployee instance also has two other variables: name and jobTitle. These two variables come from the definition of the Employee class, which you can find in Listing 8-1.

In Listing 8-4, the magic word is the word *extends*. When one class extends an existing class, the extending class automatically inherits functionality that's defined in the existing class. So, the FullTimeEmployee class *inherits* the name and jobTitle variables. The FullTimeEmployee class also inherits all the methods declared in the Employee class — setName, getName, setJobTitle, getJobTitle, and cutCheck. The FullTimeEmployee class is a *subclass* of the Employee class. That means the Employee class is the *superclass* of the FullTimeEmployee class. You can also talk in terms of blood relatives. The FullTimeEmployee class is the *child* of the Employee class, and the Employee class is the *parent* of the FullTimeEmployee class.

It's almost (but not quite) as if the FullTimeEmployee class were defined by the code in Listing 8-5.

Listing 8-5: Fake (but informative) code

```
public class FullTimeEmployee
{

    private String name;
    private String jobTitle;
    private double weeklySalary;
    private double benefitDeduction;

    public void setName(String nameIn)
    {
        name=nameIn;
    }

    public String getName()
    {
        return name;
    }

    public void setJobTitle(String jobTitleIn)
    {
        jobTitle=jobTitleIn;
    }

    public String getJobTitle()
    {
        return jobTitle;
    }

    public void setWeeklySalary(double weeklySalaryIn)
    {
        weeklySalary=weeklySalaryIn;
    }

    public double getWeeklySalary()
    {
```

```
      return weeklySalary;
   }

   public void setBenefitDeduction(double benefitDedIn)
   {
      benefitDeduction=benefitDedIn;
   }

   public double getBenefitDeduction()
   {
      return benefitDeduction;
   }

   public double findPaymentAmount()
   {
      return weeklySalary-benefitDeduction;
   }

   public void cutCheck(double amountPaid)
   {
      java.text.NumberFormat currency =
         java.text.NumberFormat.getCurrencyInstance();

      System.out.print("Pay to the order of " + name);
      System.out.print(" (" + jobTitle +")  ***");
      System.out.println(currency.format(amountPaid));
   }

}
```

Why does the title for Listing 8-5 call that code fake? (Should the code feel insulted?) Well, the main difference between Listing 8-5 and the inheritance situation in Listings 8-1 and 8-4 is this: A child class can't directly reference the private variables of its parent class. To do anything with the parent class's private variables, the child class has to call the parent class's accessor methods. Back in Listing 8-4, calling `setName("Rufus")` would be legal, but the code `name="Rufus"` wouldn't be legal. If you believe everything you read in Listing 8-5, then you'll think that code in the FullTimeEmployee class can do `name="Rufus"`. Well, it can't. (My, what a subtle point this is!)

You don't need the `Employee.java` file on your hard drive to write code that extends the Employee class. All you need is the file `Employee.class`.

Creating subclasses is habit-forming

After you're accustomed to extending classes, you can get extend-happy. If you created a FullTimeEmployee class, you might as well create a PartTimeEmployee class, as shown in Listing 8-6.

Listing 8-6:   What is a PartTimeEmployee?

```
public class PartTimeEmployee extends Employee
{

   private double hourlyRate;

   public void setHourlyRate(double rateIn)
   {
      hourlyRate=rateIn;
   }

   public double getHourlyRate()
   {
      return hourlyRate;
   }

   public double findPaymentAmount(int hours)
   {
      return hourlyRate*hours;
   }

}
```

Unlike the FullTimeEmployee class, PartTimeEmployee has no salary or deduction. Instead PartTimeEmployee has an hourlyRate variable. (Adding a numberOfHoursWorked variable would also be a possibility. I chose not to do this, figuring that the number of hours a part-time employee works will change drastically from week to week.)

Using Subclasses

The previous section tells a story about creating subclasses. It's a good story, but it's incomplete. Creating subclasses is fine, but you gain nothing from these subclasses unless you write code to use them. So in this section, you explore code that uses subclasses.

Now the time has come for you to classify yourself as either a type-F person or a type-P person. A type-F person wants to see the fundamentals. (The letter *F* stands for *fundamentals.*) "Show me a program that lays the principles out in their barest, most basic form," says the type-F person. A type F person isn't worried about bells and whistles. The bells come later, and the whistles may never come at all. If you're a type-F person, you want to see a program that uses subclasses, and then moves out of your way so you can get some work done.

On the other hand, a type-P person wants practical applications. (The letter *P* stands for *practical.*) Type-P people need to see ideas in context; otherwise the ideas float away too quickly. "Show me a program that demonstrates the usefulness of subclasses," says the type-P person. "I have no use for your stinking abstractions. I want real-life examples, and I want them now!"

Because I'm always aiming to please my reader, this section has two (count 'em — two) examples that make use of the last section's subclasses. The first example, which is for the type-F crowd, is lean and simple and makes good bedtime reading. On the other hand, the second example, which is for type-P fanatics, shows how subclasses fit into a useful context.

So that's it. Choose your poison and read on.

A program for the minimalist

Listing 8-7 shows you a bare-bones program that uses the subclasses FullTimeEmployee and PartTimeEmployee. Figure 8-5 shows the program's output.

Listing 8-7:   Use subclasses and then leave me alone

```
class DoPayrollTypeF
{

    public static void main(String args[])
    {
        FullTimeEmployee ftEmployee = new FullTimeEmployee();

        ftEmployee.setName("Barry Burd");
        ftEmployee.setJobTitle("CEO");
        ftEmployee.setWeeklySalary(5000.00);
        ftEmployee.setBenefitDeduction(500.00);

        ftEmployee.cutCheck(ftEmployee.findPaymentAmount());
        System.out.println();

        PartTimeEmployee ptEmployee = new PartTimeEmployee();

        ptEmployee.setName("Steve Surace");
        ptEmployee.setJobTitle("Driver");
        ptEmployee.setHourlyRate(7.53);

        ptEmployee.cutCheck(ptEmployee.findPaymentAmount(10));
    }

}
```

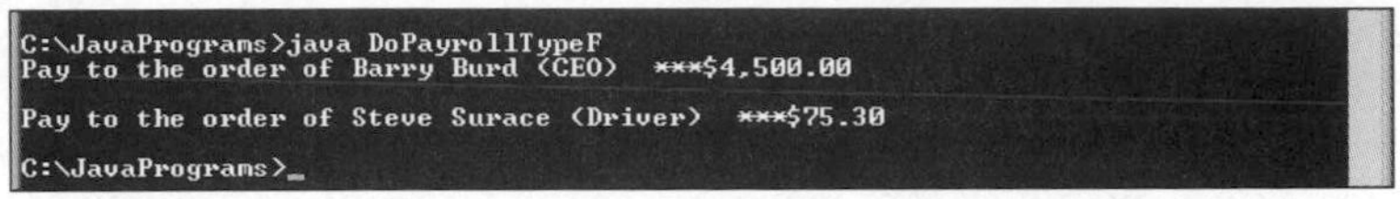

Figure 8-5:
The output
of the
program in
Listing 8-7.

```
C:\JavaPrograms>java DoPayrollTypeF
Pay to the order of Barry Burd (CEO)    ***$4,500.00

Pay to the order of Steve Surace (Driver)  ***$75.30

C:\JavaPrograms>_
```

To understand Listing 8-7, you need to keep an eye on three classes: Employee, FullTimeEmployee, and PartTimeEmployee. (For a look at the code that defines these classes, see Listings 8-1, 8-4, and 8-6.)

The first half of Listing 8-7 deals with a full-time employee. Notice how so many methods are available for use with the ftEmployee variable. For instance, you can call ftEmployee.setWeeklySalary, because ftEmployee has type FullTimeEmployee. You can also call ftEmployee.setName, because the FullTimeEmployee class extends the Employee class.

Because cutCheck is declared in the Employee class, you can call ftEmployee.cutCheck. But you can also call ftEmployee.findPaymentAmount, because a findPaymentAmount method is in the FullTimeEmployee class.

Making types match

Look again at the first half of Listing 8-7. Take special notice of that last statement — the one in which the full-time employee is actually cut a check. The statement forms a nice, long chain of values and their types. You can see this by reading the statement from the inside out.

✔ Method ftEmployee.findPaymentAmount is called with an empty parameter list (Listing 8-7).

✔ That's good, because the findPaymentAmount method takes no parameters (Listing 8-4).

✔ The findPaymentAmount method returns a value of type double (again, Listing 8-4).

✔ The double value that ftEmployee.findPaymentAmount returns is passed to method ftEmployee.cutCheck (Listing 8-7). That's good, because the cutCheck method takes one parameter of type double (Listing 8-1).

For a fanciful graphic illustration, see Figure 8-6.

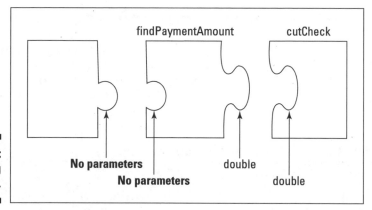

Figure 8-6:
Matching
parameters.

Always feed a method the value types that it wants in its parameter list.

The second half of the story

In the second half of Listing 8-7, the code creates an object of type
PartTimeEmployee. A variable of type PartTimeEmployee can do some of the
same things a FullTimeEmployee variable can do. But the PartTimeEmployee
class doesn't have the setWeeklySalary and setBenefitDeduction methods.
Instead, PartTimeEmployee class has the setHourlyRate method. (See Listing
8-6.) So, in Listing 8-7, the next-to-last line is a call to the setHourlyRate
method.

The last line of Listing 8-7 is, by far, the most interesting. On that line,
the code hands the number 10 (the number of hours worked) to the
findPaymentAmount method. Compare this with the earlier call to
findPaymentAmount — the call for the full-time employee in the first half
of Listing 8-7. Between the two subclasses, FullTimeEmployee and
PartTimeEmployee, are two different findPaymentAmount methods. The
two methods have two different kinds of parameter lists:

- ✔ The FullTimeEmployee class's findPaymentAmount method takes no
  parameters (Listing 8-4).
- ✔ The PartTimeEmployee class's findPaymentAmount method takes one
  int parameter (Listing 8-6).

This is par for the course. Finding the payment amount for a part-time
employee isn't the same as finding the payment amount for a full-time
employee. A part-time employee's pay changes each week, depending on the
number of hours the employee works in a week. The full-time employee's pay
stays the same each week. So both the FullTimeEmployee and
PartTimeEmployee classes have findPaymentAmount methods, but each
class's method works quite differently.

A program for the maximalist

If you crave useful results and practical applications, then you either skipped over the last listing or gritted your teeth while you read through it. Listing 8-8 gives you the same information with a more practical point of view. Of course, there's a price. Listing 8-8 is longer and more complicated than the listing in the previous section. Oh, well!

Listing 8-8:   Big-time payroll program

```java
import java.io.BufferedReader;


class DoPayrollTypeP
{

    public static void main(String args[])
    {
        BufferedReader inFile =
            DummiesIO.open("c:\\JavaPrograms\\EmployeeInfo");
        for (int emplNum=1; emplNum<=3; emplNum++)
            payOneFTEmployee(inFile);
        for (int emplNum=4; emplNum<=6; emplNum++)
            payOnePTEmployee(inFile);
    }

    public static void payOneFTEmployee(BufferedReader inFile)
    {
        FullTimeEmployee employee = new FullTimeEmployee();

        employee.setName(DummiesIO.getString(inFile));
        employee.setJobTitle(DummiesIO.getString(inFile));
        employee.setWeeklySalary(DummiesIO.getDouble(inFile));
        employee.setBenefitDeduction
                                (DummiesIO.getDouble(inFile));
        DummiesIO.getString(inFile);

        employee.cutCheck(employee.findPaymentAmount());
        System.out.println();
    }


    public static void payOnePTEmployee(BufferedReader inFile)
    {
        PartTimeEmployee employee = new PartTimeEmployee();

        employee.setName(DummiesIO.getString(inFile));
        employee.setJobTitle(DummiesIO.getString(inFile));
        employee.setHourlyRate(DummiesIO.getDouble(inFile));

        System.out.print("Enter ");
```

```
        System.out.print(employee.getName());
        System.out.print("'s hours worked this week: ");
        int hours = DummiesIO.getInt();

        DummiesIO.getString(inFile);

        employee.cutCheck(employee.findPaymentAmount(hours));
        System.out.println();
    }
}
```

For all its complexity, the code in Listing 8-8 still isn't a full-blown payroll program. It's a toy program, but it's a bit more realistic than the program in Listing 8-7. The code in Listing 8-8 writes checks for six employees — three full-time employees and three part-time employees. Calls to payOneFTEmployee and payOnePTEmployee make sure each employee receives a check. Each of these payOneEmployee methods reads data from a file and uses the data to fill the employee object's variables with values. Listing 8-9 shows the file I used to test Listing 8-8, and the resulting run is shown in Figure 8-7.

Listing 8-9:   Input for the big-time payroll program

```
Barry Burd
CEO
5000.00
500.00
---
Harriet Ritter
Captain
7000.00
700.00
---
Your Name Here
Honorary Exec of the Day
10000.00
200.00
---
Steve Surace
Driver
7.53
---
Bernard Smith
Messenger
9.26
---
Chris Apelian
Computer Book Author
3.54
```

```
C:\JavaPrograms>java DoPayrollTypeP
Pay to the order of Barry Burd (CEO)   ***$4,500.00

Pay to the order of Harriet Ritter (Captain)  ***$6,300.00

Pay to the order of Your Name Here (Honorary Exec of the Day)  ***$9,800.00

Enter Steve Surace's hours worked this week: 10
Pay to the order of Steve Surace (Driver)  ***$75.30

Enter Bernard Smith's hours worked this week: 15
Pay to the order of Bernard Smith (Messenger)  ***$138.90

Enter Chris Apelian's hours worked this week: 65
Pay to the order of Chris Apelian (Computer Book Author)  ***$230.10

C:\JavaPrograms>
```

Figure 8-7:
Paying your
employees.

Compared with its full-time cousin, the payOnePTEmployee method pulls one extra idea out of its bag of tricks. When the time comes to get the number of hours the employee worked, the payOnePTEmployee method doesn't consult a disk file. Instead, the method asks the user for live keyboard input. The thought here is that the disk file is where all the long-term information about employees lives. Because the number of hours an employee worked this week isn't long-term information, the payOnePTEmployee method gets the user to enter this information on the fly.

Overriding Existing Methods (Changing the Payments for Some of Your Employees)

Wouldn't you know it! Some knucklehead in the human resources department offered double pay for overtime to one of your part-time employees. Now word is getting around, and some of the other part-timers want double pay for their overtime work. If this keeps up, you'll end up in the poorhouse, so you need to send out a memo to all the part-time employees, explaining why earning more money is not to their benefit.

In the meantime, you have two kinds of part-time employees — the ones who receive double pay for overtime hours and the ones who don't — so you need to modify your payroll software. What are your options?

✔ Well, you can dig right into the PartTimeEmployee class code, make a few changes, and hope for the best. (Not a good idea!)

✔ You can follow the previous section's advice and create a subclass of the existing PartTimeEmployee class. "But wait," you say. "The existing PartTimeEmployee class already has a findPaymentAmount method. Do I need some tricky way of bypassing this existing findPaymentAmount method for each double-pay-for-overtime employee?"

At this point, you can thank your lucky stars that you're doing object-oriented programming in Java. With object-oriented programming, you can create a subclass that overrides the functionality of its parent class. Listing 8-10 has just such a subclass.

Listing 8-10: Yet another subclass

```
public class PartTimeWithOver extends PartTimeEmployee
{
    public double findPaymentAmount(int hours)
    {
        if (hours<=40)
            return getHourlyRate()*hours;
        else
            return getHourlyRate()*40 +
                    getHourlyRate()*2*(hours-40);
    }
}
```

Figure 8-8 shows the relationship between the code in Listing 8-10 and other pieces of code in this chapter. In particular, PartTimeWithOver is a subclass of a subclass. In object-oriented programming, a chain of this kind is not the least bit unusual. In fact, as subclasses go, this chain is rather short.

The PartTimeWithOver class extends the PartTimeEmployee class, but PartTimeWithOver picks and chooses what it wants to inherit from the PartTimeEmployee class. Because PartTimeWithOver has its own declaration for the findPaymentAmount method, the PartTimeWithOver class doesn't inherit a findPaymentAmount method from its parent. (See Figure 8-9.)

According to the official terminology, the PartTimeWithOver class *overrides* its parent class's findPaymentAmount method. If you create an object from the PartTimeWithOver class, then that object has the name, jobTitle, hourlyRate, and cutCheck of the PartTimeEmployee class, but the object has the findPaymentAmount method that's defined in Listing 8-10.

If you need clarification on the stuff that you just read, look at the code in Listing 8-11. A run of that code is shown in Figure 8-10.

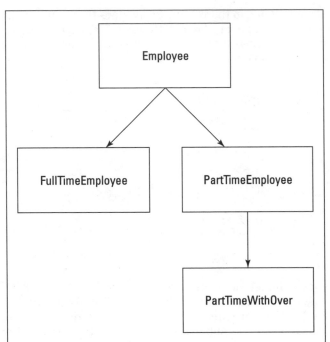

Figure 8-8:
A tree of
classes.

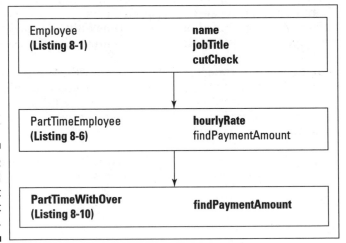

Figure 8-9:
Method
findPayment
Amount isn't
inherited.

Listing 8-11:   Testing the code from Listing 8-10

```
class DoPayrollTypeF
{

    public static void main(String args[])
    {
        FullTimeEmployee ftEmployee = new FullTimeEmployee();

        ftEmployee.setName("Barry Burd");
        ftEmployee.setJobTitle("CEO");
        ftEmployee.setWeeklySalary(5000.00);
        ftEmployee.setBenefitDeduction(500.00);

        ftEmployee.cutCheck(ftEmployee.findPaymentAmount());
        System.out.println();

        PartTimeEmployee ptEmployee = new PartTimeEmployee();

        ptEmployee.setName("Chris Apelian");
        ptEmployee.setJobTitle("Computer Book Author");
        ptEmployee.setHourlyRate(7.53);

        ptEmployee.cutCheck(ptEmployee.findPaymentAmount(50));
        System.out.println();

        PartTimeWithOver ptoEmployee = new PartTimeWithOver();

        ptoEmployee.setName("Steve Surace");
        ptoEmployee.setJobTitle("Driver");
        ptoEmployee.setHourlyRate(7.53);

        ptoEmployee.cutCheck
                        (ptoEmployee.findPaymentAmount(50));
    }

}
```

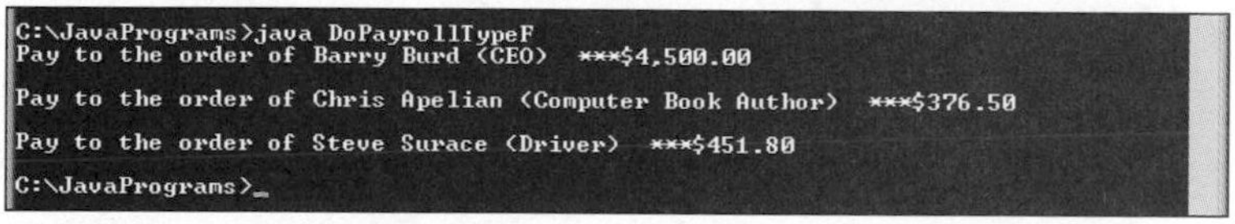

Figure 8-10:
Running the
code of
Listing 8-11.

```
C:\JavaPrograms>java DoPayrollTypeF
Pay to the order of Barry Burd (CEO)   ***$4,500.00
Pay to the order of Chris Apelian (Computer Book Author)   ***$376.50
Pay to the order of Steve Surace (Driver)   ***$451.80
C:\JavaPrograms>_
```

The code in Listing 8-11 writes checks to three employees. The first employee is a full-timer. The second is one of those part-time employees who hasn't yet gotten wind of the overtime payment scheme. The third employee knows about the overtime payment scheme and demands a fair wage.

With the subclasses, all three of these employees coexist in Listing 8-11. Sure, one subclass comes from the old PartTimeEmployee class, but that doesn't mean you can't create an object from the PartTimeEmployee class. In fact, Java is very smart about this. Listing 8-11 has three calls to the findPaymentAmount method, and each call reaches out to a different version of the method.

- ✔ In the first call, `ftEmployee.findPaymentAmount`, the ftEmployee variable is an instance of the FullTimeEmployee class. So the method that's called is the one in Listing 8-4.

- ✔ In the second call, `ptEmployee.findPaymentAmount`, the ptEmployee variable is an instance of the PartTimeEmployee class. So the method that's called is the one in Listing 8-6.

- ✔ In the third call, `ptoEmployee.findPaymentAmount`, the ptoEmployee variable is an instance of the PartTimeWithOver class. So the method that's called is the one in Listing 8-10.

This code is fantastic. It's clean, elegant and efficient. With all the money you save on software, you can afford to pay everyone double for overtime hours. (Whether you do that or keep the money for yourself is another story.)

Chapter 9

Constructing New Objects

● ●

In This Chapter

▶ Defining constructors

▶ Using constructors in subclasses

▶ Using Java's default constructor features

▶ Constructing a simple GUI

● ●

Ms. Jennie Rebekah Burd
121 Schoolhouse Lane
Anywhere, Kansas

Dear Ms. Burd,

In response to your letter of June 21, I believe I can say, with complete assurance, that objects are not created spontaneously from nothing. Although I have never actually seen an object being created (and no one else in this office can claim to have seen an object in its moment of creation), I have every confidence that some process or other is responsible for the building of these interesting and useful thingamajigs. We here at ClassesAndObjects.com support the unanimous opinions of both the scientific community and the private sector on matters of this nature. Furthermore, we agree with the recent finding of a Blue Ribbon Presidential Panel, which concludes beyond any doubt that spontaneous object creation would impede the present economic outlook.

Please be assured that I have taken all steps necessary to ensure the safety and well being of you, our loyal customer. If you have any further questions, please do not hesitate to contact our complaint department. The department's manager is Mr. Blake Wholl. You can contact him by visiting our company's Web site.

Once again, let me thank you for your concern, and I hope you continue to patronize ClassesAndObjects.com.

Yours truly,

Mr. Scott Brickenchicker
The one who couldn't get on the elevator in Chapter 4

Defining Constructors (What It Means to be a Temperature)

Here's a statement that creates an object.

```
Account myAccount = new Account();
```

I know this works, because I got it from one of my own examples in Chapter 7. Anyway, in Chapter 7, I say, "when the computer executes `new Account()`, you're creating an object by calling the Account class's constructor." What does this mean?

Well, when you ask the computer to create a new object, the computer responds by performing certain actions. For starters, the computer finds a place in its memory to store information about the new object. If the object has variables, then these variables should eventually have meaningful values.

So one question is, when you ask the computer to create a new object, can you control what's placed in the object's variables? And what if you're interested in doing more than filling variables? Perhaps, when the computer creates a new object, you have a whole list of jobs for the computer to carry out. For instance, when the computer creates a new window object, you want the computer to realign the sizes of all the buttons in that window.

Creating a new object can involve all kinds of tasks, so in this chapter, you create constructors. A constructor tells the computer to perform a new object's startup tasks.

What is a temperature?

"Good morning, and welcome to Object News. The local temperature in your area is a pleasant 73 degrees Fahrenheit."

Each temperature consists of two things — a number and a temperature scale. The code in Listing 9-1 makes this fact abundantly clear.

Listing 9-1:   The Temperature class

```
public class Temperature
{
    private double number;
    private char scale;

    public Temperature()
    {
```

```
        number=0.0;
        scale='F';
    }

    public Temperature(double number)
    {
        this.number=number;
        scale='F';
    }

    public Temperature(char scale)
    {
        number=0.0;
        this.scale=scale;
    }

    public Temperature(double number, char scale)
    {
        this.number=number;
        this.scale=scale;
    }

    public void setNumber(double number)
    {
        this.number=number;
    }

    public double getNumber()
    {
        return number;
    }

    public void setScale(char scale)
    {
        this.scale=scale;
    }

    public char getScale()
    {
        return scale;
    }

}
```

At the top of the code in Listing 9-1 are two variables: number and scale. A number is just a double value, such as 32.0 or 70.52. A scale is a char value, like 'F' for Fahrenheit or 'C' for Celsius. The code also has the usual setter and getter methods. There are accessor methods for the number and scale variables.

On top of all that, Listing 9-1 has three other method-like looking things. Each of these method-like things has the name *Temperature,* which happens to be the same as the name of the class. None of these Temperature method-like things has a return type of any kind — not even void, which is the copout return type.

Each of these method-like things is called a *constructor*. A constructor is like a method, except that a constructor has a very special purpose — creating new objects.

Whenever the computer creates a new object, the computer executes the statements inside a constructor.

What you can do with a temperature

Listing 9-2 gives form to some of the ideas described above. In Listing 9-2, you call the constructors that were declared back in Listing 9-1. Figure 9-1 shows what happens when you run all this code.

Listing 9-2: Using the Temperature class

```
class UseTemperature
{
    public static void main(String args[])
    {
        Temperature temp;

        temp = new Temperature();
        temp.setNumber(70.0);
        temp.setScale('F');
        System.out.print(temp.getNumber());
        System.out.print(" degrees ");
        System.out.println(temp.getScale());

        temp = new Temperature(32.0);
        System.out.print(temp.getNumber());
        System.out.print(" degrees ");
        System.out.println(temp.getScale());

        temp = new Temperature('C');
        System.out.print(temp.getNumber());
        System.out.print(" degrees ");
        System.out.println(temp.getScale());

        temp = new Temperature(2.73, 'K');
        System.out.print(temp.getNumber());
        System.out.print(" degrees ");
        System.out.println(temp.getScale());
    }
}
```

Figure 9-1:
Running the
code from
Listing 9-2.

```
C:\JavaPrograms>java UseTemperature
70.0 degrees F
32.0 degrees F
0.0 degrees C
2.73 degrees K
C:\JavaPrograms>
```

In Listing 9-2, each statement of the kind

```
temp = new Temperature(blah,blah,blah);
```

calls one of the constructors from Listing 9-1. So, by the time the code in
Listing 9-2 is done running, it creates four instances of the Temperature class.
Each instance is created by calling a different constructor from Listing 9-1.

Calling new Temperature (32.0): A case study

When the computer executes one of the `new Temperature` statements in
Listing 9-2, the computer has to decide which of the constructors in Listing
9-1 to use. The computer decides by looking at the parameter list (the stuff
in parentheses) after the words `new Temperature`. For instance, when the
computer executes

```
temp = new Temperature(32.0);
```

from Listing 9-2, the computer says to itself, "The number 32.0 in parentheses
is a double value. One of the Temperature constructors in Listing 9-1 has just
one parameter with type double. The constructor's header looks like this.

```
public Temperature(double number)
```

"So, I guess I'll execute the statements inside that particular constructor."
The computer goes on to execute the following statements:

```
        this.number=number;
        scale='F';
```

As a result, you get a brand-new object, whose number variable has the value
`32.0`, and whose scale variable has the value `'F'`.

In the two lines shown above, you have two statements that set values for the
variables number and scale. Take a look at the second of these statements,
which is a bit easier to understand. The second statement sets the new
object's scale variable to `'F'`. You see, the constructor's parameter list is
`(double number)`, and that list doesn't include a scale value. So whoever

programmed this code had to make a decision about what value to use for the scale variable. The programmer could have chosen 'F' or 'C', but she could also have chosen 'K' for Kelvin or 'R' for Rankine. (This programmer happens to live in New Jersey, in the United States, where people commonly use the old Fahrenheit temperature scale.)

Marching back to the first of the two statements, this first statement assigns a value to the new object's number variable. The statement uses a cute trick that you'll see in many constructors (and in other methods that assign values to objects' variables). To understand the trick, take a look at Listing 9-3. The listing shows you two ways I could have written the same constructor code.

Listing 9-3:   Two ways to accomplish the same thing

```
//Use this constructor ...

    public Temperature(double whatever)
    {
        number=whatever;
        scale='F';
    }

//... or use this constructor ...

    public Temperature(double number)
    {
        this.number=number;
        scale='F';
    }

//... but don't put both constructors in your code.
```

Listing 9-3 has two constructors in it. In the first constructor, I use two different names — number and whatever. In the second constructor, I don't need two names. Instead of making up a new name for the constructor's parameter, I reuse an existing name by writing this.number.

So here's what's going on in Listing 9-1:

   ✔ In the statement this.number=number, the name *this.number* refers to the new object's number variable — the variable that's declared near the very top of Listing 9-1. (See Figure 9-2.)

   ✔ In the statement this.number=number, the word *number* (on its own, without *this*) refers to the constructor's parameter. (Again, see Figure 9-2.)

In general, this.someName refers to a variable belonging to the object that contains the code. In contrast, plain old *someName* refers to the closest place where someName happens to be declared. In the statement this.number=number (Listing 9-1), that closest place happens to be the Temperature constructor's parameter list.

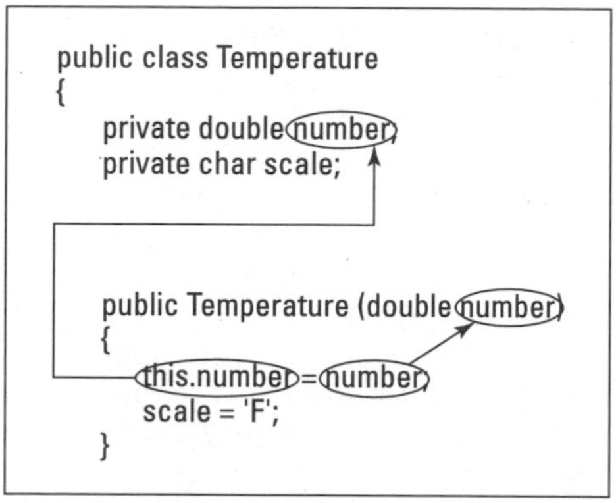

```
public class Temperature
{
    private double number
    private char scale;

    public Temperature (double number)
    {
        this.number = number
        scale = 'F';
    }
}
```

Figure 9-2:
What
this.number
and number
mean.

More Subclasses (Doing Something about the Weather)

In Chapter 8, I make a big fuss over the notion of subclasses. That's the right thing to do. Subclasses make code reusable, and reusable code is good code. With that in mind, it's time to create a subclass of the Temperature class (the class that I develop in this chapter's first section).

What's this all about?

Let's say your code contains a constructor — the first of the two constructors in Listing 9-3. The whatever parameter is passed a number like 32.0 for instance. Then the first statement in the constructor's body assigns that value, 32.0, to the new object's number variable. The code works. But, in writing this code, you had to make up a new name for a parameter — the name *whatever.* And the only purpose for this new name is to hand a value to the object's number variable. What a waste! To distinguish between the parameter and the number variable, you gave a name to something that was just momentary storage for the number value.

Making up names is an art, not a science. I've gone through plenty of naming phases. Years ago, whenever I needed a new name for

a parameter, I picked a confusing misspelling of the original variable name. (I'd name the parameter something like *numbr* or *nuhmber.*) I've also tried changing a variable name's capitalization to come up with a parameter name. (I'd use parameter names like *Number* or *nUMBER.*) In Chapter 8, I name all my parameters by adding the suffix *In* to their corresponding variable names. (The jobTitle variable matched up with the jobTitleIn parameter.) None of these naming schemes works very well. I can never remember the quirky new names that I've created. The good news is that this parameter naming effort isn't necessary. You can give the parameter the same name as the variable. To distinguish between the two, you use the Java keyword *this.*

Building better temperatures

After perusing the code in Listing 9-2, you decide that the responsibility for displaying temperatures has been seriously misplaced. Listing 9-2 has several tedious repetitions of the lines to print temperature values. A 1970s programmer would tell to you to collect those lines into one place and turn them into a method. (The 1970s programmer wouldn't have used the word *method,* but that's not important right now.) Collecting lines into methods is fine, but with today's object-oriented programming methodology, you think in broader terms. Why not get each temperature object to take responsibility for displaying itself? After all, if you develop a display method, you'll probably want to share the method with other people who use temperatures. So put the method right inside the declaration of a temperature object. That way, anyone who uses the code for temperatures has easy access to your display method.

Now replay the tape from Chapter 8. "Blah, blah, blah . . . don't want to modify existing code. . . Blah, blah, blah . . . too costly to start again from scratch. . . . Blah, blah, blah . . . extend existing functionality." It all adds up to one thing:

> Don't abuse it. Instead, reuse it.

So you decide to create a subclass of the Temperature class, which is in Listing 9-1. Your new subclass will complement the Temperature class's functionality by having methods to display values in a nice, uniform fashion. The new class, TemperatureNice, is shown in Listing 9-4.

Listing 9-4:   The TemperatureNice class

```java
import java.text.NumberFormat;

public class TemperatureNice extends Temperature
{

    public TemperatureNice ()
    {
        super();
    }

    public TemperatureNice (double number)
    {
        super(number);
    }

    public TemperatureNice (char scale)
    {
        super(scale);
    }

    public TemperatureNice (double number, char scale)
    {
```

```
        super(number, scale);
    }


    public String getScaleString()
    {
        switch (getScale())
        {
            case 'C':  return "Celsius";
            case 'F':  return "Fahrenheit";
            case 'K':  return "Kelvin";
            case 'R':  return "Rankine";
            default:   return "Unknown";
        }
    }


    public void display()
    {
        NumberFormat numFormat =
          NumberFormat.getNumberInstance();
        numFormat.setMinimumFractionDigits(2);
        numFormat.setMaximumFractionDigits(2);

        System.out.print(numFormat.format(getNumber()));
        System.out.print(" degrees ");
        System.out.println(getScaleString());
    }

}
```

Going beyond the functionality of the Temperature class, the TemperatureNice class has the getScaleString and display methods. The getScaleString method takes a single letter and returns with the name of a temperature scale. The display method takes an object's number and scale values and prints these values in a nicely formatted way.

In the getScaleString method, notice the call to the Temperature class's getScale method. Along the same lines, the display method has a call to the Temperature class's getNumber method. Why do I need to do this? Well, inside the TemperatureNice class's code, any direct references to the number and scale variables would generate error messages. It's true that every TemperatureNice object has its own number and scale variables. (After all, TemperatureNice is a subclass of the Temperature class, and the code for the Temperature class defines the number and scale variables.) But because number and scale are declared to be private inside the Temperature class, only code that's right inside the Temperature class can directly use these variables.

Don't put additional declarations of the number and scale variables inside the TemperatureNice class's code. If you do, then you'll inadvertently create four different variables (two called *number,* and another two called *scale*). You'll assign values to one pair of variables. Then you'll be shocked when, displaying the other pair of variables, those values seem to have disappeared.

The display method in Listing 9-4 has two features worth noting. First, the method gets help from another method in the TemperatureNice class — namely, the getScaleString method. This kind of inner-class cooperation is usual and normal. Second, the display method makes use of the handy NumberFormat class, which is in the API. To show numbers with exactly two digits beyond the decimal point, just cut and paste the formatting code from this display method.

When an object's code contains a call to one of the object's own methods, you don't need to preface the call with a dot. For instance, in the last statement of Listing 9-4, the object calls one of its own methods with `getScaleString()`, not with `somethingOrOther.getScaleString()`. If going "dotless" makes you queasy, you can compensate by taking advantage of yet another use for the keyword, this. Just write `this.getScaleString()` in the last line of Listing 9-4.

Constructors for subclasses

By far, the biggest news in Listing 9-4 is the way the code declares constructors. The TemperatureNice class has four of its own constructors. If you've gotten in gear thinking about subclass inheritance, then you'll wonder why these constructor declarations are necessary. Doesn't TemperatureNice inherit the parent Temperature class's constructors? No, subclasses don't inherit constructors.

Subclasses don't inherit constructors.

That's right. Subclasses don't inherit constructors. In one oddball case, a constructor may look like it's being inherited, but that oddball situation is a fluke, not the norm. (That oddball case is described later in this chapter, in the section, "The default constructor.") In general, when you define a subclass, you need to declare new constructors to go with the subclass.

So the code in Listing 9-4 has four constructors. Each constructor has the name *TemperatureNice,* and each constructor has its own, uniquely identifiable parameter list. That's the boring part. The interesting part is that each constructor makes a call to something named *super,* which is a Java keyword.

In Listing 9-4, super stands for a constructor in the parent class.

✔ The statement `super()` in Listing 9-4 calls the parameterless `Temperature()` constructor that's in Listing 9-1. That parameterless constructor assigns `0.0` to the number variable and `'F'` to the scale variable.

✔ The statement `super(number, scale)` in Listing 9-4 calls the constructor `Temperature(double number, char scale)` that's in Listing 9-1. In turn, the constructor assigns values to the number and scale variables.

✔ In a similar way, the statements `super(number)` and `super(scale)` in Listing 9-4 call constructors from Listing 9-1.

The computer decides which of the Temperature class's constructors is being called by looking at the parameter list after the word *super*. For instance, when the computer executes

```
super(number, scale);
```

from Listing 9-4, the computer says to itself, "The number and scale variables in parentheses have types double and char. Only one of the Temperature constructors in Listing 9-1 has two parameters with types double and char. The constructor's header looks like this.

```
public Temperature(double number, char scale)
```

"So, I guess I'll execute the statements inside that particular constructor."

Using all this stuff

In Listing 9-4, I defined what it means to be in the TemperatureNice class. Now it's time to put this TemperatureNice class to some good use. Listing 9-5 has code that uses TemperatureNice. Figure 9-3 shows you what happens when this code runs.

Listing 9-5:   Using the TemperatureNice class

```
class UseTemperatureNice
{
    public static void main(String args[])
    {
        TemperatureNice temp;

        temp = new TemperatureNice();
        temp.setNumber(70.0);
        temp.setScale('F');
        temp.display();

        temp = new TemperatureNice(32.0);
```

(continued)

Listing 9-5 *(continued)*

```
        temp.display();

        temp = new TemperatureNice('C');
        temp.display();

        temp = new TemperatureNice(2.73, 'K');
        temp.display();
    }
}
```

The code in Listing 9-5 is very much like its cousin code in Listing 9-2. The big differences are as follows.

✔ Listing 9-5 creates instances of the TemperatureNice class. That is, Listing 9-5 calls constructors from the TemperatureNice class, not the Temperature class.

✔ Listing 9-5 takes advantage of the display method in the TemperatureNice class. So the code in Listing 9-5 is much more tidy than its counterpart in Listing 9-2.

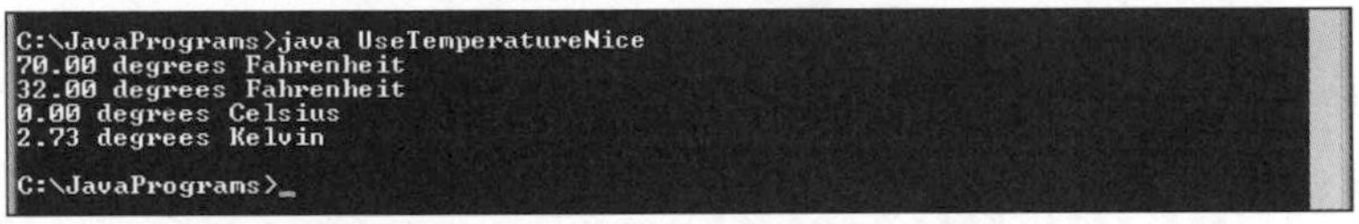

Figure 9-3:
Using the
Temperature-
Nice class.

```
C:\JavaPrograms>java UseTemperatureNice
70.00 degrees Fahrenheit
32.00 degrees Fahrenheit
0.00 degrees Celsius
2.73 degrees Kelvin

C:\JavaPrograms>_
```

The default constructor

The main message in the previous section is that subclasses don't inherit constructors. So what gives with all the listings back in Chapter 8? In Listing 8-7, a statement says

```
FullTimeEmployee ftEmployee = new FullTimeEmployee();
```

But, here's the problem: The code defining FullTimeEmployee (Listing 8-4) doesn't seem to have any constructors declared inside it. So, in Listing 8-7, how can you possibly call the FullTimeEmployee constructor?

Here's what's going on. When you create a subclass and don't put any explicit constructor declarations in your code, then Java creates one constructor for you. It's called a *default constructor*. If you're creating the public FullTimeEmployee subclass, then the default constructor looks like the one in Listing 9-6.

Listing 9-6:   A default constructor

```
public FullTimeEmployee()
{
   super();
}
```

The constructor in Listing 9-6 takes no parameters, and its one statement calls the constructor of whatever class you're extending. (Woe be to you if the class that you're extending doesn't have a parameterless constructor.)

You've just read some stuff about default constructors, but watch out! Notice one thing that this talk about default constructors *doesn't* say. It doesn't say that you always get a default constructor. In particular, if you create a subclass and define any constructors yourself, then Java doesn't add a default constructor for the subclass (and the subclass doesn't inherit any constructors either).

So how can this business trip you up? Listing 9-7 has a copy of the code from Listing 8-4, but with one constructor added to it. Take a look at this modified version of the FullTimeEmployee code.

Listing 9-7:   Look, I have a constructor!

```
public class FullTimeEmployee extends Employee
{

   private double weeklySalary;
   private double benefitDeduction;

   public FullTimeEmployee(double weeklySalary)
   {
      this.weeklySalary=weeklySalary;
   }

   public void setWeeklySalary(double weeklySalaryIn)
   {
      weeklySalary=weeklySalaryIn;
   }

   public double getWeeklySalary()
   {
      return weeklySalary;
   }

   public void setBenefitDeduction(double benefitDedIn)
   {
      benefitDeduction=benefitDedIn;
   }

   public double getBenefitDeduction()
```

(continued)

Listing 9-7 *(continued)*

```
    {
        return benefitDeduction;
    }

    public double findPaymentAmount()
    {
        return weeklySalary-benefitDeduction;
    }

}
```

Using the FullTimeEmployee code in Listing 9-7, a line like the following doesn't work.

```
FullTimeEmployee ftEmployee = new FullTimeEmployee();
```

It won't work because, having declared a FullTimeEmployee constructor that takes one double parameter, you no longer get a default parameterless constructor for free.

So what do you do about this? If you need to declare any constructors, declare all the constructors that you're possibly going to need. Take the constructor in Listing 9-6 and add it to the code in Listing 9-7. Then the call new FullTimeEmployee() will start working again.

An invisible constructor call

Here's a program that I like to yank out and show people at Java parties. (Believe me, it surprises some of the veteran Java programmers.) The program is in Listing 9-8.

Listing 9-8:   What's my output?

```
class MyClass
{
    MyClass()
    {
        System.out.println
            ("MyClass constructor being called.");
    }
}


class MySubclass extends MyClass
{
    MySubclass()
    {
```

```
        System.out.println
           ("MySubclass constructor being called.");
    }
}


class UseMyClasses
{
    public static void main(String args[])
    {
        new MySubclass();
    }
}
```

So what's the output when you run the code in Listing 9-8? Huh? You think you'll get just one line of output? Sorry, that's not the way it works. The output you'll get is shown in Figure 9-4.

Figure 9-4:
Surprise!

```
C:\JavaPrograms>java UseMyClasses
MyClass constructor being called.
MySubclass constructor being called.

C:\JavaPrograms>_
```

Under certain circumstances, Java automatically adds an invisible call to super, which is at the top of a constructor body. It's as if the MySubclass constructor in Listing 9-8 really looks like this:

```
MySubclass()
{
    super();
    System.out.println
       ("MySubclass constructor being called.");
}
```

In Listing 9-8, the invisible super call fires up the MyClass constructor, which prints the message `MyClass constructor being called`. This automatic addition of a super call is a tricky bit of business that doesn't appear often, so when it does appear, it may seem quite mysterious.

A Constructor That Does More

Here's a quote from someplace near the start of this chapter. "What if you're interested in doing more than filling variables? Perhaps, when the computer creates a new object, you have a whole list of jobs for the computer to carry out." Okay, what if?

This section's example has a constructor that does more than just assign values to variables. The example is in Listing 9-9, and the result of running the example's code is shown in Figure 9-5.

Listing 9-9:   Displaying a frame

```java
import java.awt.*;


public class SimpleFrame extends Frame
{
    public SimpleFrame()
    {
        setTitle("Don't click the button!");
        setLayout(new FlowLayout());
        add(new Button("Panic"));
        setSize(300,100);
        show();
    }
}


class ShowAFrame
{
    public static void main(String args[])
    {
        new SimpleFrame();
    }
}
```

Figure 9-5:
Don't panic.

The code in Listing 9-9 is made up mostly of calls to Java API methods. What this means to you is that the code contains lots of names that are probably unfamiliar to you. When I was first becoming acquainted with Java, I foolishly believed that learning Java meant learning all these names. Quite the contrary, these names are just carry-on baggage. The real Java is the way the language implements object-oriented concepts.

Anyway, the code's anorexic main method has only one statement — a call to the constructor in the SimpleFrame class. Notice how the object that this call creates isn't even assigned to a variable. That's okay, because the code doesn't need to refer to the object anywhere else.

Up in the SimpleFrame class is only one constructor declaration. Far from just setting variables' values, this constructor calls method after method from the Java API.

All the methods called in the SimpleFrame class's constructor come from the parent class, Frame. The Frame class lives in the package named `java.awt`. (For some gossip about the notion of a Java package, see Chapters 8 and 13.) The letters *awt* stand for *abstract windowing toolkit*. This package and another package named `javax.swing` have classes that help you put windows, images, drawings, and other gizmos on a computer screen.

In the Java API, what people normally call a *window* is an instance of the `java.awt.Frame` class.

Looking at Figure 9-5, you can probably tell that an instance of the SimpleFrame class doesn't do much. The frame has only one button and, when you click the button, nothing happens. The frame doesn't even close when you click the little × in its upper right-hand corner. I made the frame this way to keep the example from becoming too complicated. Even so, the code in Listing 9-5 uses a number of API classes and methods. The setTitle, setLayout, add, setSize, and show methods all belong to the `java.awt.Frame` class. Here's a list of names used in the code:

- **setTitle:** Calling setTitle puts words in the frame's title bar. (The new object is calling its own setTitle method.)

- **FlowLayout:** An instance of the FlowLayout class positions objects on the frame in centered, typewriter fashion. Because the frame in Figure 9-5 has only one button on it, that button is centered near the top of the frame. If the frame had eight buttons, then five of them may be lined up in a row across the top of the frame, and the remaining three would be centered along a second row.

- **setLayout:** Calling setLayout puts the new FlowLayout object in charge of arranging components, such as buttons, on the frame. (The new SimpleFrame object is calling its own setLayout method.)

- **Button:** The Button class lives in the java.awt package. One of the class's constructors takes a String instance (such as `"Panic"`) for its parameter. Calling this constructor makes that String instance be the label on the face of the new button.

- **add:** The new SimpleFrame object calls its add method. Calling the add method places the button on the object's surface (in this case, the surface of the frame).

- **setSize:** The frame becomes 300 pixels wide and 100 pixels tall. (In the `java.awt` package, whenever you specify two dimension numbers, the width number always comes before the height number.)

- **show:** When it's first created, a new frame is invisible. But when the new frame calls its show method, the frame appears on your computer screen.

Chapter 10

Putting Variables and Methods Where They Belong

*H*ello, again. You're listening to radio station WWW, and I'm your host, Sam Burd. It's the start again of the big baseball season, and today station WWW brought you live coverage of the Hankees versus Socks game. At this moment, I'm awaiting news of the game's final score.

If you remember from earlier this afternoon, the Socks looked like they were going to take those Hankees to the cleaners. Then, the Hankees were belting ball after ball, giving the Socks a run for their money. Those Socks! I'm glad I wasn't in their shoes.

Anyway, as the game went on, the Socks pulled themselves up. Now the Socks are nose to nose with the Hankees. We'll get the final score in a minute, but first, a few reminders. Stay tuned after this broadcast for the big Jersey's game. And don't forget to tune in next week when the Cleveland Gowns play the Bermuda Shorts.

Okay, here's the final score. Which team has the upper hand? Which team will come out a head? And the winner is . . . Oh, no! It's a tie!

Defining a Class (What It Means to Be a Baseball Player)

As far as I'm concerned, a baseball player has a name and a batting average. Listing 10-1 puts my feeling about this into Java program form.

Listing 10-1:   The Player class

```java
import java.text.NumberFormat;

public class Player
{
  private String name;
  private double average;

  public Player(String name, double average)
  {
    this.name=name;
    this.average=average;
  }

  public String getName()
  {
    return name;
  }

  public double getAverage()
  {
    return average;
  }

  public String getAverageString()
  {
    NumberFormat numFormat =
            NumberFormat.getNumberInstance();
    numFormat.setMaximumIntegerDigits(0);
    numFormat.setMaximumFractionDigits(3);
    numFormat.setMinimumFractionDigits(3);
    return numFormat.format(average);
  }

}
```

So here I go, picking apart the code in Listing 10-1. Lucky for both of us, earlier chapters cover lots of stuff in this code. The code defines what it means to be an instance of the Player class. Here's what's in the code:

- ✔ **Declarations of the variables name and average.** For bedtime reading about variable declarations, see Chapter 4.

- ✔ **A constructor to make new instances of the Player class.** For the lowdown on constructors, see Chapter 9.

- ✔ **Getter methods for the variables name and average.** For chitchat about accessor methods (that is, setter and getter methods), see Chapter 7.

- ✔ **A method that returns the player's batting average in String form.** For the good word about methods, see Chapter 7.

The last method in Listing 10-1 takes the value from the average variable (a player's batting average), converts that value (normally of type double) into a String, and then sends that String value right back to the method caller. The use of NumberFormat, which comes right from the Java API, makes sure that the String value looks like a baseball player's batting average. That is, the String value has no digits to the left of the decimal point and exactly three digits to the right of the decimal point.

Using the Player class

Listing 10-2 has code that uses the Player class — the class that's defined way back in Listing 10-1.

Listing 10-2:   Using the Player class

```
import java.awt.*;
import java.io.*;

public class TeamFrame extends Frame
{

    public TeamFrame()
    {
        Player player;
        BufferedReader hankees =
            DummiesIO.open("c:\\JavaPrograms\\Hankees");

        for (int num=1; num<=9; num++)
        {
            player =
                new Player (DummiesIO.getString(hankees),
                                DummiesIO.getDouble(hankees));
            addPlayerInfo(player);
        }

        setTitle("The Hankees");
        setLayout(new GridLayout(9,2));
        pack();
        show();
    }


    void addPlayerInfo(Player player)
    {
        add(new Label(player.getName()));
        add(new Label(player.getAverageString()));
```

(continued)

Listing 10-2 *(continued)*

```
    }

}


class ShowTeamFrame
{
    public static void main(String args[])
    {
        new TeamFrame();
    }
}
```

For a run of the code in Listing 10-2, see Figure 10-1. To run this program yourself, you need three extra files in your JavaPrograms directory:

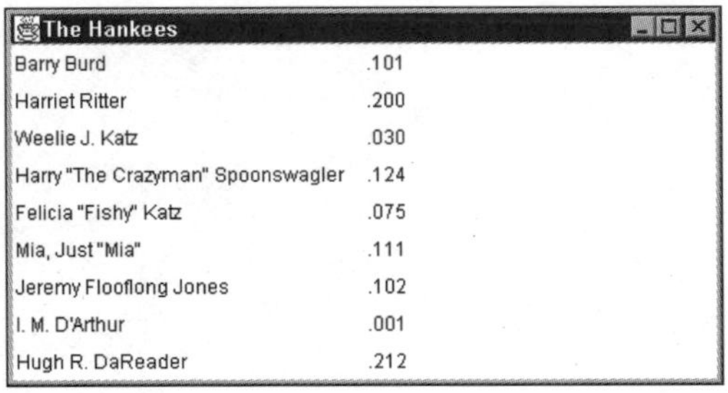

Figure 10-1:
Would you
bet money
on these
people?

> ✔ **You need the** `Player.class` **file.**
>
>   Put a compiled copy of the code from Listing 10-1 in your JavaPrograms directory.
>
> ✔ **You need the** `DummiesIO.class` **file.** I discuss your friend, the DummiesIO class, in more detail in Chapter 5. You can get the file from this book's CD-ROM.
>
> ✔ **You also need the Hankees file.** This file contains data on your favorite baseball players. (See Listing 10-3.) You can copy the Hankees file from this book's CD-ROM. Or, if you're in just the right mood, you can make up your own silly names and put them all in a brand-new Hankees file.

Listing 10-3:   What a team!

```
Barry Burd
.101
Harriet Ritter
.200
Weelie J. Katz
.030
```

```
Harry "The Crazyman" Spoonswagler
.124
Felicia "Fishy" Katz
.075
Mia, Just "Mia"
.111
Jeremy Flooflong Jones
.102
I. M. D'Arthur
.001
Hugh R. DaReader
.212
```

The window created by the code in Listing 10-2 doesn't close when you click the little × in its upper right-hand corner. I made it this way to keep the example from becoming too complicated. To close the program, just swear at it a few times and then do whatever you do on your system to close your most persistent and stubborn applications.

Nine, count 'em, nine

The code in Listing 10-2 calls the Player constructor nine times. This means the code creates nine instances of the Player class. Each instance has its own name and average variables. Each instance also has its own Player constructor, and its own getName, getAverage, and getAverageString methods. Look at Figure 10-2 and think of the Player class with its nine incarnations.

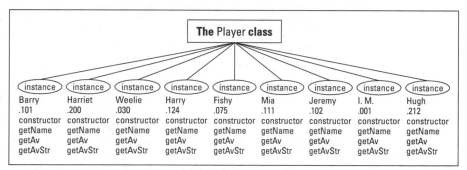

Figure 10-2:
A class and
its objects.

Don't get all GUI on me

The code in Listing 10-2 uses several names from the Java API. Some of these names are explained in the last section of Chapter 9. Others are explained right here:

✔ **Label:** A Label is an object with some text in it. One of the ways to display text inside the frame is to add an instance of the Label class to the frame.

In Listing 10-2, the addPlayerInfo method is called nine times, once for each player on the team. Each time addPlayerInfo is called, the method adds two new Label objects to the frame. The text for each Label object comes from a player object's getter method.

✔ **GridLayout:** A GridLayout arranges things in evenly spaced rows and columns. This constructor for the GridLayout class takes two parameters — the number of rows and the number of columns.

In Listing 10-2, the call to the GridLayout constructor takes parameters (9,2). So, in Figure 10-1, the display has nine rows (one for each player) and two columns (one for a name, and another for an average).

✔ **pack:** When you pack a frame, you set the frame's size. That's the size the frame has when it appears on your computer screen. Packing a frame shrink-wraps the frame around whatever objects you've added inside the frame.

In Listing 10-2, by the time you've reached the call to pack, you've already called addPlayerInfo nine times and added eighteen labels to the frame. In executing the pack method, the computer picks a nice size for each label, given whatever text you've put inside the label. Then, the computer picks a nice size for the whole frame, given that the frame has these eighteen labels inside it.

The things you use to build windows in the Java API are called *components*. More precisely, classes such as Frame, Button, and Label are (directly or indirectly) subclasses of the java.awt.Component class. When you find a nice size for a component, you're really finding the component's *preferred* size. For an instance of the Frame class, calling the pack method is the same as calling setSize(getPreferredSize()).

When you plop stuff onto frames, you have quite a bit of leeway with the order in which you do things. For instance, you can set the layout before or after you've added labels and other stuff to the frame. If you call setLayout and then add labels, the labels appear in nice, orderly positions on the frame. If you reverse this order (add labels and then call setLayout), the calling of setLayout rearranges the labels in a nice, orderly fashion. It works fine either way.

In setting up a frame, the one thing you shouldn't do is violate the following sequence:

```
Add things to the frame, then
pack();
show();
```

If you call pack and then add more things to the frame, then the pack method doesn't take the more recent things you've added into consideration. If you call show before you've added things or called pack, then the user sees the frame as it's being constructed. Finally, if you forget to set the frame's size (by calling pack or some other sizing method), then the frame you see will look like the one in Figure 10-3. (Normally, I wouldn't show you an anomalous run like the one in Figure 10-3, but I've made the mistake so many times, that I feel as if this puny frame is an old friend of mine.)

Figure 10-3:
An under-
nourished
frame.

Making Static (Finding the Team Average)

Thinking about the code in Listings 10-1 and 10-2, you decide that you'd like to find the team's overall batting average. Not a bad idea! The Hankees in Figure 10-1 have an average of about .106, so the team needs some intensive training. While the players are out practicing on the ball field, you have a philosophical hurdle to overcome.

In Listings 10-1 and 10-2, you have three classes: a Player class and two other classes that help display data from the Player class. So in this class morass, where do the variables storing your overall, team-average tally go?

- ✔ It makes no sense to put tally variables in either of the displaying classes (TeamFrame and ShowTeamFrame). After all, the tally has something or other to do with players, teams, and baseball. The displaying classes are about creating windows, not about playing baseball.

- ✔ You're uncomfortable putting an overall team average in an instance of the Player class, because an instance of the Player class represents just one player on the team. What business does a single player have storing overall team data? Sure, you could make the code work, but it wouldn't be an elegant solution to the problem.

Finally, you learn about the keyword *static*. Anything that's declared to be static belongs to the whole class, not to any particular instance of the class. When you create the static variable, totalOfAverages, you create just one copy of the variable. This copy stays with the entire Players class. No matter how many instances of the Player class you create — one, nine, or none — you have just one totalOfAverages variable. And, while you're at it, you create other static variables (playerCount and numFormat) and static methods (findTeamAverage and findTeamAverageString). To see what I mean, look at Figure 10-4.

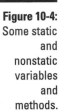

Figure 10-4:
Some static
and
nonstatic
variables
and
methods.

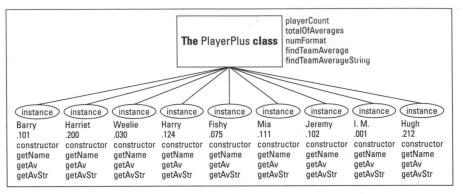

Going along with your passion for subclasses, you put code for team-wide tallies in a subclass of the Player class. The code is in Listing 10-4.

Listing 10-4: Creating a team batting average

```java
import java.text.NumberFormat;

public class PlayerPlus extends Player
{
  static int playerCount=0;
  static double totalOfAverages=.000;
  static NumberFormat numFormat =
          NumberFormat.getNumberInstance();


  public PlayerPlus (String name, double average)
  {
    super(name,average);
    playerCount++;
    totalOfAverages += average;
  }


  public static double findTeamAverage()
  {
      return totalOfAverages/playerCount;
  }


  public static String findTeamAverageString()
  {
      numFormat.setMaximumIntegerDigits(0);
      numFormat.setMaximumFractionDigits(3);
      numFormat.setMinimumFractionDigits(3);
      return numFormat.format(totalOfAverages/playerCount);
  }

}
```

Why is there so much static?

Maybe you've noticed — the code in Listing 10-4 is overflowing with the word *static*. That's because nearly everything in this code belongs to the entire PlayerPlus class, and not to individual instances of the class. That's good because something like playerCount (the number of players on the team) shouldn't belong to individual players, and having each PlayerPlus object keep track of its own count would be silly. ("I know how many players I am. I'm just one player!") If you had nine, individual playerCount variables, then either each variable would store the number 1 (which is useless) or you would have nine different copies of the count, which is wasteful and prone to error. So, by making playerCount static, you're keeping the playerCount in just one place, where it belongs.

The same kind of reasoning holds for the totalOfAverages. Eventually, the totalOfAverages variable will store the sum of the players' batting averages. For all nine members of the Hankees, this adds up to .956. It's not until someone calls the findTeamAverage or findTeamAverageString methods that the computer actually finds the overall Hankee team batting average.

You also want the methods findTeamAverage and findTeamAverageString to be static. Without the word *static,* there would be nine findTeamAverage methods — one for each instance of the PlayerPlus class. This wouldn't make much sense. Each instance would have the code to calculate `totalOfAverages/playerCount` on its own, and each of the nine calculations would yield the very same answer.

In general, any task that all the instances have in common (and that yields the same result for each instance) should be coded as a static method.

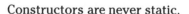

Constructors are never static.

In Listing 10-4, the numFormat variable is static. This makes sense, because numFormat makes `totalOfAverages/playerCount` look nice, and both variables in the expression `totalOfAverages/playerCount` are static. Thinking more directly, the code needs only one thing for formatting numbers. If you have several numbers to format, the same numFormat thing that belongs to the entire class can format each number. Creating a numFormat for each player is not only inelegant, but also wasteful.

In this book, my first serious use of the word *static* is way back in Listing 3-1. I use static as part of every main method (and lots of main methods are in this book's listings). So why does main have to be static? Well, remember that nonstatic things belong to objects, not classes. If the main method isn't static, then you can't have a main method until you create an object. But, when you start up a Java program, no objects have been created yet. The statements executed in the main method start creating objects. So, if the main method isn't static, then you have a big chicken-and-egg problem.

Displaying the overall team average

You may be noticing a pattern. When you create code for a class, you generally write two pieces of code. One piece of code defines the class, and the other piece of code uses the class. (The ways to "use" a class include calling the class's constructor, referencing the class's nonprivate variables, calling the class's methods, and so on.) Listing 10-4 contains code that defines the PlayerPlus class, and Listing 10-5 contains code that uses this PlayerPlus class.

Listing 10-5:   Using the code from Listing 10-4

```java
import java.awt.*;
import java.io.*;

public class TeamFrame extends Frame
{

    public TeamFrame()
    {
        PlayerPlus player;
        BufferedReader hankees =
            DummiesIO.open("c:\\JavaPrograms\\Hankees");

        for (int num=1; num<=9; num++)
        {
            player =
                new PlayerPlus (DummiesIO.getString(hankees),
                                DummiesIO.getDouble(hankees));
            addPlayerInfo(player);
        }

        add (new Label());
        add (new Label(" ------"));
        add (new Label("Team Batting Average:"));
        add (new Label(PlayerPlus.findTeamAverageString()));

        setTitle("The Hankees");
        setLayout(new GridLayout(11,2));
        pack();
        show();
    }


    void addPlayerInfo(Player player)
    {
        add(new Label(player.getName()));
        add(new Label(player.getAverageString()));
```

```
        }

    }


class ShowTeamFrame
{
    public static void main(String args[])
    {
        new TeamFrame();
    }
}
```

Figure 10-5 shows a run of the code from Listing 10-5. This run depends on the availability of two files — `DummiesIO.class` and `Hankees`. The code in Listing 10-5 is almost an exact copy of the code from Listing 10-2. (So close is the copy that, if I could afford it, I'd sue myself for theft of intellectual property.) The only thing new in Listing 10-5 is the stuff shown in bold.

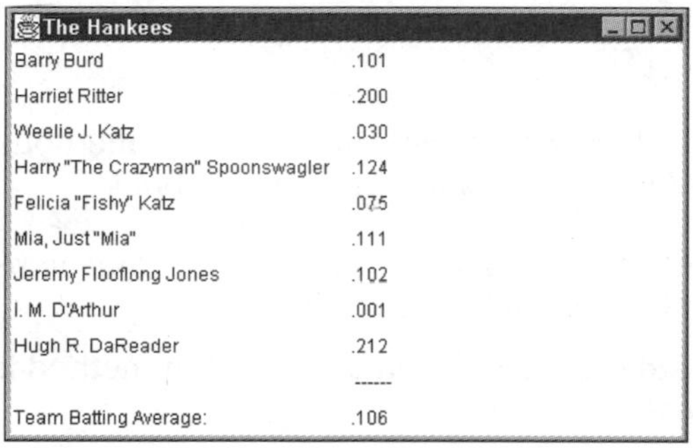

Figure 10-5:
A run of
the code in
Listing 10-5.

The Hankees	
Barry Burd	.101
Harriet Ritter	.200
Weelie J. Katz	.030
Harry "The Crazyman" Spoonswagler	.124
Felicia "Fishy" Katz	.075
Mia, Just "Mia"	.111
Jeremy Flooflong Jones	.102
I. M. D'Arthur	.001
Hugh R. DaReader	.212

Team Batting Average:	.106

In Listing 10-5, the GridLayout has two extra rows: one row for spacing and another row for the Hankee team's average. Each of these rows has two Label objects in it.

   ✔ **The spacing row has a blank label and a label with a dashed line.** The blank label is a placeholder. When you add components to a GridLayout, the components are added row by row, starting at the left end of a row and working toward the right end of the row. Without this blank label, the dashed line label would appear at the left end of the row, under Hugh R. DaReader's name.

   ✔ **The other row has a label displaying the words** Team Batting Average**, and another label displaying the number** .106. The method call that gets the number .106 is interesting. The call looks like this:

```
PlayerPlus.findTeamAverageString()
```

Take a look at that method call. That call has the following form:

```
ClassName.methodName()
```

That's new and different. In earlier chapters, I say that you normally preface a method call with an object's name, not a class's name. So why do I use a class name here? The answer: When you call a static method, you preface the method's name with the name of the class that contains the method. The same holds true whenever you reference another class's static variable. This makes sense. Remember, the whole class that defines a static variable or method owns that variable or method. So, to refer to a static variable or method, you preface the variable or method's name with the class's name.

When you're referring to a static variable or method, you can cheat and use an object's name in place of the class name. For instance, in Listing 10-5, with judicious rearranging of some other statements, you can use the expression `player.findTeamAverageString()`.

Static is old hat

This section makes a big noise about static variables and methods, but static things have been part of the picture since early in this book.

- ✔ Chapter 3 introduced System.out.println. The name *System* refers to a class, and *out* is a static variable in that class.

- ✔ Chapter 5 introduced DummiesIO.getInt. The getInt method is static in the DummiesIO class.

- ✔ Listings 10-1 and 10-4 have calls to NumberFormat.getNumberInstance. Guess what! The getNumberInstance method is declared to be static in the Java API NumberFormat class.

In Java, static variables and methods show up all over the place. When they're declared in someone else's code and you're making use of them in your code, you hardly ever have to worry about them. But, when you're declaring your own variables and methods and must decide whether to make them static, you have to think a little harder.

Could cause static; handle with care

When I first started learning Java, I had recurring dreams about getting a certain error message. The message was `non-static variable or method cannot be referenced from a static context`. So often did I see this message, so thoroughly was I perplexed, that the memory of this message became burned into my unconscious existence.

These days, I know why I get the error message so often. I can even make the message occur if I want. But I still feel a little shiver whenever I see this message on my screen.

Before you can understand why the message occurs and how to fix the problem, you need to get some terminology under your belt. If a variable or method isn't static, then it's called *nonstatic*. (Real surprising, hey?) Given that terminology, there are at least two ways to make the dreaded message appear.

- Put `Class.nonstaticThing` somewhere in your program.
- Put `nonstaticThing` somewhere inside a static method.

In either case, you're getting yourself into trouble. You're taking something that belongs to an object (the nonstatic thing) and putting it in a place where no objects are in sight.

Take, for instance, the first of the two situations listed above. To see this calamity in action, go back to Listing 10-5. Toward the end of the listing, change `player.getName()` to `Player.getName()`. That'll do the trick. What could `Player.getName` possibly mean? If it meant anything, the expression `Player.getName` would mean "call the getName method that belongs to the entire Player class." But look back at Listing 10-1. The getName method isn't static. Each instance of the Player (or PlayerPlus) class has a getName method. None of the getName methods belong to the entire class. So the call `Player.getName` doesn't make any sense. (Maybe the computer is pulling punches when it displays the inoffensive `cannot be referenced . . .` message. Perhaps a harsh `nonsensical expression` message would be more fitting.)

For a taste of the second situation (in the list I gave above), go back to Listing 10-4. While no one's looking, quietly remove the word *static* from the declaration of the numFormat variable (near the top of the listing). This turns numFormat into a nonstatic variable. Suddenly, each player on the team has a separate numFormat variable.

Well, things are just hunky-dory until the computer reaches the findTeamAverageString method. That static method has four `numFormat.SuchAndSuch` statements in it. Once again, you're forced to ask what a statement of this kind could possibly mean. Method findTeamAverageString belongs to no instance in particular. (The method is static, so the entire PlayerPlus class has one findTeamAverageString method.) But with the way you've just butchered the code, plain old numFormat, without reference to a particular object, has no meaning. So again, you're referencing the nonstatic variable, numFormat, from inside a static method's context. Shame!

A static initializer

Here's one of the things I've learned in my many years of computer programming. If something doesn't feel comfortable, then I either don't understand it, or do understand it and need to change it. In short, comfort level matters. If you find a solution to a problem and then step back and say, "There must be a better way to put all these pieces together," then you can probably find a better way.

So take one more look at the code in Listing 10-4. The listing contains the following startup statements for numFormat, the object that makes numbers look like batting averages:

```
numFormat.setMaximumIntegerDigits(0);
numFormat.setMaximumFractionDigits(3);
numFormat.setMinimumFractionDigits(3);
```

Before you can make reasonable use of numFormat, you have to call the setMaximumDigits and setMinimumDigits methods. In Listing 10-4, I put calls to these setDigits methods inside the findTeamAverageString method. But is that the best place for them? What if someone writes a program that uses your PlayerPlus class and calls findTeamAverageString five times in the same program? Then that person's program sets the number of digits in the same old numFormat object to the same old values over and over again. Setting these values once would be just fine.

When you call the setDigits methods over and over again, the processing time you're wasting may be measured in nanoseconds, but that's not the point. The question is, have you really found *"the right place"* to put these method calls? This is where my talk about comfort level kicks into gear.

Well, if the body of the findTeamAverageString method isn't exactly the right place for these calls, then what is? Ideally, you should execute these method calls just once for the whole class. And I don't see any place in Listing 10-4 for code that's going to get executed just once. Or do I?

Well, Java has a feature called the *static initializer*. A static initializer is like a constructor — it's executed once at the start of something. But, for a static initializer, that something is the entire class, not just one instance of the class.

Listing 10-6 shows you how to use a static initializer. After reading about Listing 10-6, you'll be able to sleep at night knowing that the startup statements for the code's number format are finally in their rightful place.

Listing 10-6:   Using a static initializer

```
import java.text.NumberFormat;

public class PlayerPlus extends Player
{
  static int playerCount=0;
  static double totalOfAverages=.000;
  static NumberFormat numFormat =
            NumberFormat.getNumberInstance();

  static
  {
    numFormat.setMaximumIntegerDigits(0);
    numFormat.setMaximumFractionDigits(3);
    numFormat.setMinimumFractionDigits(3);
  }


  public PlayerPlus (String name, double average)
  {
    super(name,average);
    playerCount++;
    totalOfAverages += average;
  }


  public static double findTeamAverage()
  {
      return totalOfAverages/playerCount;
  }


  public static String findTeamAverageString()
  {
      return numFormat.format(totalOfAverages/playerCount);
  }

}
```

You get the same display using the code from Listings 10-4 and 10-6. The difference is a matter of efficiency, not correctness.

To create a static initializer, just write a block of code, and put the word *static* before the block. (A block is a bunch of statements enclosed in curly braces. For a refresher course on blocks, see Chapter 5.) The statements you put inside the block are executed when the computer starts running code from your class.

Don't put a static initializer inside a method's body. That just messes up everything.

Experiments with Variables

One summer during my college days, I was sitting on the front porch, loafing around, talking with someone I'd just met. I think her name was Janine. "Where are you from?" I asked. "Mars," she answered. She paused to see if I'd ask a follow-up question.

As it turned out, Janine was from Mars, Pennsylvania, a small town about 20 miles north of Pittsburgh. Okay, so what's my point? The point is that the meaning of a name depends on the context. If you're just north of Pittsburgh and ask, "How do I get to Mars from here?" then you may get a sensible, nonchalant answer. But if you ask the same question standing on a street corner in Manhattan, you'll probably arouse some suspicion. (Okay, knowing Manhattan, people would probably just ignore you.)

Of course, the people who live in Mars, Pennsylvania, are very much aware that their town has an oddball name. Fond memories of teenage years in Mars High School don't prevent a person from knowing about the big red planet. On a clear evening in August, you can still have the following conversation with one of the local residents:

> *You:* How do I get to Mars?
>
> *Local resident:* You're in Mars, pal. What particular part of Mars are you looking for?
>
> *You:* No, I don't mean Mars, Pennsylvania. I mean the planet Mars.
>
> *Local resident:* Oh, the planet! Well, then, catch the 8:19 train leaving for Cape Canaveral . . . No, wait, that's the local train. That'd take you through West Virginia . . .

So the meaning of a name depends on where you're using the name. Although most English-speaking people think of Mars as a place with a carbon dioxide atmosphere, some folks in Pennsylvania think about all the shopping they can do in Mars. And those folks in Pennsylvania really have two meanings for the name *Mars*. In Java, those names may look like this: `Mars` and `planets.Mars`.

Putting a variable in its place

Your first experiment is shown in Listing 10-7. The listing code highlights the difference between variables declared inside and outside methods.

Listing 10-7:   Two meanings for Mars

```
public class EnglishSpeakingWorld
{
   String mars="   red planet";

   void visitPennsylvania()
   {
      System.out.println("visitPA is running:");

      String mars="   Janine's home town";

      System.out.println(mars);
      System.out.println(this.mars);
   }

}




class GetGoing
{
   public static void main(String args[])
   {
      System.out.println("main is running:");

      EnglishSpeakingWorld e = new EnglishSpeakingWorld();

      //System.out.println(mars);   cannot resolve symbol
      System.out.println(e.mars);
      e.visitPennsylvania();
   }
}
```

Figure 10-6 shows a run of the code in Listing 10-7, and Figure 10-7 shows a diagram of the code's structure. In the GetGoing class, the main method creates an instance of the EnglishSpeakingWorld class. The new instance is an object with a variable named *mars* inside it. That mars variable has value "red planet". The mars variable is called an *instance variable,* because the variable belongs to an object — an instance of the EnglishSpeakingWorld class.

Now look at the main method in Listing 10-7. Inside the GetGoing class's main method, you aren't permitted to write System.out.println(mars). In other words, a bare-faced reference to any mars variable is a definite no-no. The mars variable mentioned in the previous paragraph belongs to the EnglishSpeakingWorld object, not the GetGoing class.

But, inside the GetGoing class's main method, you can certainly write e.mars, because the e variable refers to your EnglishSpeakingWorld object. That's nice.

Figure 10-6:
A run of
the code in
Listing 10-7.

```
C:\JavaPrograms>java GetGoing
main is running:
    red planet
visitPA is running:
    Janine's home town
    red planet
C:\JavaPrograms>
```

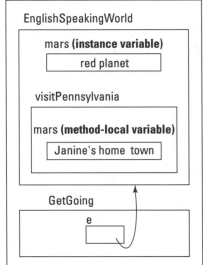

Figure 10-7:
The
structure of
the code in
Listing 10-7.

Near the bottom of the code, the visitPennsylvania method is called. When you're inside visitPennsylvania, you have another declaration of a mars variable, whose value is `"Janine's home town"`. This particular mars variable is called a *method-local variable,* because it belongs to just one method — the visitPennsylvania method.

So now you have two variables, both with the name *mars.* One mars variable, an instance variable, has the value `"red planet"`. The other mars variable, a method-local variable, has the value `"Janine's home town"`. In the code, when you use the word *mars,* which of the two variables are you referring to?

The answer is, when you're visiting Pennsylvania, the variable with value `"Janine's home town"` wins. When in Pennsylvania, think the way the Pennsylvanians think. When you're executing code inside the visitPennsylvania method, resolve any variable name conflicts by going with variables that are declared right inside the visitPennsylvania method.

So what if you're in Pennsylvania and need to refer to that two-mooned celestial object? More precisely, how does code inside the visitPennsylvania method refer to the variable with value `"red planet"`? The answer is, use `this.mars`. The word *this* points to whatever object contains all this code (and not to any methods inside the code). That object, an instance of the EnglishSpeakingWorld class, has a big, fat mars variable, and that variable's value is "red planet". So that's how you can force code to see outside of the method it's in — you use the Java keyword *this*. (For more information on the keyword *this*, see Chapter 9.)

Telling a variable where to go

Years ago, when I lived in Milwaukee, Wisconsin, I made frequent use of the local bank's automatic teller machines. Machines of this kind were just beginning to become standardized. The local teller machine system was named *TYME,* which stood for *Take Your Money Everywhere.*

I remember traveling by car out to California. At one point I got hungry and stopped for a meal, but I was out of cash. So I asked a gas station attendant, "Do you know where there's a TYME machine around here?"

So you see, a name that works well in one place may work terribly, or not at all, in another place. In Listing 10-8, I illustrate this point (with more than just an anecdote about teller machines).

Listing 10-8:   Tale of Atomic City

```
public class EnglishSpeakingWorld2
{
   String mars;

   void visitIdaho()
   {
      System.out.println("visitID is running:");

      mars = "   red planet";
      String atomicCity="   Population: 25";

      System.out.println(mars);
      System.out.println(atomicCity);
   }

   void visitNewJersey()
   {
      System.out.println("visitNJ is running:");

      System.out.println(mars);
      //System.out.println(atomicCity);
      //   cannot resolve symbol
```

(continued)

Listing 10-8 *(continued)*

```
    }

}


class GetGoing2
{
    public static void main(String args[])
    {
        EnglishSpeakingWorld2 e = new EnglishSpeakingWorld2();

        e.visitIdaho();
        e.visitNewJersey();
    }
}
```

Figure 10-8 shows a run of the code in Listing 10-8, and Figure 10-9 shows a diagram of the code's structure. The code for EnglishSpeakingWorld2 has two variables. The mars variable, which isn't declared inside a method, is an instance variable. The other variable, atomicCity, is a method-local variable and is declared inside the visitIdaho method.

In Listing 10-8, notice where each variable can, and cannot, be used. When you try to use the atomicCity variable inside the visitNewJersey method, you get an error message. Literally, the message says `cannot resolve symbol`. Figuratively the message says, "Hey, buddy, Atomic City is in Idaho, not New Jersey." Technically, the message says that the method-local variable atomicCity is available only in the visitIdaho method because that's where the variable was declared.

So back inside the visitIdaho method, you're free to use the atomicCity variable as much as you want. After all, the atomicCity variable is declared inside the visitIdaho method.

Figure 10-8:
A run of
the code in
Listing 10-8.

```
C:\JavaPrograms>java GetGoing2
visitID is running:
   red planet
   Population: 25
visitNJ is running:
   red planet

C:\JavaPrograms>_
```

And what about Mars? Have you forgotten about your old friend, that lovely eighty-degrees-below-zero planet? Well, both the visitIdaho and visitNewJersey methods can access the mars variable. That's because the mars variable is an instance variable. The mars variable is declared in the code for the EnglishSpeakingWorld2 class, but not inside any particular method. (In my stories about the names for things, remember that people who live in both states, Idaho and New Jersey, have heard of the planet Mars.)

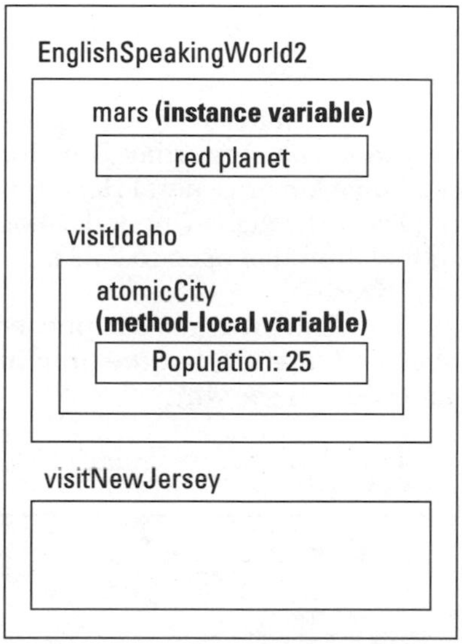

Figure 10-9:
The structure of the code in Listing 10-8.

```
┌─────────────────────────────────────────────┐
│ EnglishSpeakingWorld2                         │
│   ┌───────────────────────────────────────┐  │
│   │     mars (instance variable)          │  │
│   │   ┌─────────────────────────────┐     │  │
│   │   │         red planet          │     │  │
│   │   └─────────────────────────────┘     │  │
│   │                                       │  │
│   │   visitIdaho                          │  │
│   │   ┌─────────────────────────────┐     │  │
│   │   │  atomicCity                 │     │  │
│   │   │  (method-local variable)    │     │  │
│   │   │  ┌───────────────────────┐  │     │  │
│   │   │  │   Population: 25       │  │     │  │
│   │   │  └───────────────────────┘  │     │  │
│   │   └─────────────────────────────┘     │  │
│   └───────────────────────────────────────┘  │
│   ┌───────────────────────────────────────┐  │
│   │  visitNewJersey                       │  │
│   │  ┌─────────────────────────────────┐  │  │
│   │  │                                 │  │  │
│   │  └─────────────────────────────────┘  │  │
│   └───────────────────────────────────────┘  │
└─────────────────────────────────────────────┘
```

The lifecycle of the mars variable has three separate steps:

✔ When the EnglishSpeakingWorld2 class first flashes into existence, the computer sees `String mars` and creates space for the variable.

✔ When the visitIdaho method is executed, the method assigns the value `"red planet"` to the mars variable. (The visitIdaho method also prints the value of the mars variable.)

✔ When the visitNewJersey method is executed, the method prints the mars value once again.

In this way, the mars variable's value is passed from one method to another.

Passing Parameters

A method can communicate with another part of your Java program in several ways. One of the ways is through the method's parameter list. Using a parameter list, you pass on-the-fly information to a method as the method is being called.

So imagine that the information you pass to the method is stored in one of your program's variables. What, if anything, does the method actually do with that variable? This section presents a few interesting case studies.

Pass by value

According to my Web research, the town of Smackover, Arkansas, has 2,232 people in it. But my research isn't current. Just yesterday, Dora Kermongoos celebrated a joyous occasion over at Smackover General Hospital — the birth of her healthy, blue-eyed baby girl. (The girl weighs 7 pounds, 4 ounces, and is 21 inches tall.) Now the town's population has risen to 2,233.

Listing 10-9 has a very bad program in it. The program is supposed to add 1 to a variable that stores Smackover's population, but the program doesn't work. Take a look at Listing 10-9, and you can see why.

Listing 10-9: This program doesn't work

```
class TrackPopulation
{

    public static void main(String args[])
    {
        int smackoverARpop = 2232;

        birth(smackoverARpop);
        System.out.println(smackoverARpop);
    }


    public static void birth(int cityPop)
    {
        cityPop++;
    }

}
```

When you run the program in Listing 10-9, the program displays the number 2232 on the computer screen. After nine months of planning and anticipation and a whopping seven hours in labor, the Kermongoos family's baby girl wasn't registered in the system. What a shame!

The improper use of parameter passing caused the problem. In Java, when you pass a parameter that has one of the eight primitive types to a method, then that parameter is *passed by value*. (For a review of Java's eight primitive types, see Chapter 4.) Here's what this means in plain English: Any changes that the method makes to the value of its parameter don't affect the values of variables back in the calling code. In Listing 10-9, the birth method can apply the ++ operator to cityPop all it wants — the application of ++ to the cityPop parameter has absolutely no effect on the value of the smackoverARpop variable back in the main method.

Technically, what's happening is the copying of a value. (See Figure 10-10.) When the main method calls the birth method, the value stored in smackoverARpop is copied to another memory location — a location reserved for the cityPop parameter's value. During the birth method's execution, 1 is added to the cityPop parameter. But the place where the original 2232 value was stored — the memory location for the smackoverARpop variable — remains unaffected.

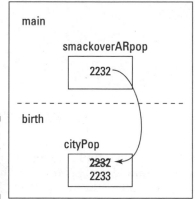

Figure 10-10:
Pass by
value, under
the hood.

When you do parameter passing with any of the eight primitive types, the computer uses pass by value. The value stored in the calling code's variable remains unchanged. This happens even if the calling code's variable and the called method's parameter happen to have the exact same name.

Returning a result

You must fix the problem that the code in Listing 10-9 poses. After all, a young baby Kermongoos can't go through life untracked. To record this baby's existence, you have to add 1 to the value of the smackoverARpop variable. You can do this in plenty of ways, and the way presented in Listing 10-10 is not the simplest. Even so, the way shown in Listing 10-10 illustrates a point: Returning a value from a method call can be an acceptable alternative to parameter passing. Look at Listing 10-10, and you can see what I mean.

Listing 10-10:   This program works

```
class TrackPopulation2
{

   public static void main(String args[])
   {
      int smackoverARpop = 2232;

      smackoverARpop = birth(smackoverARpop);
      System.out.println(smackoverARpop);
   }


   public static int birth(int cityPop)
   {
      return cityPop+1;
   }

}
```

After running the code in Listing 10-10, the number you see on your computer screen is the correct number, 2233.

The code in Listing 10-10 has no new features in it (unless you call "working correctly" a new feature). The most important idea in Listing 10-10 is the return statement, which also appears in Chapter 7. Even so, Listing 10-10 presents a nice contrast to Listing 10-9's approach, which had to be discarded.

Pass by reference

In the last section or two, I took great pains to emphasize a certain point — that when a parameter has one of the eight primitive types, then the parameter is passed by value. If you read this, you probably missed the emphasis on the parameter's having one of the eight primitive types. The emphasis is needed, because passing objects (reference types) doesn't quite work the same way.

When you pass an object to a method, the object is passed by reference. What this means to you is that statements in the called method *can* change any values stored in the object's variables. Those changes *do* affect the values that are seen by whatever code called the method. Listing 10-11 illustrates the point.

Listing 10-11:   Passing an object to a method

```
public class City
{
   int population;
```

```
}


class TrackPopulation3
{

  public static void main(String args[])
  {
    City smackoverAR = new City();
    smackoverAR.population = 2232;
    birth(smackoverAR);
    System.out.println(smackoverAR.population);
  }


  public static void birth(City aCity)
  {
    aCity.population++;
  }

}
```

When you run the code in Listing 10-11, the output you get is the number 2233. That's good, because the code has things like ++ and the word *birth* in it. The deal is, adding 1 to aCity.population inside the birth method actually changes the value of smackoverAR.population as it's known in the main method.

To see how the birth method changes the value of smackoverAR.population, look at Figure 10-11. When you pass an object to a method, the computer doesn't make a copy of the entire object. Instead, the computer makes a copy of a reference to that object. (Think of it the way it's pictured in Figure 10-11. The computer makes a copy of an arrow that points to the object.)

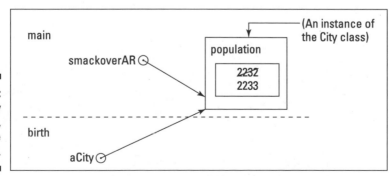

Figure 10-11:
Pass by reference, under the hood.

In Figure 10-11, you see just one instance of the City class, with a population variable inside it. Now keep your eye on that object as you read the following steps:

✔ Just before the birth method is called, the smackoverAR variable refers to that object — the instance of the City class.

✔ When the birth method is called and smackoverAR is passed to the birth method's aCity parameter, the computer copies the reference from smackoverAR to aCity. Now aCity refers to that same object — the instance of the City class.

✔ When the statement aCity.population++ is executed inside the birth method, the computer adds 1 to the object's population variable. Now the program's one and only City instance has 2233 stored in its population variable.

✔ The flow of execution goes back to the main method. The value of smackoverAR.population is printed. But smackoverAR refers to that one instance of the City class. So smackoverAR.population has the value 2233. The Kermongoos family is so proud.

Returning an object from a method

Believe it or not, there's one nook and cranny of Java methods that the previous sections on parameter passing didn't explore. When you call a method, the method can return something right back to the calling code. In previous chapters and sections, I return primitive values, such as int values, or nothing (otherwise known as *void*). In this section, I return a whole object. It's an object of type City. The code that makes this happen is in Listing 10-12.

Listing 10-12:   Here, have a City

```
public class City
{
    int population;
}


class TrackPopulation4
{
    public static void main(String args[])
    {
        City smackoverAR = new City();
        smackoverAR.population = 2232;
        smackoverAR = doBirth(smackoverAR);
        System.out.println(smackoverAR.population);
```

```
      }

      public static City doBirth(City aCity)
      {
          City myCity = new City();
          myCity.population = aCity.population+1;
          return myCity;
      }
  }
```

If you run the code in Listing 10-12, you get the number 2233. That's good. The code works by telling the doBirth method to create another City instance. In the new instance, the value of population is 2333 (Figure 10-12).

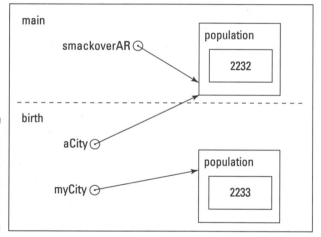

Figure 10-12: The doBirth method creates a City instance.

When the doBirth method is finished being executed, that City instance is returned to the main method. Then, back in the main method, that instance (the one that doBirth returns) is assigned to the smackoverAR variable (Figure 10-13). Now smackoverAR refers to a brand new City instance — an instance with whose population is 2233.

In Listing 10-12, notice the type consistency in the calling and returning of the doBirth method.

- ✔ The smackoverAR variable has type City. The smackoverAR variable is passed to the aCity parameter, which is also of type City.

- ✔ The myCity variable is of type City. The myCity variable is sent back in the doBirth method's return statement. That's consistent, because the doBirth method's header begins with the promise public static City — the promise to return an object of type City.

✔ The doBirth method returns an object of type City. Back in the main method, the object that the call to doBirth returns is assigned to the smackoverAR variable, and (you guessed it) the smackoverAR variable is of type City.

Aside from being very harmonious, all this type agreement is absolutely necessary. If you write a program, and your types don't agree with one another in the program, then javac will spit out an unsympathetic `incompatible types` message.

Epilogue

Dora Kermongoos and her newborn baby daughter are safe, healthy, and resting happily in their Smackover, Arkansas, home.

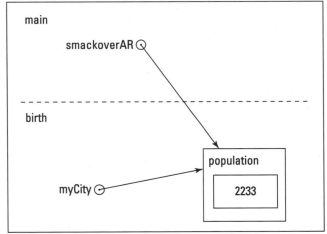

Figure 10-13: The new City instance is assigned to the smackoverAR variable.

Part IV
Savvy Java Techniques

The 5th Wave — By Rich Tennant

HERE'S THE DEAL—MANAGEMENT IS WILLING TO PAY BIG BUCKS TO ANY PROGRAMMER WHO CAN WORK WITH APPLETS.

AWRIGHT!!

In this part . . .

If you've read this far, then you're ready for some big-time Java concepts. This part of the book describes the tricky things, the little nooks and crannies, the special rules, and the not-so-special exceptions. As usual, you shouldn't feel intimidated. I take you one step at a time and keep the whole thing light, interesting, and manageable.

Chapter 11

Using an Array to Juggle Several Values at Once

• •

• •

Welcome to the Java Motel! No haughty bellhops, no overpriced room service, none of the usual silly puns. Just a clean double room at a darn good value.

Getting Your Ducks All in a Row

The Java Motel, with its ten comfortable rooms, sits in a quiet place off the main highway. Aside from a small, separate office, the motel is just one long row of ground floor rooms. Each room is easily accessible from the spacious front parking lot.

Oddly enough, the motel's rooms are numbered 0 through 9. I could say that the numbering is a fluke — something to do with the builder's original design plan. But the truth is, starting with 0 makes the examples in this chapter easier to write.

Anyway, you're trying to keep track of the number of guests in each room. Because you have ten rooms, you may think about declaring ten variables.

```
int guestsInRoomNum0, guestsInRoomNum1, guestsInRoomNum2,
    guestsInRoomNum3, guestsInRoomNum4, guestsInRoomNum5,
    guestsInRoomNum6, guestsInRoomNum7, guestsInRoomNum8,
    guestsInRoomNum9;
```

Doing it this way may seem a bit inefficient. But inefficiency isn't the only thing wrong with this code. Even more problematic is the fact that you can't loop through these variables. To read a value for each variable, you have to copy the getInt method ten times.

```
guestsInRoomNum0 = DummiesIO.getInt(guestList);
guestsInRoomNum1 = DummiesIO.getInt(guestList);
guestsInRoomNum2 = DummiesIO.getInt(guestList);
... and so on.
```

Surely, there's a better way.

That better way involves an array. An *array* is a row of values, like the row of rooms in a one-floor motel. To picture the array, just picture the Java Motel.

✔ First, picture the rooms, lined up next to one another.

✔ Next, picture the same rooms with their front walls missing. Inside each room you can see a certain number of guests.

✔ If you can, forget that the two guests in Room 9 are putting piles of bills into a big briefcase. Ignore the fact that the guest in Room 6 hasn't moved away from the TV set in a day and a half. Instead of all these details, just see numbers. In each room, see a number representing the count of guests in that room. (If freeform visualization isn't your strong point, then look at Figure 11-1.)

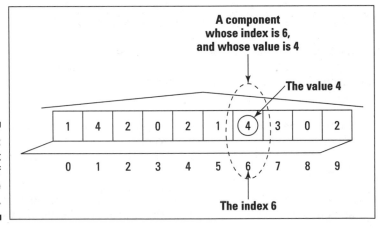

Figure 11-1:
An abstract snapshot of rooms in the Java Motel.

In the lingo of this chapter, the entire row of rooms is called an *array*. Each room in the array is called a *component* of the array (also known as an array *element*). Each component has two numbers associated with it:

> ✔ The room number (a number from 0 to 9), which is called an *index* of the array
>
> ✔ A number of guests, which is a *value* stored in a component of the array

Using an array saves you from all the repetitive nonsense in the sample code shown above. For instance, to declare an array with ten values in it, you can write two, fairly short statements:

```
int guests[];
guests = new int[10];
```

You can even squish the two statements into one longer statement:

```
int guests[] = new int[10];
```

In either of these code snippets, notice the use of the number 10. This number tells the computer to make the guests array have ten components. Each component of the array has a name of its own. The starting component is named *guests[0],* the next is named *guests[1],* and so on. The last of the ten components is named *guests[9].*

In creating an array, you always specify the number of components. The array's indices start with 0 and end with the number that's one less than the total number of components.

The snippets shown above give you two ways to create an array. One way uses two lines. The other way uses one line. If you take the single line route, then you can put that line inside or outside a method. The choice is yours. On the other hand, if you use two separate lines, then the second line, `guests = new int[10]`, should be inside a method.

In an array declaration, you can put the square brackets either before or after the variable name. In other words, you can write `int guests[]` or `int[] guests`. The computer creates the same guests variable, no matter which form you use.

Creating an array in two easy steps

Look once again at the two lines that you can use to create an array:

```
int guests[];
guests = new int[10];
```

Each line serves its own distinct purpose:

✔ `int guests[]`: This first line is a declaration. The declaration reserves the array name (a name like *guests*) for use in the rest of the program. In the Java Motel metaphor, this line says, "I plan to build a motel here and put a certain number of guests in each room." (See Figure 11-2.)

Never mind what the declaration `int guests[]` does. It's more important to notice what the declaration `int guests[]` *doesn't* do. The declaration doesn't reserve ten memory locations. Indeed, a declaration like `int guests[]` doesn't really create an array. All the declaration does is set up the guests variable. At that point in the code, the guests variable still doesn't refer to a real array. (In other words, the motel hasn't been built yet.)

✔ `guests = new int[10]`: This second line is an assignment statement. The assignment statement reserves space in the computer's memory for ten int values. In terms of real estate, this line says, "I've finally built the motel. Go ahead and put guests in each room." (Again, see Figure 11-2.)

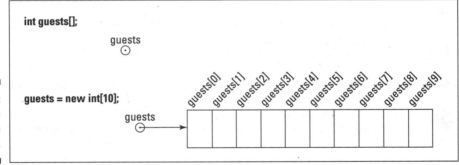

Figure 11-2:
Two steps in
creating an
array.

Storing values

After you've created an array, you can put values into the array's components. For instance, you would like to store the fact that Room 6 contains 4 guests. To put the value 4 in the component with index 6, you write `guests[6]=4`.

Now business starts to pick up. A big bus pulls up to the motel. On the side of the bus is a sign that says "Noah's Ark." Out of the bus come 25 couples, each walking, stomping, flying, hopping, or slithering to the motel's small office. Only 10 of the couples can stay at the Java Motel, but that's okay, because you can send the other 15 couples down the road to the old C-Side Resort and Motor Lodge.

Anyway, to register 10 couples into the Java Motel, you put a couple (2 guests) in each of your 10 rooms. Having created an array, you can take advantage of the array's indexing and write a for loop, like this:

```
for (int roomNum=0; roomNum<10; roomNum++)
   guests[roomNum] = 2;
```

This loop takes the place of ten assignment statements. Notice how the loop's counter goes from 0 to 9. Compare this with Figure 11-2, and remember that the indices of an array go from 0 to one less than the number of components in the array.

Now, given the way the world works, your guests won't always arrive in neat pairs, and you'll have to fill each room with a different number of guests. You probably store information about rooms and guests in a database. If you do, you can still loop through an array, gathering numbers of guests as you go. The code to perform such a task may look like this:

```
resultset =
   statement.executeQuery("SELECT GUESTS FROM RoomData");
for (int roomNum=0; roomNum<10; roomNum++)
{
   resultset.next();
   guests[roomNum]=resultset.getInt("GUESTS");
}
```

But, because this book doesn't cover databases until Bonus Chapter C (on the CD-ROM), you may be better off reading numbers of guests from a plain text file. If you're a Windows user, you can use Notepad to deposit numbers into the file. (A sample file is shown in Listing 11-1.) After you've made a file, you can call on this book's DummiesIO class to get values from the file. The code is shown in Listing 11-2, and the resulting output is in Figure 11-3.

Listing 11-1:   The GuestList file

```
1
4
2
0
2
1
4
3
0
2
```

Listing 11-2:   Filling an array with values

```java
import java.io.BufferedReader;

public class ShowGuests
{

    public static void main(String args[])
    {
        int guests[] = new int[10];
        BufferedReader guestList =
            DummiesIO.open("c:\\JavaPrograms\\GuestList");

        for(int roomNum=0; roomNum<10; roomNum++)
            guests[roomNum] = DummiesIO.getInt(guestList);

        System.out.println("Room\tGuests");
        for(int roomNum=0; roomNum<10; roomNum++)
        {
            System.out.print(roomNum);
            System.out.print("\t");
            System.out.println(guests[roomNum]);
        }
    }

}
```

Figure 11-3:
Running the
code from
Listing 11-2.

```
C:\JavaPrograms>java ShowGuests
Room    Guests
0       1
1       4
2       2
3       0
4       2
5       1
6       4
7       3
8       0
9       2

C:\JavaPrograms>
```

The code in Listing 11-2 has two for loops. The first loop reads numbers of guests, and the second loop writes numbers of guests.

In the writing loop, a few calls to print use the \t escape sequence. It's called an *escape sequence* because you escape from displaying the letter t on the screen. Instead, the characters \t stand for a tab. The computer moves forward to the next tab stop before printing any more characters. Java has a few of these handy escape sequences. Some of them are shown in Table 11-1.

Table 11-1	Escape Sequences
Sequence	*Meaning*
\b	backspace
\t	horizontal tab
\n	linefeed
\f	form feed
\r	carriage return
\"	double quote "
\'	single quote '
\\	backslash \

There's another way to fill an array in Java. It's with an *array initializer*. When you use an array initializer, you don't even have to tell the computer how many components the array has. The computer figures this out for you.

Listing 11-3 shows a new version of the code to fill an array. The program's output is the same as the output of Listing 11-2. (It's the stuff shown in Figure 11-3.) The only difference is that the code in Listing 11-3 uses an array initializer.

Listing 11-3: Using an array initializer

```java
public class ShowGuests
{
   public static void main(String args[])
   {
      int guests[] = {1,4,2,0,2,1,4,3,0,2};

      System.out.println("Room\tGuests");
      for(int roomNum=0; roomNum<10; roomNum++)
      {
         System.out.print(roomNum);
         System.out.print("\t");
         System.out.println(guests[roomNum]);
      }
   }
}
```

An array initializer can contain expressions as well as literals. In plain English, this means that you can put all kinds of things between the commas in the initializer. For instance, an initializer like {1+3, DummiesIO.getInt(), 2,0,2,1,4,3,0,2} works just fine.

Every array has a built-in length field. An array's length is the number of components in the array. So, in Listing 11-3, if you print the value of guests.length, you get 10.

Searching

You're sitting behind the desk at the Java Motel. Look! Here comes a party of five. These people want a room, so you need software that checks to see if a room is vacant. If there is, then the software needs to modify the GuestList file (Listing 11-1) by replacing the number 0 with the number 5. As luck would have it, the software is right on your hard drive. The software is shown in Listing 11-4.

Listing 11-4:   Do you have a room?

```java
import java.io.BufferedReader;
import java.io.PrintStream;

public class FindVacancy
{
    public static void main(String args[])
    {
        int guests[] = new int[10];
        int roomNum;

        BufferedReader guestList =
            DummiesIO.open("c:\\JavaPrograms\\GuestList");
        for(roomNum=0; roomNum<10; roomNum++)
            guests[roomNum] = DummiesIO.getInt(guestList);

        for (roomNum=0; roomNum<=10; roomNum++)
            if(roomNum==10 || guests[roomNum]==0)
                break;

        if (roomNum==10)
            System.out.println("Sorry, no v cancy");
        else
        {
            System.out.print("How many people for room ");
            System.out.print(roomNum);
            System.out.print("? ");
            guests[roomNum] = DummiesIO.getInt();

            PrintStream listOut =
```

```
          DummiesIO.create("c:\\JavaPrograms\\GuestList");
       for (roomNum=0; roomNum<10; roomNum++)
          listOut.println(guests[roomNum]);
    }

  }

}
```

Figure 11-4 shows several runs of the Listing 11-4's code. In the figure, the motel starts with two vacant rooms — Rooms 3 and 8. (Remember, the rooms start with Room 0.) The first time you run the code in Listing 11-4, the program tells you that Room 3 is vacant and puts five people into the room. The second time you run the code, the program finds the remaining vacant room (Room 8) and puts a party of ten in the room. (What a party!) The third time you run the code, you don't have any more vacant rooms. When the program discovers this, it displays the message Sorry, no v cancy, omitting at least one letter in the tradition of all motel neon signs.

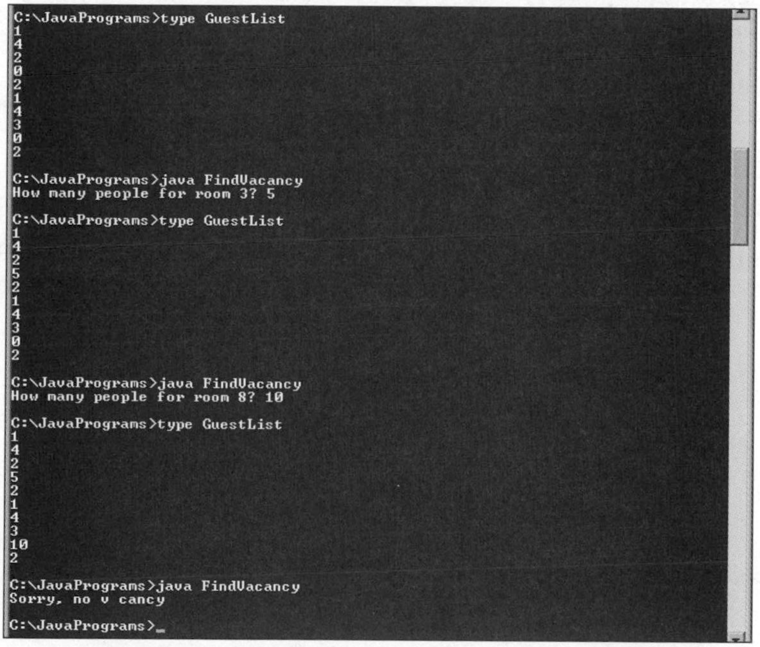

Figure 11-4:
Filling
vacancies.

The code uses tricks from other chapters and sections of this book. The code's only brand-new feature is the use of DummiesIO to write to a disk file. Because the DummiesIO class isn't standard Java (and, heaven knows, it should be!), I don't need to belabor the details. All you need to know is that, by calling the DummiesIO.create method, you destroy anything that was already in the GuestList file.

After calling create and assigning the method's result value to a variable, you can use that variable's println method. In Listing 11-4 calls `listOut.println(guests[roomNum])` to write the number of guests in a room to the new GuestList file.

You can find `DummiesIO.java` on this book's CD-ROM. Just copy the code to your local hard drive.

Like many other methods of its kind, the DummiesIO.create method doesn't pussyfoot around with files. If it can't find a GuestList file, the method creates one and starts writing values into it. But, if a GuestList file already exists, the method clobbers the existing file and starts writing to its new, empty GuestList file. If you don't like it when files are clobbered, then take precautions before calling a method like DummiesIO.create.

To use PrintStream (a class in the Java API), be sure to import java.io.PrintStream at the top of your Java file.

Short-circuit evaluation

The if statement in Listing 11-4 uses an interesting trick. To see the trick in action, try defeating it. Change the condition in the if statement so that the tests are reversed:

```
if(guests[roomNum]==0 || roomNum==10)
```

If the motel has a vacant room when you do this, things are okay. But, if the motel doesn't have a free room, then running the program gives you a lovely error message like this one:

```
Exception in thread "main"
        java.lang.ArrayIndexOutOfBoundsException
        at FindVacancy.main(FindVacancy.java:17)
```

What's going on here? Well, Java's || and && operators use something called *short-circuit evaluation*. If, in the middle of evaluating an expression, the computer figures that it already knows the final outcome, then the computer stops evaluating the expression.

To understand this, think about the expression `roomNum==10 || guests[roomNum]==0` in Listing 11-4. If there's really no room at the inn, then the loop reaches an iteration in which roomNum is 10. The computer tests the condition `roomNum==10` and finds the condition to be true. At that point, the computer doesn't need to test the rest of the condition `guests[roomNum]==0`, because if half of the || expression is true, then the whole || expression is true, no matter what the other half says.

In fact, it's a good thing that the computer doesn't bother testing guests[roomNum]==0. If the computer tried to perform the test, then it would be checking guests[10], but indices of the guests array don't go all the way up to 10. The indices go from 0 to 9. You'd get an ArrayIndexOutOfBoundsException.

And that's what happens when you accidentally reverse the tests inside the if statement. With the tests reversed, the computer always checks first to see if guests[roomNum]==0. If roomNum happens to be 10, then the program crashes with an ArrayIndexOutOfBoundsException before the computer ever gets to test for roomNum==10.

As they say at Java programmer gatherings, "What's good for the || is good for the &&." Java's && operator uses short-circuit evaluation too. Imagine that you write firstTest && secondTest. What if the computer evaluates firstTest and finds it to be false? Then the whole && condition can't possibly be true. When one of the two tests is false, the whole && expression is false. So, again, the computer uses short-circuit evaluation. The computer doesn't bother going on to evaluate secondTest. You can take advantage of this in writing your code.

Arrays of Objects

The Java Motel is open for business, now with improved guest registration software! The people who brought you this chapter's first section are always scratching their heads, looking for the best ways to improve their services. Now, with some ideas from object-oriented programming, they've started thinking in terms of a Room class.

"And what," you ask, "is a Room instance?" That's easy. A Room instance has three properties — the number of guests in the room, the room rate, and a smoking/nonsmoking stamp. Figure 11-5 illustrates the situation.

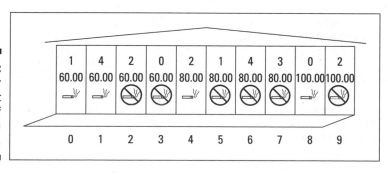

Figure 11-5: Another abstract snapshot of rooms in the Java Motel.

Listing 11-5 shows the code that describes the Room class. As promised, each instance of the Room class has three variables: the guests, rate, and smoking variables. (A false value for the boolean variable, smoking, indicates a nonsmoking room.) In addition, the entire Room class has a static variable named *currency*. This currency object makes room rates look like dollar amounts. (To find out what static means, see Chapter 10.)

Listing 11-5:   So this is what a Room looks like!

```java
import java.io.BufferedReader;
import java.text.NumberFormat;

public class Room
{
    private int guests;
    private double rate;
    private boolean smoking;

    private static NumberFormat currency =
                NumberFormat.getCurrencyInstance();


    public void readRoom(BufferedReader roomList)
    {
        guests = DummiesIO.getInt(roomList);
        rate = DummiesIO.getDouble(roomList);
        smoking = DummiesIO.getBoolean(roomList);
    }


    public void writeRoom()
    {
        System.out.print(guests);
        System.out.print("\t");
        System.out.print(currency.format(rate));
        System.out.print("\t");
        if(smoking)
            System.out.println("yes");
        else
            System.out.println("no");
    }
}
```

So now you need an array of rooms. The code to create such a thing is in Listing 11-6. To run the code, you need the usual DummiesIO.class file and the RoomList file. (The code in Listing 11-6 reads data from the RoomList file. Listing 11-7 shows the contents of the RoomList file.) Figure 11-6 shows a run of Listing 11-6's code.

Listing 11-6:   Would you like to see a Room?

```java
import java.io.BufferedReader;

public class ShowRooms
{

    public static void main(String args[])
    {
        Room rooms[];
        rooms = new Room[10];
        BufferedReader roomList =
            DummiesIO.open("c:\\JavaPrograms\\RoomList");


        for(int roomNum=0; roomNum<10; roomNum++)
        {
            rooms[roomNum] = new Room();
            rooms[roomNum].readRoom(roomList);
        }


        System.out.println("Room\tGuests\tRate\tSmoking?");
        for(int roomNum=0; roomNum<10; roomNum++)
        {
            System.out.print(roomNum);
            System.out.print("\t");
            rooms[roomNum].writeRoom();
        }
    }

}
```

Listing 11-7:   A file of Room data

```
1
60.00
true
4
60.00
true
2
60.00
false
0
60.00
false
2
80.00
true
```

(continued)

Listing 11-7 *(continued)*

```
1
80.00
false
4
80.00
false
3
80.00
false
0
100.00
true
2
100.00
false
```

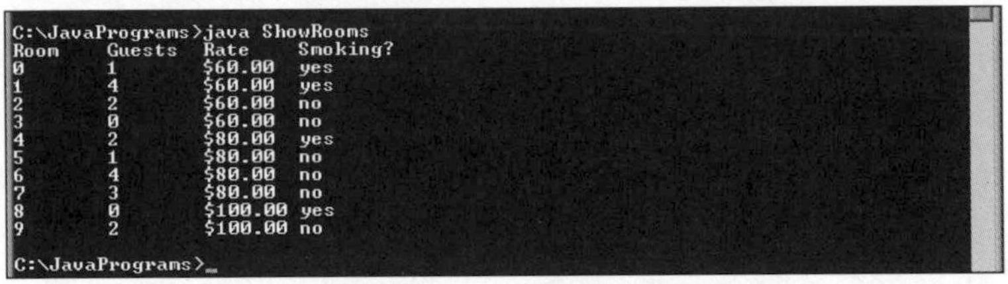

Figure 11-6:
A run of the code in Listing 11-6.

```
C:\JavaPrograms>java ShowRooms
Room    Guests  Rate    Smoking?
0       1       $60.00  yes
1       4       $60.00  yes
2       2       $60.00  no
3       0       $60.00  no
4       2       $80.00  yes
5       1       $80.00  no
6       4       $80.00  no
7       3       $80.00  no
8       0       $100.00 yes
9       2       $100.00 no

C:\JavaPrograms>_
```

Say what you want about the code in Listing 11-6. As far as I'm concerned, only one issue in the whole listing should concern you. And what, you ask, is that issue? Well, to create an array of objects, you have to do three things — make the array variable, make the array itself, and then construct each individual object in the array. This is different from creating an array of int values or an array containing any other primitive type values. When you create an array of primitive type values, you do only the first two of these three things.

To help make sense of all this, follow along in Listing 11-6 and Figure 11-7 as you read the following points.

✔ Room rooms[];: This declaration creates a rooms variable. This variable is destined to refer to an array (but doesn't yet refer to anything at all).

✔ rooms = new Room[10];: This statement reserves ten slots of storage in the computer's memory. The statement also makes the rooms variable refer to the group of storage slots. Each slot is destined to refer to an object (but doesn't yet refer to anything at all).

✔ rooms[roomNum] = new Room();: This statement is inside of a for loop. The statement is executed once for each of the ten room numbers. For example, the first time through the loop, this statement says rooms[0] = new Room(). That first time around, the statement makes the slot rooms[0] refer to an actual object (an instance of the Room class).

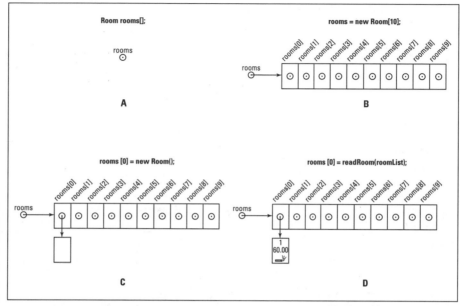

Figure 11-7:
Steps in
creating an
array of
objects.

Although it's technically not considered a step in "array making," you still have to fill each object's variables with values. For instance, the first time through the loop, the readRoom call says `rooms[1].readRoom(roomList)`, which means, "Read data from the roomList file into the rooms[1] object's variables." Each time through the loop, the program creates a new object and reads data into that new object's variables.

Similar to creating arrays of primitive values, you can squeeze the steps together. For instance, you can do the first two steps in one fell swoop, like this:

```
Room rooms[] = new Room[10];
```

You can also use an array initializer. (For an introduction to array initializers, see the section, "Storing values," earlier in this chapter. Also, the upcoming section has a cool array initializer example.)

An Array of Strings

Suppose you want to keep track of the happenings on various days of the week. You'd like 1 to stand for Sunday, 2 to stand for Monday, and so on. What's the best way to go back and forth between numbers and day names? Sure, you can write a big if statement, but big if statements are clunky. You can write a switch statement to go from number to day name, but the other way won't work. (It's not legal for the expression in a switch to be a string of characters.)

Hey, how about making an array of strings? To go back and forth between numbers and day names, you just look up the one you know in the array. When you find what you're looking for, you print that item's counterpart in the array. The array that makes this strategy work is pictured in Figure 11-8. To see the strategy in action, look at Listing 11-8.

Figure 11-8:
A lookup
table,
implemented
as an array.

0	1	2	3	4	5	6	7
Noday	Sunday	Monday	Tuesday	Wednesday	Thursday	Friday	Saturday

Listing 11-8:   Using an array of strings

```
public class DayOfTheWeek
{
    public static void main(String args[])
    {
        int dayNum;
        String aDayName;
        String dayNames[] = {"Noday", "Sunday", "Monday",
                             "Tuesday","Wednesday", "Thursday",
                             "Friday", "Saturday"};

        System.out.print("Enter a number from 1 to 7: ");
        dayNum = DummiesIO.getInt();

        if (dayNum<1 || dayNum>7)
            dayNum=0;

        System.out.println(dayNames[dayNum]);
        System.out.println();

        System.out.print("Enter a day name: ");
        aDayName = DummiesIO.getString();

        for (dayNum=1; dayNum<=7; dayNum++)
            if (aDayName.equals(dayNames[dayNum]))
            {
                System.out.println(dayNum);
                System.exit(0);
            }
        System.out.println("That's not a day of the week.");
    }
}
```

Figure 11-9 has two runs of the code from Listing 11-8. In the first run, the user types two sensible values (**3** and **Friday**). In the second run, the user types garbage (**8** and **Wensday**). In both cases, the computer responds appropriately.

Figure 11-9:
What day
is it?

```
C:\JavaPrograms>java DayOfTheWeek
Enter a number from 1 to 7: 3
Tuesday

Enter a day name: Friday
6
C:\JavaPrograms>java DayOfTheWeek
Enter a number from 1 to 7: 8
Noday

Enter a day name: Wensday
That's not a day of the week.

C:\JavaPrograms>_
```

Things like "Tuesday" are objects — instances of Java's String class. So, in Listing 11-8, dayNames is an array of objects. Going from number to day name is easy — just plug the number between brackets in the dayNames array.

Going the other way (from day name back to number) is a little bit tougher. Given a day name, you loop through the array components looking for a match. If you find a match, then you display the index of the matching component. That index is the day number. After you've displayed this index, you want to skedaddle out of the program. (You want to avoid getting to the end of the loop, and displaying That's not a day of the week.) To make a quick getaway from a running program, call the System class's exit method.

When you call the exit method, you always feed the method an int parameter. If the program ends happily and normally, it's customary to give the method the value 0. On the other hand, if the method ends sadly and abnormally (with an error of some kind), then you're expected to feed the method a number that isn't 0.

Now notice that, in creating numbers for days of the week, I didn't start with 0. In my code, Sunday is 1 and Saturday is 7. I did this for two reasons. First, I couldn't stomach the idea of having a zero day of the week. Second, I wanted to show you that the crazy room numbering for the Java Motel (which you see in earlier examples in this chapter) isn't absolutely necessary. You can use all kinds of tricks to ignore the 0 index and use indices starting from 1 in a Java array.

Command-Line Arguments

Since you first started learning Java, you've been seeing this `String args[]` business in the header of every main method. Well, it's high time you learned what that business is all about.

When you want to run a Java program, you can get the program going by typing

```
java ClassName
```

That works well in plenty of situations. But sometimes, you want to add a little extra information as you get the program going. Say, for instance, that the program puts a new file on your computer's hard drive. Maybe, when you start the program, you want to tell the program what it should name that new file.

```
java ClassName FileName
```

Hey, maybe you give the program even more information. Imagine this file of yours has random numbers in it. (It's a list of numbers to be read aloud at your motel's weekly Bingo game.) When you get the program running, you tell the program the name of the new file and how many numbers you want the new file to contain.

```
java ClassName FileName howMany
```

All this leads to one big question. How do you get the program to see the extra things that you're typing along with your java command?

That's where this `String args[]` business enters the picture. Anything extra that you type on the command line is fed to the main method by way of its parameter list. The parameter `args[]` is an array of String values. Each String value is one of the words that you typed when you issued the java command. These words are called *command-line arguments*. Listing 11-9 shows you how to do it.

Listing 11-9:   Generate a file of numbers

```
import java.io.PrintStream;


public class MakeRandomNumsFile
{
    public static void main(String args[])
    {
        PrintStream fileOut;
```

```
    int numLines;

    if (args.length < 2)
    {
        System.out.println
            ("Usage: MakeRandomNumsFile filename number");
        System.exit(1);
    }

    fileOut = DummiesIO.create(args[0]);
    numLines = Integer.parseInt(args[1]);

    for (int count=1; count<=numLines; count++)
        fileOut.println(DummiesRandom.getInt());
    }
}
```

Figure 11-10 shows some runs of the code in Listing 11-9. Before running the code yourself, make sure you've copied DummiesRandom.class from this book's CD-ROM to your JavaPrograms directory. Then, to get the code in Listing 11-9 running, you type

```
java MakeRandomNumsFile MyNumberedFile 5
```

If you work with a Java development environment, and not with the command line, you probably run a Java program by clicking a menu item. Somewhere within your environment's menus, you can find an option to add command-line arguments.

Figure 11-10: Running the code in Listing 11-9.

```
C:\JavaPrograms>type MyNumberedFile
The system cannot find the file specified.

C:\JavaPrograms>java MakeRandomNumsFile MyNumberedFile 5

C:\JavaPrograms>type MyNumberedFile
10
2
2
7
8
C:\JavaPrograms>java MakeRandomNumsFile YourNumberedFile
Usage: MakeRandomNumsFile filename number

C:\JavaPrograms>
```

In the main method, the array component args[0] automatically takes on the value "MyNumberedFile", and args[1] automatically becomes "5". So the program's two assignment statements end up having the following meaning:

```
fileOut = DummiesIO.create("MyNumberedFile");
numLines = Integer.parseInt("5");
```

The program creates a file named *MyNumberedFile,* and sets numLines to 5. (Later in the code, the program puts five values into the MyNumberedFile.)

Notice how each command-line argument is a String value. When you look at `args[1]`, you don't see the number 5, you see the string `"5"` with a digit character in it. Unfortunately, you can't use that `"5"` to do any counting. To get an int value from `"5"`, you have to apply the Integer.parseInt method.

The parseInt method, which lives inside the Integer class, is static. So, to call parseInt, you preface the name *parseInt* with the word *Integer*. The Integer class has all kinds of handy methods for doing things with int values. The Integer class is part of a package named java.lang. But notice — you don't need to put `import java.lang.Integer` at the top of your program file. The java.lang package is special. Everything from the java.lang package is imported automatically whenever you run a Java program.

In Java, *Integer* is the name of a class, and *int* is the name of a primitive (simple) type. The two things are related, but they're not the same. The Integer class has methods and other tools for dealing with int values.

Toward the end of the goings-on in Figure 11-10, the user makes a mistake and types

```
java MakeRandomNumsFile YourNumberedFile
```

The problem is that the command line has no second argument. The computer assigns `"YourNumberedFile"` to `arg[0]`, but it doesn't assign anything to `arg[1]`. This is bad. If the computer ever reaches the statement

```
numLines = Integer.parseInt(args[1]);
```

then the program will crash with an unfriendly `ArrayIndexOutOfBoundsException`.

So, what do you do about this? You check the length of the args array. You compare args.length with 2. If the args array has fewer than two components, then you get out while the getting out is still good. (In other words, you exit from the program.)

Despite the checking of args.length in Listing 11-9, the code still isn't crash-proof. If you type **java MakeRandomNumsFile MyNumberedFile five**, then the program takes a nosedive with a `NumberFormatException`. The second command-line argument can't be a word. The argument has to be a number (and a whole number at that). I can add statements to Listing 11-9 to make the code more bulletproof, but checking for the `NumberFormatException` is better done in Chapter 12.

When you're working with command-line arguments, you can enter a String value with a blank space in it. Just enclose the value in double quote marks. For instance, you can run the code of Listing 11-9 with arguments `"My File.txt"` 7.

Two-Dimensional Arrays

Great news! What used to be the old one-floor Java Motel has just been reno-vated! The new, five-floor Java Hotel features a free continental breakfast and, at absolutely no charge, a free newspaper delivered to your door every morn-ing. That's a 50-cent value, absolutely free!

Speaking of things that are continental, the designers of the new Java Hotel took care to number floors the way people do in France. The ground floor (in French, "le rez-de-chaussée") is the zero floor, the floor above that is the first floor, and so on. Figure 11-11 shows the newly renovated hotel.

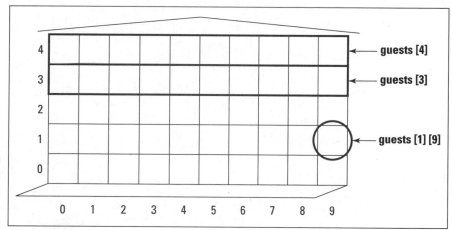

Figure 11-11: A big, high-rise hotel.

A two-dimensional array of primitive values

You can think of the hotel as an array with two indices — a *two-dimensional array*. You declare the array this way.

```
int guests[][] = new int[5][10];
```

The guests array has five rows (numbered 0 to 4, inclusive) and ten columns (numbered 0 to 9, inclusive). To register two guests in Room 9 on the first floor, you write

```
guests[1][9] = 2;
```

The people who do serious Java like to think of a two-dimensional array as an array of rows (that is, an array of ordinary one-dimensional arrays). With this thinking, the rows of the guests array (above) are denoted guests[0], guests[1], guests[2], guests[3], and guests[4]. For a picture of all this, refer to Figure 11-11.

A complete program that uses this guest array is shown in Listing 11-10.

Listing 11-10:   An array of arrays

```
import java.io.BufferedReader;

public class ShowGuests
{

    public static void main(String args[])
    {
        int guests[][] = new int[5][10];
        BufferedReader guestList =
            DummiesIO.open("c:\\JavaPrograms\\GuestList");

        for (int floor=0; floor<5; floor++)
            for (int roomNum=0; roomNum<10; roomNum++)
                guests[floor][roomNum] =
                                DummiesIO.getInt(guestList);


        for (int floor=4; floor>=0; floor--)
        {
            System.out.print("Floor " + floor + ":");
            for (int roomNum=0; roomNum<10; roomNum++)
            {
                System.out.print("   ");
                System.out.print(guests[floor][roomNum]);
            }
            System.out.println();
        }


        System.out.println();
        System.out.print("Room:     ");
        for (int roomNum=0; roomNum<10; roomNum++)
        {
            System.out.print("    ");
            System.out.print(roomNum);
        }
    }

}
```

Figure 11-12 shows a run of the code from Listing 11-10. The input file, GuestList, looks like the file in Listing 11-1, except that the file for this section's program has 50 lines in it.

ON THE CD

You can snare a 50-line GuestList file off this book's CD-ROM.

Figure 11-12:
Guest
counts.

```
C:\JavaPrograms>java ShowGuests
Floor 4:    5    2    2    1    0    3    3    0    0    0
Floor 3:    1    1    4    5    0    0    0    2    2    3
Floor 2:    2    3    1    1    1    2    3    3    2    1
Floor 1:    4    5    0    2    2    0    0    0    1    1
Floor 0:    1    3    2    0    4    3    3    2    1    0

Room:       0    1    2    3    4    5    6    7    8    9
C:\JavaPrograms>_
```

In Listing 11-10, notice the primary way you handle a two-dimensional array — by putting a for loop inside another for loop. For instance, when you read values into the array, you have a room number loop within a floor number loop.

```
for (int floor=0; floor<5; floor++)
    for (int roomNum=0; roomNum<10; roomNum++)
```

Because the roomNum loop is inside the floor loop, the roomNum variable changes faster than the floor variable. In other words, the program prints guest counts for all the rooms on a floor before marching on to the next floor.

REMEMBER

The outer loop's variable changes slower; the inner loop's variable changes faster.

In displaying the hotel's numbers, I could have chosen to start with floor 0 and go up to floor 4. But then the output would have looked like an upside-down hotel. In the program's output, you want the top floor's numbers to be displayed first. To make this work, I created a loop whose counter goes backwards.

```
for (int floor=4; floor>=0; floor--)
```

So notice that the loop's counter starts at 4, goes downward each step of the way, and keeps going down until the counter's value is equal to 0.

A two-dimensional array of objects

This section does "one better" on the stuff from earlier sections. If you can make a two-dimensional array and an array of objects, then why not join these ideas to make a two-dimensional array of objects. Technically, this ends up being an array of arrays of objects. How about that!

First you define your two-dimensional array of Room objects. (The declaration of the Room class comes right from Listing 11-5.)

```
Room rooms[][] = new Room[5][10];
```

Next, you do that all-important step of constructing an object for each component in the array.

```
for (int floor=0; floor<5; floor++)
    for (int roomNum=0; roomNum<10; roomNum++)
        rooms[floor][roomNum] = new Room();
```

Then you read values into the array components' variables, write values, and so on. A complete program is shown in Listing 11-11.

Listing 11-11: A two-dimensional array of objects

```
import java.io.BufferedReader;

public class ShowRooms
{

    public static void main(String args[])
    {
        Room rooms[][] = new Room[5][10];
        BufferedReader roomList =
            DummiesIO.open("c:\\JavaPrograms\\RoomList");

        for (int floor=0; floor<5; floor++)
            for (int roomNum=0; roomNum<10; roomNum++)
            {
                rooms[floor][roomNum] = new Room();
                rooms[floor][roomNum].readRoom(roomList);
            }


        for (int floor=4; floor>=0; floor--)
        {
            System.out.println("Floor " + floor + ":");
            for (int roomNum=0; roomNum<10; roomNum++)
            {
                System.out.print("    ");
                rooms[floor][roomNum].writeRoom();
            }
            System.out.println();
        }
    }

}
```

By the time you're done, the program that uses objects is actually simpler than the code that doesn't use objects. That's because, in writing the code with an array of objects, you're taking advantage of methods that are already written as part of the Room class, such as readRoom and writeRoom.

A run of the code in Listing 11-11 displays information about all 50 of the hotel's rooms. Instead of showing you all that stuff, Figure 11-13 shows you the first several lines in the run. (You don't need to know about every room in the Java Hotel anyway.) The input to the code in Listing 11-11, the RoomList file, looks just like the stuff in Listing 11-7. The only difference is that the RoomList file for this section's code has 150 lines in it.

You can snare a 150-line RoomList file off this book's CD-ROM.

```
C:\JavaPrograms>java ShowRooms
Floor 4:
     5     $100.00  yes
     2     $100.00  yes
     2     $100.00  yes
     1     $100.00  yes
     0     $100.00  yes
     3     $100.00  no
     3     $100.00  no
     0     $100.00  no
     0     $100.00  no
     0     $100.00  no
Floor 3:
     1      $80.00  no
     1      $80.00  no
     4      $80.00  no
     5      $80.00  no
     0      $80.00  no
     0      $80.00  no
```

Figure 11-13: Starting a run of the code from Listing 11-11.

With all the examples building up to Listing 11-11, the code in the listing may be fairly uneventful. The only thing you need to notice is that the line

```
rooms[floor][roomNum] = new Room();
```

is absolutely, indubitably, 100-percent required. When you accidentally leave off this line (not "if you leave off this line," but "when you leave off this line"), you get a runtime error message saying java.lang.NullPointerException.

Chapter 12

Looking Good When Things Take Unexpected Turns

*S*eptember 9, 1945: A moth flies into one of the relays of the Harvard Mark II computer and gums up the works. This becomes the first recorded case of a real computer bug.

April 19, 1957: Herbert Bright, manager of the data processing center at Westinghouse in Pittsburgh, receives an unmarked deck of computer punch cards in the mail (which is like getting an unlabeled CD-ROM in the mail today). Mr. Bright guesses that this deck comes from the development team for FORTRAN — the first computer programming language. He's been waiting a few years for this software. (No Web downloads were available at the time.)

Armed with nothing but this good guess, Bright writes a small FORTRAN program and tries to compile it on his IBM 704. (The IBM 704 lives in its own, specially built 2,000-square-foot room. With vacuum tubes instead of transistors, the machine has a whopping 32K of RAM. The operating system has to be loaded from tape before the running of each program, and a typical program takes between two and four hours to run.) After the usual waiting time, Bright's attempt to compile a FORTRAN program comes back with a single error — a missing comma in one of the statements. Bright corrects the error, and the program runs like a charm.

July 22, 1962: Mariner I, the first U.S. spacecraft aimed at another planet, is destroyed when it behaves badly four minutes after launch. The bad behavior is attributed to a missing bar (like a hyphen) in the formula for the rocket's velocity.

Around the same time, orbit computation software at NASA is found to contain the incorrect statement `DO 10 I=1.10` (instead of the correct `DO 10 I=1,10`). In modern notation, this is like writing `do10i = 1.10` in place of `for (int i=1; i<=10; i++)`. The change from a comma to a period turns a loop into an assignment statement.

January 1, 2000: The Year 2000 Problem wreaks havoc on the modern world.

Any historically accurate facts in these notes were borrowed from the following sources: the Computer Folklore newsgroup (`alt.folklore.computers`), the Free On-line Dictionary of Computing (`www.foldoc.org`), the "Looking Back" column in *Computer* magazine (`www.computer.org/computer/`), and the Web pages of the IEEE (`www.computer.org/history/`).

Handling Exceptions

You're taking inventory. This means counting item after item, box after box, and marking the numbers of such things on log sheets, in little handheld gizmos, and into forms on computer keyboards. A particular part of the project involves entering the number of boxes you find on the Big Dusty Boxes That Haven't Been Opened Since Year One shelf. Rather than break the company's decades-old habit, you decide not to open any of these boxes. You arbitrarily assign the value $3.25 to each box.

Listing 12-1 shows the software to handle this bit of inventory. The software has a flaw, which is revealed in Figure 12-1. When the user enters a whole number value, things are okay. But when the user enters something else (like the number 3.5), the program comes crashing to the ground. Surely something can be done about this. Computers are stupid, but they're not so stupid that they should fail royally when a user enters an improper value.

Listing 12-1: Counting boxes

```java
import java.text.NumberFormat;

public class InventoryA
{
    public static void main(String args[])
    {
        String numBoxesIn;
        int numBoxes;
        double boxPrice = 3.25;
        NumberFormat currency =
            NumberFormat.getCurrencyInstance();

        System.out.print("How many boxes do we have? ");
        numBoxesIn = DummiesIO.getString();
```

```
        numBoxes = Integer.parseInt(numBoxesIn);

        System.out.print("The value is ");
        System.out.println(currency.format(numBoxes*boxPrice));
    }
}
```

```
C:\JavaPrograms>java InventoryA
How many boxes do we have? 3
The value is $9.75

C:\JavaPrograms>java InventoryA
How many boxes do we have? 3.5
Exception in thread "main" java.lang.NumberFormatException: 3.5
        at java.lang.Integer.parseInt(Integer.java:414)
        at java.lang.Integer.parseInt(Integer.java:454)
        at InventoryA.main(InventoryA.java:15)

C:\JavaPrograms>java InventoryA
How many boxes do we have? three
Exception in thread "main" java.lang.NumberFormatException: three
        at java.lang.Integer.parseInt(Integer.java:405)
        at java.lang.Integer.parseInt(Integer.java:454)
        at InventoryA.main(InventoryA.java:15)

C:\JavaPrograms>_
```

Figure 12-1:
Oops! That's
not a
number.

The key to fixing a program bug is examining the message that appears when the program crashes. The inventory program's message says java.lang. NumberFormatException. That means a class named *NumberFormatException* is in the java.lang API package. Somehow, the call to Integer.parseInt brought this NumberFormatException class out of hiding. (For a brief explanation of the Integer.parseInt method, see Chapter 11.)

Well, here's what's going on. The Java programming language has a mechanism called *exception handling*. With exception handling, a program can detect that things are about to go wrong and respond by creating a brand-new object. In the official terminology, the program is said to be *throwing* an exception. That new object, an instance of the Exception class, is passed like a hot potato from one piece of code to another, until some piece of code decides to *catch* the exception. When the exception has been caught, the program executes some recovery code, buries the exception, and moves on to the next normal statement as if nothing had ever happened. The process is illustrated in Figure 12-2.

The whole thing is done with the aid of several Java keywords. These keywords are as follows:

✔ **throw:** Creates a new exception object.

✔ **throws:** Passes the buck from a method up to whatever code called the method.

✔ **try:** Encloses code that has the potential to create a new exception object.

In the usual scenario, the code inside a try clause contains calls to methods whose code can create one or more exceptions.

✔ **catch:** Deals with the exception, buries it, and then moves on.

So, the truth is out. Through some chain of events like the one shown in Figure 12-2, the method Integer.parseInt can throw a NumberFormatException. When you call Integer.parseInt, this NumberFormatException is passed on to you.

The Java API documentation for the parseInt method says, "Throws: NumberFormatException — if the string does not contain a parsable integer." Once in a while, reading the documentation actually pays.

```
void method1()
{
    try
    {
        method2();
    }
    catch (Exception e)
    {
    }
}

void method2() throws Exception
{
    method3();
}

void method3() throws Exception
{
    method4();
}

void method4() throws Exception
{
    throw new Expection();
}
```

Figure 12-2:
Throwing,
passing, and
catching an
exception.

If you call yourself a hero, you better catch the exception so all the other code can get on with its regular business. Listing 12-2 shows the catching of an exception.

Listing 12-2:   A hero counts boxes

```
import java.text.NumberFormat;

public class InventoryB
{
    public static void main(String args[])
    {
        String numBoxesIn;
        int numBoxes;
        double boxPrice = 3.25;
        NumberFormat currency =
            NumberFormat.getCurrencyInstance();

        System.out.print("How many boxes do we have? ");
        numBoxesIn = DummiesIO.getString();

        try
        {
            numBoxes = Integer.parseInt(numBoxesIn);
            System.out.print("The value is ");
            System.out.println
                (currency.format(numBoxes*boxPrice));
        }
        catch (NumberFormatException e)
        {
            System.out.println("That's not a number.");
        }
    }
}
```

Figure 12-3 shows three runs of the code from Listing 12-2. When a misguided user types **three** instead of **3**, the program maintains its cool by displaying That's not a number. The trick is to enclose the call to Integer.parseInt inside a try clause. When you do this, the computer watches for exceptions when any statement inside the try clause is executed. If an exception is thrown, then the computer jumps from inside the try clause to a catch clause below it. In Listing 12-2, the computer jumps directly to the catch (NumberFormatException e) clause. The computer executes the println statement inside the clause, and then marches on with normal processing. (If there were statements in Listing 12-2 after the end of the catch clause, the computer would go on and execute them.)

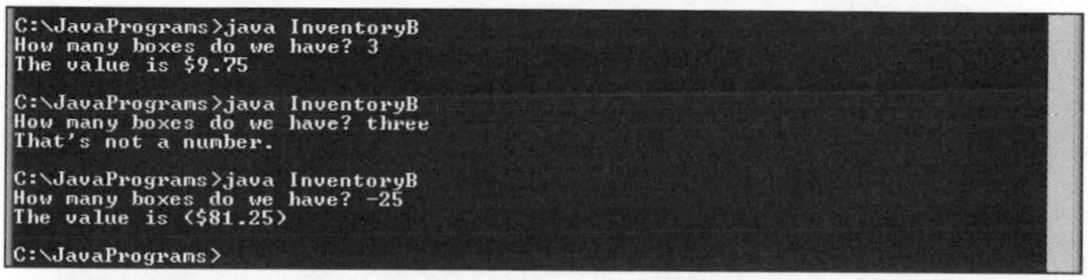

Figure 12-3:
Catch that
exception.

```
C:\JavaPrograms>java InventoryB
How many boxes do we have? 3
The value is $9.75

C:\JavaPrograms>java InventoryB
How many boxes do we have? three
That's not a number.

C:\JavaPrograms>java InventoryB
How many boxes do we have? -25
The value is ($81.25)

C:\JavaPrograms>
```

An entire try-catch assembly, complete with try clause, catch clause, and what have you, is called a *try statement*. Sometimes, for emphasis, I call it a *try-catch statement*.

The parameter in a catch clause

Take a look at the catch clause in Listing 12-2, and pay particular attention to the words (NumberFormatException e). This looks a lot like a method's parameter list, doesn't it? In fact, every catch clause is like a little mini-method with its own parameter list. The parameter list always has an exception type name and then a parameter.

In Listing 12-2, I don't do anything with the catch clause's e parameter, but I certainly could if I wanted to. Remember, the exception that's thrown is an object — an instance of the NumberFormatException class. When an exception is caught, the computer makes the catch clause's parameter refer to that exception object. In other words, the name *e* stores a bunch of information about the exception. To take advantage of this, you can call some of the exception object's methods.

```
catch (NumberFormatException e)
{
    System.out.println("That's not a number.");

    System.out.println("Message: " + e.getMessage());

    System.out.println("Here comes a stack trace: ");
    e.printStackTrace();
    System.out.println("Did you like the stack trace?");
}
```

With this enhanced catch clause, a run of the inventory program may look like the run shown in Figure 12-4. When you call getMessage, you fetch some detail about the exception. (In Figure 12-4, the detail is the fact that the user mistakenly typed the word `three`.) When you call printStackTrace, you get a display showing the methods that were running at the moment when the exception was thrown. (In Figure 12-4, the display includes Integer.parseInt and the main method.) Both getMessage and printStackTrace present information to help you find the source of the program's difficulties.

Figure 12-4:
Calling an
exception
object's
methods.

```
C:\JavaPrograms>java InventoryB
How many boxes do we have? three
That's not a number.
Message: three
Here comes a stack trace:
java.lang.NumberFormatException: three
        at java.lang.Integer.parseInt(Integer.java:405)
        at java.lang.Integer.parseInt(Integer.java:454)
        at InventoryB.main(InventoryB.java:18)
Did you like the stack trace?

C:\JavaPrograms>_
```

Exception types

So what else can go wrong today? Are there other kinds of exceptions — things that don't come from the NumberFormatException class? Sure, plenty of different exception types are out there. You can even create one of your own. You wanna try? If so, look at Listing 12-3.

Listing 12-3:   Making your own kind of exception

```
import java.text.NumberFormat;

public class InventoryC
{
    public static void main(String args[])
    {
        String numBoxesIn;
        int numBoxes;
        double boxPrice = 3.25;
        NumberFormat currency =
            NumberFormat.getCurrencyInstance();

        System.out.print("How many boxes do we have? ");
        numBoxesIn = DummiesIO.getString();

        try
        {
            numBoxes = Integer.parseInt(numBoxesIn);
            if (numBoxes < 0)
                throw new NegativeNumberException();
            System.out.print("The value is ");
            System.out.println
                (currency.format(numBoxes*boxPrice));
        }
        catch (NegativeNumberException e)
        {
            System.out.print(numBoxesIn);
            System.out.println("? That's impossible!");
        }
        catch (NumberFormatException e)
        {
            System.out.println("That's not a number.");
        }
    }
}


class NegativeNumberException extends Exception
{
}
```

The code in Listing 12-3 remedies a problem that cropped up in Figure 12-3. Look at the last of the three runs in Figure 12-3. The user reports that the shelves have −25 boxes, and the computer takes this value without blinking an eye. The truth is that you would need a black hole, or some other exotic space-time warping phenomenon, to have a negative number of boxes on any shelf in your warehouse. So the program should get all upset if the user enters a negative number of boxes, which is what the code in Listing 12-3 does. To see the upset code, look at Figure 12-5.

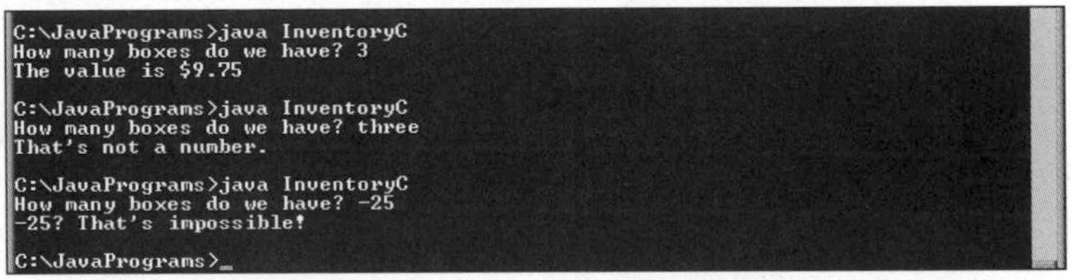

Figure 12-5:
Running the
code from
Listing 12-3.

```
C:\JavaPrograms>java InventoryC
How many boxes do we have? 3
The value is $9.75

C:\JavaPrograms>java InventoryC
How many boxes do we have? three
That's not a number.

C:\JavaPrograms>java InventoryC
How many boxes do we have? -25
-25? That's impossible!

C:\JavaPrograms>_
```

The code in Listing 12-3 declares a new kind of exception class — the NegativeNumberException. This makes a lot of sense. In many situations, typing a negative number would be just fine, so NegativeNumberException isn't built into the Java API. But, in the inventory program, a negative number should be flagged as an anomaly.

So the code in Listing 12-3 declares a NegativeNumberException. This NegativeNumberException class wins the award for the shortest self-contained piece of code in the book. The class's code is just a declaration line and an empty pair of braces. The code's operative phrase is extends Exception. Being a subclass of the Java API Exception class allows any instance of the NegativeNumberException class to be thrown.

Back inside the main method's try clause, a new NegativeNumberException instance is thrown. When this happens, the clause labeled catch (NegativeNumberException e) catches the instance. The clause echoes the user's input and displays the message That's impossible!

Who's going to catch the exception?

Take one more look at Listing 12-3. Notice that more than one catch clause can accompany a single try clause. When an exception is thrown inside a try clause, the computer starts going down the accompanying list of catch clauses. The computer starts at whatever catch clause comes immediately after the try clause and works its way down the program's text.

For each catch clause, the computer asks itself, "Is the exception that was just thrown an instance of the class in this clause's parameter list?"

✔ If not, then the computer skips this catch clause and moves on to the next catch clause in line.

✔ If so, then the computer executes this catch clause and then skips past all the other catch clauses that come with this try clause. The computer goes on and executes whatever statements come after the whole try-catch statement.

For some concrete examples, see Listing 12-4.

Listing 12-4:   Where does the buck stop?

```java
import java.text.NumberFormat;

public class InventoryD
{
    public static void main(String args[])
    {
        String numBoxesIn;
        int numBoxes;
        double boxPrice = 3.25;
        NumberFormat currency =
            NumberFormat.getCurrencyInstance();

        System.out.print("How many boxes do we have? ");
        numBoxesIn = DummiesIO.getString();

        try
        {
            if (numBoxesIn.equals(""))
                throw new NoInputException();

            numBoxes = Integer.parseInt(numBoxesIn);
            if (numBoxes < 0)
                throw new NegativeNumberException();

            System.out.print("The value is ");
            System.out.println
                (currency.format(numBoxes*boxPrice));
        }

        catch (NegativeNumberException e)
        {
            System.out.print(numBoxesIn);
            System.out.println("? That's impossible!");
        }

        catch (NumberFormatException e)
        {
```

(continued)

Listing 12-4 (continued)

```
            System.out.println("That's not a number.");
        }

        catch (Exception e)
        {
            System.out.print("Something went wrong, ");
            System.out.print("but I'm clueless about what ");
            System.out.println("it actually was.");
        }
    }
}


class NegativeNumberException extends Exception
{
}

class NoInputException extends NumberFormatException
{
}
```

What do you do if you ask the user how many boxes are on a shelf, and the user doesn't answer? Instead of typing **3**, **three**, or **–25**, the user just presses Enter? Well, you have choices. You can treat this situation the way you treat a NumberFormatException, or you can set numBoxes to some default value. You can even display a special message, like Hey, buddy, next time why don't you try typing something?

The code in Listing 12-4 takes a middle ground approach. The code declares a new NoInputException class. Although the code doesn't have a separate catch clause to handle a NoInputException, everything still works out just fine. That's because NoInputException is a subclass of NumberFormatException and NumberFormatException has a catch clause.

You see, because NoInputException is a subclass of NumberFormatException, any instance of NoInputException is just a special kind of NumberFormatException. So, when the computer sees the catch clause with parameter NumberFormatException, the computer says, "Okay, I've found a match. I'll execute the statements in this catch clause." To keep from having to write this whole story over and over again, I introduce some new terminology. I say that the catch clause with parameter NumberFormatException *matches* the NoInputException that's been thrown. I call this catch clause a *matching catch clause.*

The following bullets describe different things the user may do and how the computer will respond. As you read through the bullets, you can follow along by looking at the runs shown in Figure 12-6.

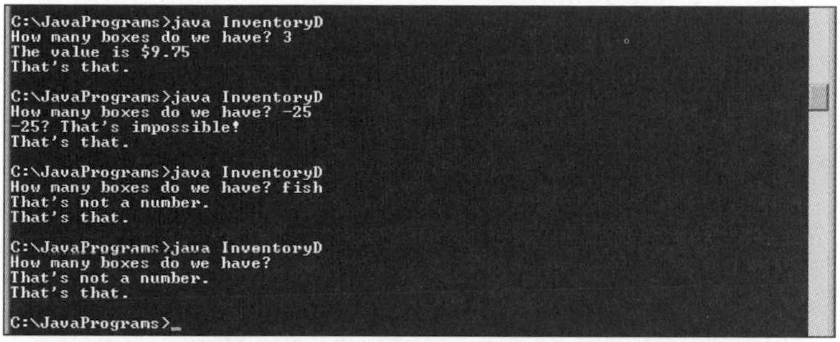

Figure 12-6:
Running the
code from
Listing 12-4.

```
C:\JavaPrograms>java InventoryD
How many boxes do we have? 3
The value is $9.75
That's that.

C:\JavaPrograms>java InventoryD
How many boxes do we have? -25
-25? That's impossible!
That's that.

C:\JavaPrograms>java InventoryD
How many boxes do we have? fish
That's not a number.
That's that.

C:\JavaPrograms>java InventoryD
How many boxes do we have?
That's not a number.
That's that.

C:\JavaPrograms>_
```

Figure 12-6:
Running the
code from
Listing 12-4.

 ✔ **The user enters an ordinary whole number, like the number 3.**

All the statements in the try clause are executed. Then, the computer skips past all the catch clauses and executes the code that comes immediately after all the catch clauses. (See Figure 12-7.)

Figure 12-7:
No
exception is
thrown.

```
try
{

      //Normal processing (throw no exception)

}
catch (NegativeNumberException e)
{
     System.out.print(numBoxesIn);
     System.out.println("? That's impossible!");
}
catch (NumberFormatException e)
{
     System.out.println("That's not a number.");
}
catch (Exception e)
{
     System.out.print("Something went wrong, ");
     System.out.print("but I'm clueless about what ");
     System.out.println("it actually was.");
}
System.out.println("That's that.");
```

 ✔ **The user enters a negative number, like the number –25.**

The code throws a NegativeNumberException. The computer skips past the remaining statements in the try clause. The computer executes the statements inside the first catch clause — the clause whose parameter is of type NegativeNumberException. Then, the computer skips past the second and third catch clauses and executes the code that comes immediately after all the catch clauses. (See Figure 12-8.)

```
try
{

    throw new NegativeNumberException();

}
catch (NegativeNumberException e)
{
    System.out.print(numBoxesIn);
    System.out.println("? That's impossible!");
}
catch (NumberFormatException e)
{
    System.out.println("That's not a number.");
}
catch (Exception e)
{
    System.out.print("Something went wrong, ");
    System.out.print("but I'm clueless about what ");
    System.out.println("it actually was.");
}

System.out.println("That's that.");
```

Figure 12-8:
A Negative-
Number-
Exception is
thrown.

✔ **The user enters something that's not a whole number, like the word *fish*.**

The code throws a NumberFormatException. The computer skips past the remaining statements in the try clause. The computer even skips past the statements in the first catch clause. (After all, a NumberFormatException isn't any kind of a NegativeNumberException. The catch clause with parameter NegativeNumberException isn't a match for this NumberFormatException.) The computer executes the statements inside the second catch clause — the clause whose parameter is of type NumberFormatException. Then, the computer skips past the third catch clause and executes the code that comes immediately after all the catch clauses. (See Figure 12-9.)

```
try
{

        throw new NegativeNumberException ();

}
catch (NegativeNumberException e)
{
    System.out.print(numBoxesIn);
    System.out.println("? That's impossible!");
}
catch (NumberFormatException e)
{
    System.out.println("That's not a number.");
}
catch (Exception e)
{
    System.out.print("Something went wrong, ");
    System.out.print("but I'm clueless about what ");
    System.out.println("it actually was.");
}

System.out.println("That's that.");
```

Figure 12-9:
A Number-
Format-
Exception is
thrown.

✔ **The user presses Enter without typing anything.**

The code throws a NoInputException. The computer skips past the remaining statements in the try clause. The computer even skips past the statements in the first catch clause. (After all, a NoInputException isn't any kind of NegativeNumberException.)

But, according to the code in Listing 12-4, NoInputException is a subclass of NumberFormatException. When the computer reaches the second catch clause, the computer says, "Hmm! A NoInputException is a kind of NumberFormatException. I'll execute the statements in this catch clause — the clause with parameter of type NumberFormatException." In other words, it's a match.

So, the computer executes the statements inside the second catch clause. Then, the computer skips the third catch clause and executes the code that comes immediately after all the catch clauses. (See Figure 12-10.)

```
try
{

        throw new NoInputException ();

}
catch (NegativeNumberException e)
{
    System.out.print(numBoxesIn);
    System.out.println("? That's impossible!");
}
catch (NumberFormatException e)
{
    System.out.println("That's not a number.");
}
catch (Exception e)
{
    System.out.print("Something went wrong, ");
    System.out.print("but I'm clueless about what ");
    System.out.println("it actually was.");
}

System.out.println("That's that.");
```

Figure 12-10:
A NoInput-
Exception is
thrown.

✔ **Something else, something very unpredictable happens (I don't know what).**

With my unending urge to experiment, I reached into the try clause of Listing 12-4 and added a statement that throws an IOException. No reason — I just wanted to see what would happen.

When the code threw an IOException, the computer skipped past the remaining statements in the try clause. Then, the computer skipped past the statements in the first and second catch clauses. When the computer reached the third catch clause, I could hear the computer say, "Hmm! An IOException is a kind of Exception. I've found a matching catch clause — a clause with a parameter of type Exception. I'll execute the statements in this catch clause."

So, the computer executed the statements inside the third catch clause. Then, the computer executed the code that comes immediately after all the catch clauses. (See Figure 12-11.)

```
try
{

         throw new IOException ();

}
catch (NegativeNumberException e)
{
     System.out.print(numBoxesIn);
     System.out.println("? That's impossible!");
}
catch (NumberFormatException e)
{
     System.out.println("That's not a number.");
}
catch (Exception e)
{
     System.out.print("Something went wrong, ");
     System.out.print("but I'm clueless about what ");
     System.out.println("it actually was.");
}

System.out.println("That's that.");
```

Figure 12-11:
An
IOException
is thrown.

When the computer looks for a matching catch clause, the computer latches on to the topmost clause that fits one of the following descriptions:

- The clause's parameter type is the same as the type of the exception that was thrown.
- The clause's parameter type is a superclass of the exception's type.

If a better match appears further down the list of catch clauses, that's just too bad. For instance, imagine that you added a catch clause with a parameter of type NoInputException to the code in Listing 12-4. Imagine, also, that you put this new catch clause after the catch clause with parameter of type NumberFormatException. Then, because NoInputException is a subclass of the NumberFormatException class, the code in your new NoInputException clause would never be executed. That's just the way the cookie crumbles.

Throwing caution to the wind

Are you one of those obsessive-compulsive types? Do you like to catch every possible exception before the exception can possibly crash your program? Well, watch out. Java doesn't let you become paranoid. You can't catch an exception if the exception has no chance of being thrown.

Consider the code shown below. The code has a very innocent i++ statement inside a try clause. That's fair enough. But then the code's catch clause is pretending to catch an IOException.

```
// Bad code!
try
{
    i++;
}
catch (IOException e)
{
    e.printStackTrace();
}
```

Who is this catch clause trying to impress? A statement like i++ doesn't do any input or output. The code inside the try clause can't possibly throw an IOException. So the compiler comes back and says, "Hey, catch clause. Get real. Get off your high horse." Well, to be a bit more precise, the compiler's reprimand reads as follows:

```
exception java.io.IOException is never thrown in body of
           corresponding try statement
```

Doing useful things

So far, each example in this chapter catches an exception, prints a "bad input" message, and then closes up shop. Wouldn't it be nice to see a program that actually carries on after an exception has been caught? Well, it's time for something nice. Listing 12-5 has a try-catch statement inside a loop. The loop keeps running until the user types something sensible.

Listing 12-5:   Keep pluggin' along

```
import java.text.NumberFormat;

public class InventoryLoop
{
```

```
public static void main(String args[])
{
    String numBoxesIn;
    int numBoxes;
    double boxPrice = 3.25;
    boolean gotGoodInput=false;
    NumberFormat currency =
        NumberFormat.getCurrencyInstance();

    do
    {
        System.out.print("How many boxes do we have? ");
        numBoxesIn = DummiesIO.getString();

        try
        {
            numBoxes = Integer.parseInt(numBoxesIn);
            System.out.print("The value is ");
            System.out.println
                (currency.format(numBoxes*boxPrice));
            gotGoodInput = true;
        }
        catch (NumberFormatException e)
        {
            System.out.println();
            System.out.println("That's not a number.");
        }
    }
    while (!gotGoodInput);

    System.out.println("That's that.");
}
}
```

Figure 12-12 shows a run of the code from Listing 12-5. In the first four attempts, the user types just about everything except a valid whole number. At last, the fifth attempt is a success. The user types **3,** and the computer leaves the loop.

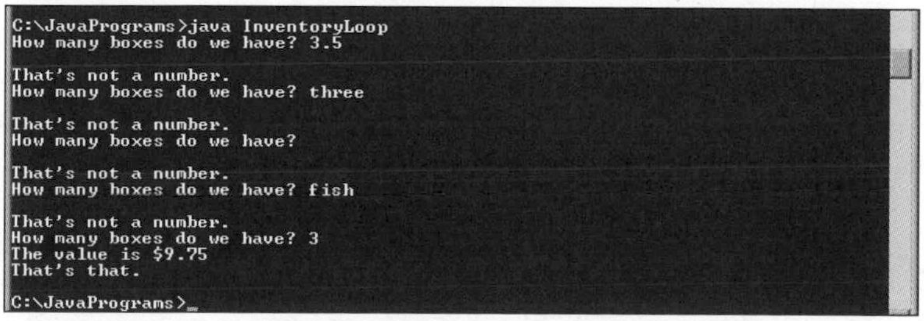

Figure 12-12:
A run of the code in Listing 12-5.

```
C:\JavaPrograms>java InventoryLoop
How many boxes do we have? 3.5

That's not a number.
How many boxes do we have? three

That's not a number.
How many boxes do we have?

That's not a number.
How many boxes do we have? fish

That's not a number.
How many boxes do we have? 3
The value is $9.75
That's that.

C:\JavaPrograms>_
```

Our friends, the good exceptions

A rumor is going around that Java exceptions always come from unwanted, erroneous situations. Although there's some truth to this rumor, the rumor isn't entirely accurate. Occasionally, an exception arises from a normal, expected occurrence. Take, for instance, the detection of the end of a file. The following code makes a copy of a file:

```
try
{
    while(true)
        dataOut.writeByte(dataIn.readByte());
}
catch (EOFException e)
{
    numFilesCopied = 1;
}
```

To copy bytes from dataIn to dataOut, you just go into a while loop. With its true condition, the while loop is seemingly endless. But, eventually, you reach the end of the dataIn file. When this happens, the readByte method throws an EOFException (and end-of-file exception). The throwing of this exception sends the computer out of the try clause and out of the while loop. From there, you do whatever you want to do in the catch clause and then proceed with normal processing.

Handle an Exception or Pass the Buck

So you're learning Java, hey? What? You say you're all the way up to Chapter 12?

I'm impressed. You must be a hard worker. But remember, all work and no play . . .

So, how about taking a break? A little nap will do you the world of good. Is ten seconds okay? Or, is that too long? Let's make it five seconds.

Listing 12-6 has a program that's supposed to pause its execution for five seconds. The problem is, the program in Listing 12-6 is incorrect. Take a look at Listing 12-6 for a minute, and then I'll tell you what's wrong with it.

Listing 12-6:   An incorrect program

```
public class NoSleepForTheWeary
{
    public static void main(String args[])
    {
```

```
        System.out.print("Excuse me while I nap ");
        System.out.println("for just five seconds...");

        takeANap();

        System.out.println("Ah, that was refreshing.");
    }


    static void takeANap()
    {
        Thread.sleep(5000);
    }
}
```

The strategy in Listing 12-6 isn't bad. The idea is to call the sleep method, which is defined in the Java API. This sleep method belongs to the API Thread class. When you call sleep, the number you feed it is a number of milliseconds. So, "take 5000" means pause for five seconds.

The problem is, the code inside the sleep method can throw an exception. This kind of exception is an instance of the InterruptedException class. When you apply javac to the code in Listing 12-6, you get the following unwanted message:

```
unreported exception java.lang.InterruptedException; must be
            caught or declared to be thrown
```

For the purpose of understanding exceptions in general, you don't need to know exactly what an InterruptedException is. All you really have to know is that a call to Thread.sleep can throw one of these InterruptedException objects. But, if you're really curious, an InterruptedException is thrown when some code interrupts some other code's sleep. Imagine that you have two pieces of code running at the same time. One piece of code calls the Thread.sleep method. At the same time, another piece of code calls the interrupt method. By calling interrupt, the second piece of code brings the first code's Thread.sleep method to a screeching halt. The Thread.sleep method responds by spitting out an InterruptedException.

Now, the Java programming language has two different kinds of exceptions. They're called *checked* and *unchecked* exceptions:

✔ The potential throwing of a checked exception must be acknowledged in the code.

✔ The potential throwing of an unchecked exception doesn't need to be acknowledged in the code.

An InterruptedException is one of Java's checked exception types. When you call a method that has the potential to throw an InterruptedException, you need to acknowledge that exception in the code.

Now, when I say that an exception is "acknowledged in the code," what do I really mean?

```
// The author wishes to thank that InterruptedException,
// without which this code could not have been written.
```

No, that's not what it means to be "acknowledged in the code." Acknowledging an exception in the code means one of two things:

- ✔ The statements (including method calls) that can throw the exception are inside a try clause. That try clause has a catch clause with a matching exception type in its parameter list.
- ✔ The statements (including method calls) that can throw the exception are inside a method that has a throws clause in its header. The throws clause contains a matching exception type.

If you're confused by the wording of these two bullets, don't worry. The next two listings illustrate the points made in the bullets.

In Listing 12-7, the method call that can throw an InterruptedException is inside a try clause. That try clause has a catch clause with exception type InterruptedException.

Listing 12-7: Acknowledging with a try-catch statement

```java
public class GoodNightsSleepA
{
    public static void main(String args[])
    {
        System.out.print("Excuse me while I nap ");
        System.out.println("for just five seconds...");

        takeANap();

        System.out.println("Ah, that was refreshing.");
    }


    static void takeANap()
    {
        try
        {
            Thread.sleep(5000);
        }
        catch (InterruptedException e)
        {
            System.out.println("Hey, who woke me up?");
        }
    }
}
```

It's my custom, at this point in a section, to remind you that a run of Listing Such-and-Such is shown in Figure So-and-So. But the problem here is, Figure 12-13 doesn't do justice to the code in Listing 12-7. When you run the program in Listing 12-7, the computer displays Excuse me while I nap for just five seconds, **pauses for five seconds,** and then displays Ah, that was refreshing. **The code works because the call to sleep, which can throw an InterruptedException, is inside a try clause. That try clause has a catch clause whose exception is of type InterruptedException.**

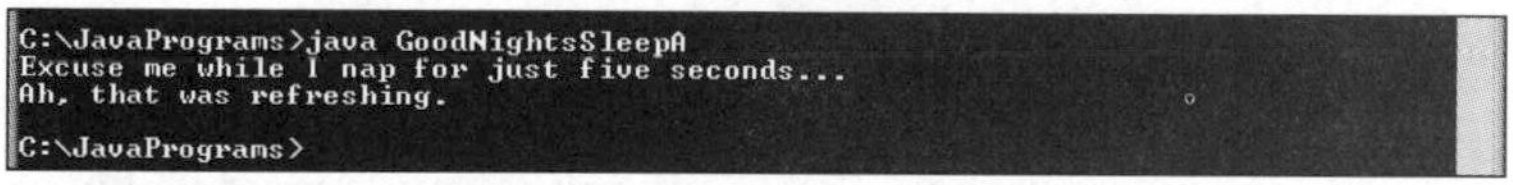

Figure 12-13:
There's a
five-second
pause
before the
"Ah" line.

```
C:\JavaPrograms>java GoodNightsSleepA
Excuse me while I nap for just five seconds...
Ah, that was refreshing.

C:\JavaPrograms>
```

So much for acknowledging an exception with a try-catch statement. You can acknowledge an exception another way, which is used in Listing 12-8.

Listing 12-8:   Acknowledging with throws

```java
public class GoodNightsSleepB
{
    public static void main(String args[])
    {
        System.out.print("Excuse me while I nap ");
        System.out.println("for just five seconds...");

        try
        {
            takeANap();
        }
        catch (InterruptedException e)
        {
            System.out.println("Hey, who woke me up?");
        }

        System.out.println("Ah, that was refreshing.");
    }

    static void takeANap() throws InterruptedException
    {
        Thread.sleep(5000);
    }
}
```

To see a run of the code in Listing 12-8, look back at Figure 12-13. Once again, Figure 12-13 fails to capture the true essence of the run, but that's okay. Just remember that, in Figure 12-13, the computer pauses for five seconds before it displays `Ah, that was refreshing`.

The important part of Listing 12-8 is in the takeANap method's header. That header ends with `throws InterruptedException`. By announcing that it throws an InterruptedException, method takeANap passes the buck. What this throws clause really says is, "I realize that a statement inside this method has the potential to throw an InterruptedException, but I'm not acknowledging the exception in a try-catch statement. Java compiler, please don't bug me about this. Instead of having a try-catch statement, I'm passing the responsibility for acknowledging the exception to the main method (the method that called the takeANap method)."

Indeed, in the main method, the call to takeANap is inside a try clause. That try clause has a catch clause with a parameter of type InterruptedException. So everything is okay. Method takeANap passes the responsibility to the main method, and the main method accepts the responsibility with an appropriate try-catch statement. Everybody's happy. Even javac is happy.

To better understand the throws clause, imagine a volleyball game in which the volleyball is an exception. When a player on the other team serves, that player is throwing the exception. The ball crosses the net and comes right to you. If you pounded the ball back across the net, that would be like catching the exception. But, if you pass the ball to another player, you're using the throws clause. In essence, you're saying, "Here, other player. You deal with this exception."

A statement in a method can throw an exception that's not matched by a catch clause. This includes situations in which the statement throwing the exception isn't even inside a try block. When this happens, execution of the program jumps out of the method that contains the offending statement. Execution jumps back to whatever code called the method in the first place.

A method can name more than one exception type in its throws clause. Just use commas to separate the names of the exception types, as in the following example:

```
throws InterruptedException, IOException,
       ArithmeticException.
```

The Java API has hundreds of exception types. Several of them are subclasses of the RuntimeException class. Anything that's a subclass of RuntimeException (or a sub-subclass, sub-sub-subclass, and so on) is unchecked. Any exception that's not a descendent of RuntimeException is checked. The unchecked exceptions include things that would be hard for the computer to predict. Such things include the NumberFormatException of Listings 12-2 through 12-5, the ArithmeticException, the IndexOutOfBoundsException, the infamous

NullPointerException, and many others. When you write Java code, much of your code is susceptible to these exceptions, but enclosing the code in try clauses (or passing the buck with throws clauses) is completely optional.

The Java API also has its share of checked exceptions. The computer can readily detect exceptions of this kind. So Java insists that, for an exception of this kind, any potential exception-throwing statement is acknowledged with either a try statement or a throws clause. Java's checked exceptions include the InterruptedException (Listings 12-7 and 12-8), the IOException, the SQLException, and a gang of other interesting exceptions.

Finishing the Job with a finally Clause

Once upon a time, I was a young fellow, living with my parents in Philadelphia, just starting to drive a car. I was heading toward a friend's house and thinking about who knows what, when another car came from nowhere and bashed my car's passenger door. This kind of thing is called a *RunARedLightException*.

Anyway, both cars were still drivable, and we were right in the middle of a busy intersection. To avoid causing a traffic jam, we both pulled over to the nearest curb. I fumbled for my driver's license (which had a very young picture of me on it), and opened the door to get out of my car.

And that's when the second accident happened. As I was getting out of my car, a city bus was coming by. The bus hit me and rolled me a few times between itself and my car. This kind of thing is called a *DealWithLawyersException*.

The truth is that everything came out just fine. I was bruised, but not battered. My parents paid for the damage to the car, so I never suffered any financial consequences. (I managed to pass on the financial burden by putting the RunARedLightException into my throws clause.)

This incident helps to explain why I think the way I do about exception handling. In particular, I wonder, "What happens if, while the computer is recovering from one exception, a second exception is thrown?" After all, the statements inside a catch clause aren't immune to calamity.

Well, the answer to this question is anything but simple. For starters, you can put a try statement inside a catch clause. This protects you against unexpected, potentially embarrassing incidents that can crop up during the execution of the catch clause. But, when you start worrying about cascading exceptions, you've opened up a very slimy can of worms. The number of scenarios is large, and things can become complicated very quickly.

One not-too-complicated thing you can do is to create a finally clause. Like a catch clause, a finally clause comes after a try clause. The big difference is that the statements in a finally clause are executed whether or not an exception is thrown. The idea is, "No matter what happens, good or bad, execute the statements inside this finally clause." Listing 12-9 has an example.

Listing 12-9: Jumping around

```java
public class DemoFinally
{
    public static void main(String args[])
    {
        try
        {
            doSomething();
        }
        catch (Exception e)
        {
            System.out.println("Exception caught in main.");
        }
    }

    static void doSomething()
    {
        try
        {
            System.out.println(0/0);
        }
        catch (Exception e)
        {
            System.out.println
                ("Exception caught in doSomething.");
            System.out.println(0/0);
        }
        finally
        {
            System.out.println("I'll get printed.");
        }

        System.out.println("I won't get printed.");
    }
}
```

Normally, when I think about a try statement, I think about the computer recovering from an unpleasant situation. The recovery takes place inside a catch clause, and then the computer marches on to whatever statements come after the try statement. Well, if something goes wrong during execution of a catch clause, then this picture can start looking different.

Listing 12-9 gets a workout in Figure 12-14. First, the main method calls doSomething. Then, the stupid doSomething method goes out of its way to cause trouble. The doSomething method divides 0 by 0, which is illegal and undoable in anyone's programming language. This foolish action by the doSomething method throws an ArithmeticException, which is caught by the try statement's one and only catch clause.

Figure 12-14:
Running the
code from
Listing 12-9.

```
C:\JavaPrograms>java DemoFinally
Exception caught in doSomething.
I'll get printed.
Exception caught in main.

C:\JavaPrograms>_
```

Inside the catch clause, that lowlife doSomething method divides 0 by 0 again. This time, the statement that does the division isn't inside a protective try clause. That's okay, because an ArithmeticException isn't checked. (It's one of those RuntimeException subclasses. It's an exception that doesn't have to be acknowledged in a try or a throws clause. For details, see the previous section.)

Well, checked or not, the throwing of another ArithmeticException causes control to jump out of the doSomething method. But, before leaving the doSomething method, the computer executes the try statement's last will and testament — namely, the statements inside the finally clause. That's why, in Figure 12-14, you see the words I'll get printed on the screen.

Interestingly enough, you don't see the words I won't get printed in Figure 12-14. Because the catch clause's execution throws its own uncaught exception, the computer never makes it down past the try-catch-finally statement.

So, the computer goes back to where it left off in the main method. Back in the main method, word of the doSomething method's ArithmeticException mishaps causes execution to jump into a catch clause. The computer prints Exception caught in main, and then this terrible nightmare of a run is finished.

Chapter 13

Sharing Names among the Parts of a Java Program

*S*peaking of private variables and methods (and I do speak about these things in this chapter) . . .

I'm eating lunch with some friends of mine at work. "They can read your e-mail," says one fellow. Another chimes in, "They know every single Web site that you visit. They know what products you buy, what you eat for dinner, what you wear, what you think. They even know your deepest darkest secrets. Why, I wouldn't be surprised if they know when you're going to die."

A third voice enters the fray. "It's getting to the point where you can't blow your nose without someone taking a record of it. I visited a Web site a few weeks ago, and the page wished me a Happy Birthday. How did they know it was me, and how did they remember that it was my birthday?"

"Yeah," says the first guy. "I have a tag on my car that lets me sail through toll booths. It senses that I'm going through and puts the charge on my credit card automatically. So every month, I get a list from the company showing where I've been, and when I was there. I'm amazed it doesn't say who I was visiting, and what I did when I got there."

I think quietly to myself. I think about saying, "That's just a bunch of baloney. Personally, I'd be flattered if my employer, the government, or some big company thought so much of me that they tracked my every move. I have enough trouble getting people's attention when I really want it. And most agencies that keep logs of all my purchasing and viewing habits can't even spell my name right when they send me junk mail. 'Hello, this is courtesy call for Larry Burg. Is Mr. Burg at home?' Spying on people is really boring. I can just see the headline on the front page of *The Times:* 'Author of *Java 2 For Dummies* Wears His Undershirt Inside Out!' Big deal!"

So, I think for a few seconds, and then I say, "They're out to get us. TV cameras! That's the next big thing — TV cameras everywhere."

Access Modifiers

If you've read this far into *Java 2 For Dummies* (or even if you're browsing the bookstore shelves and have opened right to this chapter), you probably know one thing: Object-oriented programming is big on hiding details. Programmers who write one piece of code shouldn't tinker with the details inside another programmer's code. It's not a matter of security and secrecy. It's a matter of modularity. When you hide details, you keep the intricacies inside one piece of code from being twisted and broken by another piece of code. Your code comes in nice, discrete, manageable lumps. You keep complexity to a minimum. You make fewer mistakes. You save money. You help promote world peace.

Earlier chapters have plenty of examples of the use of private variables. When a variable is declared private, it's hidden from all outside meddling. This hiding enhances modularity, minimizes complexity, and so on.

Elsewhere in the annals of *Java 2 For Dummies* are examples of things that are declared public. Just like a public celebrity, a variable that's declared public is left wide open. Plenty of people probably know what kind of toothpaste Elvis used, and any programmer can reference a public variable, even a variable that's not named Elvis.

In Java, the words *public* and *private* are called *access modifiers*. No doubt you've seen variables and methods with no access modifiers in their declarations. A method or variable of this kind is said to have *default access*. Many examples in this book use default access without making a big fuss about it. That's okay in some chapters, but not in this chapter. In this chapter, I describe the nitty-gritty details about default access.

And you can find out about yet another access modifier that isn't used in any example before this chapter. (At least, I don't remember using it in any earlier examples.) It's the protected access modifier. Yes, this chapter covers some of the slimy, grimy facts about protected access.

Classes, Access, and Multi-Part Programs

With this topic, you can become all tangled up in terminology, so you need to get some basics out of the way. (Most of the terminology you need comes from Chapter 10, but it's worth reviewing at the start of this chapter.) Here's a fake piece of Java code:

```
class MyClass
{
   int myVariable;              //an instance variable
                                // (a member)

   void myMethod()              //a method (another member)
   {
     int myOtherVariable;       //a method-local variable
   }                            // (not a member)
}
```

The comments on the right side of the code tell the whole story. There are two kinds of variables — instance variables and method-local variables. This chapter isn't about method-local variables. It's about methods and instance variables.

Believe me, it's not easy carrying around the phrase "methods and instance variables" wherever you go. It's much better to give these things one name and be done with it. That's why both methods and instance variables are called *members* of a class.

The Java class is where all the action takes place. Each instance variable is declared in a particular class, belongs to that class, and is a member of that class. The same is true of methods. Each method is declared in a particular class, belongs to that class, and is a member of that class. Can you use a certain member name in a particular place in your code? To begin answering the question, you check to see if that place is inside or outside of the member's class:

✔ If the member is private, then only code that's inside the member's class can refer directly to that member's name.

```
class SomeClass
{
   private int myVariable=10;
}


class SomeOtherClass
{
   public static void main(String args[])
   {
     SomeClass someObject = new SomeClass();

     //This doesn't work:
     System.out.println(someObject.myVariable);
   }
}
```

✔ If the name is public, then any code can refer directly to that member's name.

```
class SomeClass
{
    public int myVariable=10;
}


class SomeOtherClass
{
    public static void main(String args[])
    {
        SomeClass someObject = new SomeClass();

        //This works:
        System.out.println(someObject.myVariable);
    }
}
```

Putting a drawing on a frame

To start the ball rolling, you need a baseline example. In this baseline, almost everything is public. With public access, you don't have to worry about who can use what.

The code for this first example comes in several parts. The first part, which is in Listing 13-1, displays an ArtFrame. On the face of the ArtFrame is a Drawing. If all the right pieces are in place, running the code of Listing 13-1 displays a window like the one in Figure 13-1.

Listing 13-1: Displaying a frame

```
import com.burdbrain.drawings.*;
import com.burdbrain.frames.ArtFrame;

public class ShowFrame
{
    public static void main(String args[])
    {
        ArtFrame artFrame = new ArtFrame(new Drawing());
        artFrame.setSize(200,100);
        artFrame.show();
    }
}
```

Figure 13-1:
An
ArtFrame.

The code in Listing 13-1 creates a new ArtFrame instance. You may suspect that ArtFrame is a subclass of a Java frame class, and that's certainly the case. Chapter 9 says that Java frames are, by default, invisible. So, in Listing 13-1, to make the ArtFrame instance visible, you call the show method.

Now notice that Listing 13-1 starts with two import declarations. (For a review of import declarations, see Chapter 8.) The first import declaration allows you to abbreviate any name from the com.burdbrain.drawings package. The second import declaration allows you to abbreviate the name *ArtFrame*.

The detective in you may be thinking, "He must have written more code (code that I don't see here) and put that code in packages that he named *com.burdbrain.drawings* and *com.burdbrain.frames*." And, indeed, you are correct. To make Listing 13-1 work, I need to create something called a *Drawing*, and I'm putting all my drawings in the com.burdbrain.drawings package. I also need an ArtFrame class, and I'm putting all such classes in my com.burdbrain.frames package.

So, really, what's a Drawing? Well, if you're so anxious to know, look at Listing 13-2.

Listing 13-2:   The Drawing class

```
package com.burdbrain.drawings;

import java.awt.Graphics;

public class Drawing
{
    public int x=40, y=40, width=40, height=40;

    public void paint (Graphics g)
    {
        g.drawOval(x, y, width, height);
    }
}
```

The code for the Drawing class is pretty slim. It contains a few int variables and a paint method. That's all. Well, when I create my classes, I try to keep 'em lean. Anyway, here are some notes about my Drawing class:

✔ **At the top of the code is a *package declaration*.** Lo, and behold! I've made my Drawing class belong to a package — the com.burdbrain.drawings package. I didn't pull this package name out of the air. The convention (handed down by the people at Sun Microsystems) says that you start a package name by reversing the parts of your domain name, so I reversed `burdbrain.com`. Then, you add one or more descriptive names, separated by dots. I added the name *drawings,* because I intend to put all my drawing goodies in this package.

✔ **The code has a paint method.** This paint method uses a standard Java trick for making things appear on-screen. In the simplest terms, all you do is paint onto a Graphics buffer, and that buffer is eventually rendered on the computer screen.

Here's a little more detail: In Listing 13-2, the paint method takes a g parameter. This g parameter refers to an instance of the java.awt. Graphics class. A Graphics instance is a buffer. The things you put onto this buffer are eventually displayed on the screen. Like all instances of the java.awt.Graphics class, this buffer has several drawing methods — one of them being drawOval. When you call drawOval, you specify a starting position (*x* pixels from the left edge of the frame and *y* pixels from the top of the frame). You also specify an oval size by putting numbers of pixels in the width and height parameters. Calling the drawOval method puts a little round thing into the Graphics buffer. That Graphics buffer, round thing and all, is displayed on the computer screen.

Directory structure

The code in Listing 13-2 belongs to the com.burdbrain.drawings package. After you put a class into a package, you have to create a directory structure that mirrors the name of the package.

After you put a class into a package, you have to create a directory structure that mirrors the name of the package.

After you put . . . Okay, you get the point. The idea is that, to house code that's in the com.burdbrain.drawings package, you have to create three directories: a com directory, a subdirectory of com named *burdbrain,* and a subdirectory of burdbrain named *drawings.* The overall directory structure is shown in Figure 13-2.

If you don't heed the advice about putting package code in appropriate directories, then you get a repulsive and disgusting `NoClassDefFoundError`. Believe me, this error is never fun to get. When you see this error, you don't have any clues to help you figure out where the missing class is or where the compiler expects to find it. If you stay calm, you can figure out all this stuff on your own. If you panic, you'll be poking around for hours. As a seasoned Java programmer, I can remember plenty of scraped knuckles that came from this heinous `NoClassDefFoundError`.

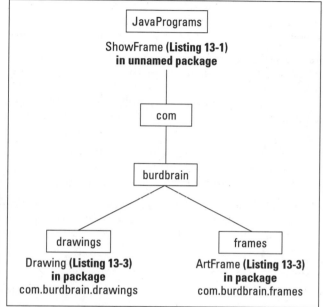

Figure 13-2:
The files and directories in your project.

Using the CLASSPATH

Was it Sigmund Freud or Johnny the Two-Fisted Drunk who said, "Everything has to start somewhere"? I don't remember. Anyway, take another look at the diagram in Figure 13-2 and ask yourself, "What's so special about that JavaPrograms directory at the top of the tree?" Well, if you insist on having a com directory, and a burdbrain subdirectory, and a drawings sub-subdirectory, then you need to mark the place where all these directories start. Indeed, the computer won't bother looking for all these sub-sub-subdirectories if it doesn't know where the root of the tree is.

And that's just where the CLASSPATH enters the scene. The CLASSPATH is a list of starting points for your computer to look for directories. If your CLASSPATH contains

```
c:\JavaPrograms;d:\Java\MyClasses;.
```

then the computer looks in the following three places for the start of the directory tree:

✔ **The computer looks in your** `c:\JavaPrograms` **directory.** For the com.burdbrain.drawings package, the computer looks in directory `c:\JavaPrograms\com\burdbrain\drawings`. If no such directory exists, or if the class the computer is looking for isn't in that directory, then the computer marches to the next item in the CLASSPATH list.

✔ **Next, the computer looks in your** `d:\Java\MyClasses` **directory.** For the com.burdbrain.drawings package, the computer looks in directory `d:\Java\MyClasses\com\burdbrain\drawings`. If no such directory exists, or if the class the computer is looking for isn't in that directory, then the computer marches to the next item in the CLASSPATH list.

✔ **Finally, the computer looks in your working directory, whatever that happens to be.** On many systems (including Windows, Unix, and Linux systems), the dot in the CLASSPATH list stands for your current *working directory,* which is the directory that you're working in at the moment.

Imagine that you're working in your system's command prompt window. (For news about the command prompt window, see Chapter 2.) The command prompt window displays

```
C:\My Documents>
```

Then your working directory is `C:\My Documents`. To look for classes that belong to the com.burdbrain.drawings package, the computer checks the `C:\My Documents\com\burdbrain\drawings` directory.

The way you change what's in your computer's CLASSPATH variable depends on the kind of computer you're running. For tips on setting your computer's CLASSPATH, see Chapters 2 and 7.

If you can, pick one directory and then stick with that directory for issuing the javac command. Using the diagram in Figure 13-2, go to your system's command prompt window and make your working directory be `c:\JavaPrograms`. Then type **javac** and the name of the file you're trying to compile. For instance, to compile `Drawing.java`, **type**

```
javac com\burdbrain\drawings\Drawing.java
```

If that doesn't work, then try reminding the computer that `c:\JavaPrograms` is in the CLASSPATH. Type the command

```
javac -classpath . com\burdbrain\drawings\Drawing.java
```

or type the following on one line:

```
javac -classpath c:\JavaPrograms
                 com\burdbrain\drawings\Drawing.java
```

Making a frame

This chapter's first three listings develop one multipart example. This section has the last of three pieces in that example. This last piece isn't crucial for the understanding of access modifiers, which is the main topic of this chapter. So, if you want to skip past the explanation of Listing 13-3, you can skip it without losing the chapter's thread. On the other hand, if you want to know a little bit about the Java Swing classes, then read on.

Listing 13-3:   The ArtFrame class

```
package com.burdbrain.frames;

import com.burdbrain.drawings.*;
import javax.swing.JFrame;
import java.awt.Graphics;

public class ArtFrame extends JFrame
{
    Drawing drawing;

    public ArtFrame(Drawing drawing)
    {
        this.drawing=drawing;
        setTitle("Abstract Art");
        setDefaultCloseOperation(JFrame.EXIT_ON_CLOSE);
    }

    public void paint(Graphics g)
    {
        drawing.paint(g);
    }
}
```

Listing 13-2 has all the gadgetry you need for putting a drawing on a Java frame. Here are some observations about the code in Listing 13-3 that can help you figure out how the code works:

✔ **The ArtFrame class extends JFrame, and the code imports the javax.swing.JFrame class.** Java's API has two packages for putting windows on a computer screen. The older of these two packages is java.awt (see Chapter 9). The newer package is javax.swing. The newer package has more features, and depends less on the features of individual platforms. (The javax.swing package is called "lightweight," because its code uses less Windows, less Unix, and more pure Java.) But, to use some of the new javax.swing classes, you have to call on some of the old java.awt classes. Go figure!

Anyway, you can usually tell when something is a javax.swing class by the thing's name. Put the letter *J* in front of a java.awt class's name, and you often get a javax.swing class's name. For example, the java.awt package contains the Frame class, and the javax.swing package contains the JFrame class.

✔ **The code calls the setDefaultCloseOperation — a method declared in the JFrame class.** Along with many other goodies, the javax.swing version of a frame can sense when the user wants to close up and go home. In Windows, when you click the little × in the frame's upper right-hand corner, the frame closes.

✔ **The paint method in Listing 13-3 defers to another paint method — the paint method belonging to a Drawing object.** The ArtFrame object creates a floating window on your computer screen. What's drawn in that floating window depends on whatever Drawing object was passed to the ArtFrame constructor.

If you trace the flow of Listings 13-1 through 13-3, you may notice something peculiar. The paint method in Listing 13-3 never seems to be called. Well, for many of Java's window-making components, you just declare a paint method, and let the method sit there quietly in the code. When the program runs, the computer calls the paint method automatically.

That's what happens with javax.swing.JFrame objects. In Listing 13-3, the frame's paint method is called from behind the scenes. Then, the frame's paint method calls the Drawing object's paint method, which in turn, draws an oval on the frame. That's how you get the stuff you see in Figure 13-1.

Sneaking Away from the Original Code

Your preferred software vendor, Burd Brain Consulting, has sold you two files — Drawing.class and ArtFrame.class. As a customer, you can't see the code inside the files Drawing.java and ArtFrame.java. So, you have to live with whatever happens to be inside these two files. (If only you'd purchased a copy of *Java 2 For Dummies*, which has the code for these files in Listings 13-2 and 13-3!) Anyway, you want to tweak the way the oval looks in Figure 13-1 so that it's a bit wider. To do this, you create a subclass of the Drawing class — DrawingWide — and put it in Listing 13-4.

Listing 13-4: A subclass of the Drawing class

```
import com.burdbrain.drawings.*;

import java.awt.Graphics;

public class DrawingWide extends Drawing
```

```
{
   int width=100, height=30;

   public void paint (Graphics g)
   {
      g.drawOval(x, y, width, height);
   }
}
```

To make use of the code in Listing 13-4, you remember to change one of the lines in Listing 13-1. You change the line to

```
ArtFrame artFrame = new ArtFrame(new DrawingWide());
```

Listing 13-4 defines a subclass of the original Drawing class. In that subclass, you override the original class's width and height variables and the original class's paint method. The frame you get is shown in Figure 13-3.

Figure 13-3:
Another art
frame.

In passing, you may notice that the code in Listing 13-4 doesn't start with a package declaration. This means that your whole collection of files comes from the following three packages:

- **The com.burdbrain.drawings package.** The original Drawing class from Listing 13-2 is in this package.

- **The com.burdbrain.frames package.** The ArtFrame class from Listing 13-3 is in this package.

- **An ever present, unnamed package.** In Java, when you don't start a file with a package declaration, all the code in that file goes into one big, unnamed package. Listings 13-1 and 13-4 are in the same unnamed package. In fact, most of the listings from the first 12 chapters of this book are in Java's unnamed package.

At this point, your project has two drawing classes — the original Drawing class and your new DrawingWide class. Similar as these classes may be, they live in two separate packages. That's not surprising. The Drawing class, developed by your friends at Burd Brain Consulting, lives in a package whose name starts with *com.burdbrain.* But you developed DrawingWide on your own, so you shouldn't put it in a com.burdbrain package. The most sensible thing to do is to put it in one of your own packages, such as com.iamthereader.drawings, but putting your class in the unnamed package will do for now.

One way or another, your DrawingWide subclass compiles and runs as planned. You go home, beaming with the confidence of having written useful, working code.

Default access

If you're reading these paragraphs in order, you know that the last example ends very happily. The code in Listing 13-4 runs like a charm. Everyone, including my wonderful editor Paul Levesque, is happy.

But, wait! Do you ever wonder what life would be like if you hadn't chosen that particular career, dated that certain someone, or read that certain *For Dummies* book? In this section, I roll back the clock a bit to show you what would have happened if one word had been omitted from the code in Listing 13-2.

Dealing with different versions of a program can give you vertigo, so I start this discussion by describing what you've got. First, you have a Drawing class. In this class, the variables aren't declared to be public and have the default access. The Drawing class lives in the com.burdbrain.drawings package. (See Listing 13-5.)

Listing 13-5:   Variables with default access

```
package com.burdbrain.drawings;

import java.awt.Graphics;

public class Drawing
{
    int x=40, y=40, width=40, height=40;

    public void paint (Graphics g)
    {
        g.drawOval(x, y, width, height);
    }
}
```

Next, you have a DrawingWide subclass (copied, for your convenience, in Listing 13-6). The DrawingWide class is in Java's unnamed package.

Listing 13-6:   A failed attempt to create a subclass

```
import com.burdbrain.drawings.*;

import java.awt.Graphics;

public class DrawingWide extends Drawing
{
    int width=100, height=30;

    public void paint (Graphics g)
    {
        g.drawOval(x, y, width, height);
    }
}
```

The trouble is, the whole thing falls apart at the seams. The code in Listing 13-6 doesn't compile. Instead, you get the following error messages:

```
x is not public in com.burdbrain.drawings.Drawing;
cannot be accessed from outside package
y is not public in com.burdbrain.drawings.Drawing;
cannot be accessed from outside package
```

The code doesn't compile, because an instance variable that has default access can't be directly referenced outside its package — not even by a subclass of the class containing the variable. The same holds true for any methods that have default access.

A class's instance variables and methods are called *members* of the class. The rules for access, default and otherwise, apply to all members of classes.

The access rules described in this chapter do not apply to method-local variables. (For the rundown on method-local variables, see Chapter 10.) A method-local variable can be accessed only within its own method.

In Java, the default access for a member of a class is package-wide access. A member declared without the word *public, private,* or *protected* in front of it is accessible in the package in which its class resides. Figure 13-4 illustrates some important ideas about access. In that figure, notice that the word *default* doesn't appear outside the "same package" oval.

The names of packages, with all their dots and subparts, can be slightly misleading. For instance, when you write a program that responds to button clicks, you normally import classes from two separate packages. On one line, you have `import java.awt.*;`. On another line, you have `import java.awt.event.*;`. Importing classes from the java.awt package does not automatically import classes from the java.awt.event package.

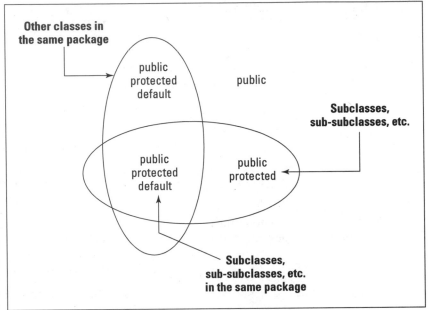

Figure 13-4:
Access in
Java.

Crawling back into the package

I love getting things in the mail. At worst, it's junk mail that I can throw right into the trash. At best, it's something I can use, a new toy, or something somebody sent specially for me.

Well, today is my lucky day. Somebody from Burd Brain Consulting sent a subclass of the Drawing class. It's essentially the same as the code in Listing 13-6. The only difference is, this new DrawingWideBB class lives inside the com.burdbrain.drawings package. The code is shown in Listing 13-7. To run this code, I have to modify Listing 13-1 with the line

```
ArtFrame artFrame = new ArtFrame(new DrawingWideBB());
```

Listing 13-7: **A subclass of the Drawing class**

```
package com.burdbrain.drawings;

import java.awt.Graphics;

public class DrawingWideBB extends Drawing
{
    int width=100, height=30;

    public void paint (Graphics g)
    {
```

```
        g.drawOval(x, y, width, height);
    }
}
```

When you run Listing 13-7 alongside the Drawing class in Listing 13-5, every-thing works just fine. The reason? It's because Drawing and DrawingWideBB are in the same package. Look at Figure 13-4 and notice how the word *default* appears with plentitude inside the "same package" oval. Being in the same package, the code in the DrawingWideBB class has every right to use the x and y variables, which are defined with default access in the Drawing class.

Protected Access

When I was first learning Java, I thought the word *protected* meant "nice and secure," or something like that. "Wow, that variable is protected. It must be hard to get at." Well, this notion turned out to be wrong. In Java, a member that's protected is less hidden, less secure, and easier to use than one that has default access. The concept is rather strange.

Think of protected access this way. You start with an instance variable that has default access (a variable without the word *public, private,* or *protected* in its declaration). That variable can be accessed only inside the package in which it lives. Now add the word *protected* to the front of the variable's decla-ration. Suddenly, classes outside that variable's package have some access to the variable. A subclass (of the class in which the variable is declared) can now reference the variable. You can also reference the variable from a sub-subclass, a sub-sub-subclass, and so on. Any descendent class will do. For an example, see Listings 13-8 and 13-9.

Listing 13-8:   Protected variables

```
package com.burdbrain.drawings;

import java.awt.Graphics;

public class Drawing
{
    protected int x=40, y=40, width=40, height=40;

    public void paint (Graphics g)
    {
        g.drawOval(x, y, width, height);
    }
}
```

Listing 13-9:   A subclass of the Drawing class

```
import com.burdbrain.drawings.*;

import java.awt.Graphics;

public class DrawingWide extends Drawing
{
    int width=100, height=30;

    public void paint (Graphics g)
    {
        g.drawOval(x, y, width, height);
    }
}
```

Listing 13-8 defines the Drawing class. Listing 13-9 defines DrawingWide, which is a subclass of the Drawing class.

In the Drawing class, the x, y, width, and height variables are protected. The DrawingWide class has its own width and height variables, but DrawingWide references the x and y variables that are defined in the parent Drawing class. That's okay, even though DrawingWide isn't in the same package as its parent Drawing class. (The Drawing class is in the com.burdbrain.drawings package; the DrawingWide class is in Java's great, unnamed package.) It's okay because the x and y variables are protected in the Drawing class.

Look at Figure 13-4 and notice the word *protected* throughout the figure's wide "subclasses" oval. A subclass can access a protected member of a class, even if that subclass belongs to some other package.

Do you work with a team of programmers? Do people from outside your team use their own team's package names? If so, when they use your code, they may make subclasses of the classes that you've defined. This is where protected access comes in handy. Use protected access when you want people from outside your team to make direct references to your code's variables or methods.

Putting non-subclasses in the same package

Those people from Burd Brain Consulting are sending you one piece of software after another. This time, they've sent an alternative to the ShowFrame class — the class in Listing 13-1. This new ShowFrameWideBB class displays a wider oval (how exciting!), but it does this without creating a subclass of the old Drawing class. Instead, the new ShowFrameWideBB code creates a Drawing instance and then changes the value of the instance's width and height variables. The code is shown in Listing 13-10.

Listing 13-10:   Drawing a wider oval

```
package com.burdbrain.drawings;

import com.burdbrain.frames.ArtFrame;

public class ShowFrameWideBB
{
    public static void main(String args[])
    {
        Drawing drawing = new Drawing();
        drawing.width=100;
        drawing.height=30;
        ArtFrame artFrame = new ArtFrame(drawing);
        artFrame.setSize(200,100);
        artFrame.show();
    }
}
```

So, here's the story. This ShowFrameWideBB class in Listing 13-10 is in the same package as the Drawing class (the com.burdbrain.drawings package). But ShowFrameWideBB isn't a subclass of the Drawing class.

Now imagine compiling ShowFrameWideBB with the Drawing class that's shown in Listing 13-8 — the class with all those protected variables. What happens? Well, everything goes smoothly, because a protected member is available in two (somewhat unrelated) places. Look at Figure 13-4, and notice the vast proliferation of the word *protected.* A protected member is available to subclasses outside the package, but the member is also available to code (subclasses or not) within the member's package.

The real story about protected access is one step more complicated than the story that I describe in this section. The Java Language Specification mentions a hair-splitting point about code being responsible for an object's implementation. When you're first figuring out how to program in Java, don't worry about this point. Wait until you've written many Java programs. Then, when you stumble upon a `variable has protected access` error message, you can start worrying. Better yet, skip the worrying and take a careful look at the protected access section in the Java Language Specification.

Using a fully qualified class name

Normally, to get a class's main method running, you type **java** and then the name of a class. For instance, to run the code in Listing 13-1, you type **java ShowFrame**.

When you do this, the computer consults its CLASSPATH variable, and looks for the ShowFrame class. (You can find a briefing on the CLASSPATH variable earlier in this chapter.) After the computer finds the ShowFrame class, the computer looks for a main method.

So how does this story play out when the class with the main method is in a named package? For instance, how do you get the code in Listing 13-10 to run? The code has a main method, and the code is in a named package — the com.burdbrain.drawings package. You can proceed in several ways, but the idea is to make sure the computer can find all the classes that you're trying to use. This means that the computer must know two important things:

✔ **The computer must know where to look for the top of the directory tree.** If the code in Listing 13-10 lives in your `c:\JavaPrograms\ com\burdbrain\drawings` directory, then the directory named `c:\JavaPrograms` must be part of your computer's CLASSPATH variable. Figure 13-5 shows an illustration of the directory tree.

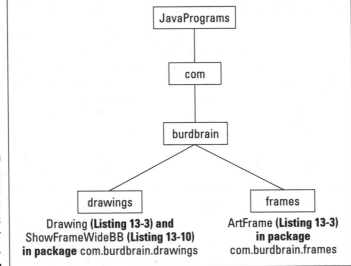

Figure 13-5:
The files and directories in your project.

✔ **The computer must know where to find the class containing the main method.** Again, assume the lineup of files and directories shown in Figure 13-5. Starting from the `c:\JavaPrograms` directory, the fully qualified name of the ShowFrameWideBB class is `com.burdbrain. drawings.ShowFrameWideBB`. So, to get the code running, you type

```
java com.burdbrain.drawings.ShowFrameWideBB
```

For more information about fully qualified names, see Chapter 8.

When you run java, you type the name of a class, not the name of a file. A class's fully qualified name uses dots, not slashes.

Access Modifiers for Java Classes

Maybe the things you read about access modifiers for members make you a tad dizzy. After all, member access in Java is a very complicated subject, with lots of plot twists and cliffhangers. Well, the dizziness is over. Compared with the saga for variables and methods, the access story for classes is rather simple.

A class can be either public or nonpublic. If you see something like

```
public class ShowFrame
```

then you're looking at the declaration of a public class. But, if you see plain old

```
class UseAccount
```

then the class that's being declared isn't public.

Public classes

If a class is public, then you can refer to the class from anywhere in your code. Of course, some restrictions apply. For instance, the computer has to be able to locate the class through the CLASSPATH variable. You also have to name the class properly. If the class is inside a named package that's not the package you're currently working in, you need to call the class by the class's fully qualified name. Here's an example:

```
java.text.NumberFormat currency =
    java.text.NumberFormat.getCurrencyInstance();
```

Alternatively, you can start your file with an import declaration and be on a first-name basis with a Java class, like this:

```
import java.text.NumberFormat;

NumberFormat numFormat =
    NumberFormat.getNumberInstance();
```

Nonpublic classes

If a class isn't public, then you can refer to the class only from code within the class's package.

I tried it. First, I went back to Listing 13-2 and deleted the word *public*. I turned `public class Drawing` into plain old `class Drawing`, like this:

```
package com.burdbrain.drawings;

import java.awt.Graphics;

class Drawing
{
    public int x=40, y=40, width=40, height=40;

    public void paint (Graphics g)
    {
        g.drawOval(x, y, width, height);
    }
}
```

Then I compiled the code in Listing 13-7. Everything was peachy, because Listing 13-7 starts with the following lines:

```
package com.burdbrain.drawings;

public class DrawingWideBB extends Drawing
```

Because both pieces of code are in the same com.burdbrain.drawings package, access from DrawingWideBB back to the nonpublic Drawing class was no problem at all.

But then, I tried to compile the code in Listing 13-3. The code in Listing 13-3 begins with

```
package com.burdbrain.frames;
```

That code isn't in the com.burdbrain.drawings package. So, when the computer reached the line

```
Drawing drawing;
```

from Listing 13-3, the computer went "poof!" To be more precise, the computer displayed this message:

```
com.burdbrain.drawings.Drawing is not public
in com.burdbrain.drawings;
cannot be accessed from outside package
```

Well, I guess I got what was coming to me.

Things are never as simple as they seem. The rules described in this section apply to the kinds of classes described in this book. Java has other classes, called *inner classes*, which follow a different set of rules. Fortunately, the use of inner classes makes up a rather isolated niche of the entire Java realm. Even veteran Java programmers use inner classes very sparingly. Most of the time, you can live very happily without such things.

Part V
The Part of Tens

In this part . . .

You're near the end of the book, and the time has come to sum it all up. This part of the book is your slam-bam, two-thousand-words-or-less resource for Java. What? You didn't read every word in the chapters before this one? That's okay. You can pick up a lot of useful information in this Part of Tens.

Chapter 14

Ten Ways to Avoid Mistakes

"The only people who never make mistakes are the people who never do anything at all." One of my college professors said that. I don't remember the professor's name, so I can't give him proper credit. I guess that's my mistake.

Reloading an Applet

You've created an applet and tested it with your Web browser. Everything's fine, but you want to change the label on the face of a button. So you go back to your editor and make a change in your Java program file. You run javac again — that's good.

But then, when you press the Web browser's Refresh or Reload button, you don't see the change you made. The button still has the old label. What went wrong?

The Java Virtual Machine is playing its usual tricks on you. After you load an applet into your Web browser's window, you have to jump through hoops to load a different version of the same applet. To make sure you see the updated applet, you can try these three things:

✔ Hold down the Shift key while you click Refresh.

✔ Hold down the Ctrl key while you click Refresh.

✔ Close your Web browser and then reopen it again.

For the real story on running Java applets, see Chapter 2.

Putting Capital Letters Where They Belong

Java is a case-sensitive language, so you really have to mind your Ps and Qs — along with every other letter of the alphabet. Here are some things to keep in mind as you create Java programs:

✔ Java's keywords are all completely lowercase. For instance, in a Java if statement, the word *if* can't be *If* or *IF*.

✔ When you use names from the Java API, the case of the names has to match what appears in the API.

✔ You also need to make sure that the names you make up yourself are capitalized the same way throughout your entire program. If you declare a myAccount variable, then you can't refer to it as MyAccount, myaccount, or Myaccount. If you capitalize the variable name two different ways, then Java thinks you're referring to two completely different variables.

For more info, see Chapter 3.

Breaking Out of a switch Statement

If you don't break out of a switch statement, then you get fall-through. For instance, if the value of verse is 3, then the following code prints all three lines — Last refrain, He's a pain, and Has no brain.

```
switch (verse)
{
   case 3: System.out.print  ("Last refrain, ");
           System.out.println("last refrain,");
   case 2: System.out.print  ("He's a pain, ");
           System.out.println("he's a pain,");
   case 1: System.out.print  ("Has no brain, ");
           System.out.println("has no brain,");
}
```

For the full story, see Chapter 5.

Comparing Values with a Double Equal Sign

When you compare two values with one another, you use a double equal sign. The line

```
if(inputNumber==randomNumber)
```

is correct, but the line

```
if(inputNumber=randomNumber)
```

is not correct. For a full report, see Chapter 5.

Adding Components to a GUI

Here's a constructor for a Java frame.

```
public SimpleFrame()
{
    Button b = new Button("Thank you...");
    setTitle("...Jill Byus Schorr");
    setLayout(new FlowLayout());
    add(b);
    b.addActionListener(this);
    setSize(300,100);
    show();
}
```

Whatever you do, don't forget the call to the add method. Without this call, you go to all the work of creating a button, but the button doesn't show up on your frame. For an introduction to such issues, see Chapter 9.

Adding Listeners to Handle Events

Look again at the previous section's code to construct a SimpleFrame. If you forget the call to addActionListener, then when you click the button, nothing happens. Clicking the button a second time and clicking it harder don't help. For the rundown on listeners, see Bonus Chapter A, which is on the CD-ROM.

Defining the Required Constructors

When you define a constructor with parameters, as in

```
public Temperature(double number)
```

then the computer no longer creates a default parameterless constructor for you. In other words, you can no longer call

```
Temperature roomTemp = new Temperature();
```

unless you explicitly define your own parameterless Temperature constructor. For all the gory details, see Chapter 9.

Fixing Nonstatic References

If you try to compile the following code, you get an error message.

```
public class WillNotWork
{
    String greeting = "Hello";

    public static void main(String args[])
    {
        System.out.println(greeting);
    }
}
```

You get an error message because main is static, but greeting isn't static. For the complete guide to finding and fixing this problem, see Chapter 10.

Staying within Bounds in an Array

When you declare an array with ten components, the components have indices 0 through 9. In other words, if you declare

```
int guests[] = new int[10];
```

then you can refer to the guests array's components by writing guests[0], guests[1], and so on, all the way up to guests[9]. You can't write guests[10], because the guests array has no component with index 10.

For the latest gossip on arrays, see Chapter 11.

Dealing with the CLASSPATH

You're compiling Java code, minding your own business, when the computer gives you a `NoClassDefFoundError`. All kinds of things can be going wrong. But chances are that the computer can't find your .class file. To fix this, you must align all the planets correctly. That is, your computer's CLASSPATH has to point to a particular directory, and your .class file has to be in the right place relative to that directory. For specific guidelines, see Chapters 2 and 13.

Chapter 15

Ten Sets of Web Resources for Java

*N*o wonder the Web is so popular. It's both useful and fun. This chapter has ten bundles of resources. Each bundle has Web sites for you to visit. Each Web site has resources to help you use Java more effectively.

The Horse's Mouth

Sun's official Web site for Java is `java.sun.com` (also known as `www.javasoft.com`). This site has all the latest development kits, and many of them are free. The site also has a great section with online tutorials and mini-courses. The tutorial/mini-course section's Web address is `developer.java.sun.com/developer/onlineTraining/`.

Finding News, Reviews, and Sample Code

The Web has plenty of sites devoted exclusively to Java. Many of these sites feature reviews, links to other sites, and best of all, oodles of sample Java code. They may also offer free mailing lists that keep you informed of the latest Java developments. Here's a brief list of such sites:

- **EarthWeb:** `softwaredev.earthweb.com/java`
- **JavaFile.com:** `www.javafile.com`
- **The Giant Java Tree:** `www.gjt.org`
- **The Java Boutique:** `javaboutique.internet.com`
- **Digital Cat's Java Resource Center:** `www.javacats.com`
- **FreewareJava.com:** `www.freewarejava.com`
- **JavaPowered:** `www.javapowered.com`
- **The JavaRanch:** `www.javaranch.com`
- **JavaToys:** `www.nikos.com/javatoys`
- **Java Shareware:** `www.javashareware.com`

Improving Your Code with Tutorials

To find out more about Java, you can visit Sun's online training pages. Some other nice sets of tutorials are available at the following Web sites:

- **Richard Baldwin's Web site:** `www.phrantic.com/scoop/tocadv.htm`
- **1001 tutorials:** `www.1001tutorials.com/java`
- **IBM developerWorks:** `www-105.ibm.com/developerworks/education.nsf/dw/java-onlinecourse-bytitle`
- **ProgrammingTutorials.com:** `www.programmingtutorials.com`

Finding Help on Newsgroups

Have a roadblock you just can't get past? Try posting your question on an Internet newsgroup. Almost always, some friendly expert will post just the right reply.

With or without Java, you should definitely start exploring newsgroups. You can find thousands of newsgroups — groups on just about every conceivable topic. (Yes, there are more newsgroups than *For Dummies* titles!) To get started with newsgroups, visit `groups.google.com`. For postings specific to Java, look for the groups whose names begin with `comp.lang.java`. As a novice, you'll probably find the following three groups to be the most useful:

- ✔ comp.lang.java.programmer
- ✔ comp.lang.java.help
- ✔ comp.lang.java.api

Checking the FAQs for Useful Info

Has the acronym FAQ made it to the Oxford English Dictionary yet? Everybody seems to be using FAQ as an ordinary English word. In case you don't already know, FAQ stands for *Frequently Asked Questions.* In reality, a FAQ should be called ATQTWTOSPOTN. This acronym stands for *Answers to Questions That We're Tired of Seeing Posted on This Newsgroup.*

You can find several FAQs at the official Sun Web site. You can also check out the FAQ for the comp.lang.java newsgroups that I discuss in the previous section. To read this wealth of information, go to www.afu.com/javafaq.html.

Opinions and Advocacy

Java isn't just techie stuff. The field has issues and opinions of all shapes and sizes. To find out more about them, visit www.javalobby.org. After you've hovered for a while and learned the etiquette, you can even join the discussion.

Looking for Java Jobs

Are you looking for work? Would you like to have an exciting, lucrative career as a Java programmer? Then try visiting a Web site designed specially for people like you. Point your Web browser to www.javajobs.com or java.computerwork.com. Then, to hobnob and network with other Java professionals visit www.teamjava.com. The site's mission is "to promote and advance Java and assist Java consultants the world over in locating and completing contract work." Sounds good.

Becoming Certified in Java

These days, everybody is anxious to become certified. If you're one of these people, you can find plenty of resources about Java certification on the Web. Just start by visiting www.jcert.org and www.javacert.com. Both of these sites link to other interesting sites, including sites with practice certification exams.

Developing Servlets

This book has all the tools you need to start using Java. When you've finished being started, you may want to start continuing. This may involve writing Java servlets.

A *servlet* is program that responds to a Web request. For instance, a user sitting at a computer in Ong's Hat, New Jersey, clicks a link. The link-click is sent to a host computer in Chicken, Alaska. Sophisticated as it is, that host computer in Chicken composes an entire Web page on the fly. The host computer sends the newly composed page back to the visitor's computer in Ong's Hat, New Jersey.

Composing a Web page on the fly is something you can do with a Java servlet. The only extra thing you need is a cooperative host computer. Fortunately for cheapskates, you can use some host computers for free. For a list of free servlet-enabled hosts, visit `www.jspin.com/home/sites/jsphosts/freejsph`.

Finding Out about Related Technologies

The world of Java is always growing. When it started, Java programmers were big on applets. They used lots of HTML code. Nowadays, the hot topic is the merger of Java and XML. (The acronym XML stands for *Extensible Markup Language.*)

For a wealth of information on HTML and XML, visit the official sites for these technologies. The official HTML Web site is `www.w3.org/MarkUp`. The official XML site is `www.xml.org`.

Part VI

Appendix

In this part . . .

The appendix tells you how to use the book's CD-ROM. And, by the way, if you haven't cracked open the seal on the book's CD-ROM yet, then please do so. (Of course, you should pay for the book first.) The CD-ROM has some wonderful things on it — all the code from the book, my favorite pieces of shareware, plus three additional chapters! That's right. If you just can't get enough *Java 2 For Dummies*, you can read the encore chapters available on the CD-ROM. So what are you waiting for? Whip out that CD, shove it into your computer, and have some fun.

Appendix
Using the CD-ROM

Sure, you can read, read, read until your eyes bug out. But you won't learn Java until you write and run some code. Besides, it's no fun to just read about programming. You've got to experiment, try things, make some mistakes, and discover some things on your own.

So this book's CD-ROM has everything you need to get going interactively. First, read the little warning about all the legal consequences of your breaking the seal on this book's disk pack. Then, throw caution to the wind and rip that pack open. Put the CD-ROM in the drive, and you're ready to go.

System Requirements

This CD-ROM has two kinds of files on it:

- ✔ **Files that I, the author, created:** For the most part, these files contain all the listings in this book (Listing 3-1 in Chapter 3, for instance). Most of these listings are Java program files.

- ✔ **Various pieces of freeware, shareware, and whateverware:** I generally lapse into laziness and call all these things by the name *shareware,* but the legal department tells me that I should be more careful.

Anyway, these two kinds of files have two different sets of system requirements. For the files that I created, you can use almost any computer. Sure, a Pentium with Windows 95 is nice. And, if you want to use the current Java Software Development Kit from Sun, you probably need at least 32MB of RAM. But because Java has been ported to so many different platforms, you can probably find a way to run this book's examples on your grandfather's old Victrola. There's definitely a Java compiler that runs on Windows 3.1.

For some lists of Java compiler versions (versions for computers not officially supported by the folks at Sun Microsystems), visit the following Web addresses:

```
www.javasoft.com/cgi-bin/java-ports.cgi

www-105.ibm.com/developerworks/tools.nsf/dw/java-devkits-
           byname?OpenDocument&Count=100
```

Of course, the shareware on this CD-ROM is a whole different story. To run the shareware, make sure that your computer meets the minimum system requirements in the following list:

- A PC with a Pentium or faster processor, or a Mac OS computer with a 68040 or faster processor.
- Microsoft Windows 95 or later, or Mac OS system software 7.6.1 or later.
- At least 32MB of total RAM installed on your computer; for best performance, I recommend at least 64MB.
- You'd better have a CD-ROM drive. Otherwise, you'll have difficulty grabbing software off this book's CD-ROM.
- A monitor capable of displaying at least 256 colors or grayscale.

If your computer doesn't match up to most of these requirements, you may have problems using the shareware on the CD. For the latest and greatest information, please refer to the ReadMe file located at the root of the CD-ROM.

If you need more information on the basics, check out these books published by Hungry Minds, Inc.: *PCs For Dummies,* by Dan Gookin; *Macs For Dummies,* by David Pogue; *iMacs For Dummies,* by David Pogue; and *Windows 95 For Dummies, Windows 98 For Dummies, Windows 2000 Professional For Dummies, Microsoft Windows ME Millennium Edition For Dummies,* all by Andy Rathbone.

Using the CD with Microsoft Windows

To install items from the CD to your hard drive (and you have the Autorun feature enabled), follow these steps:

1. **Insert the CD into your computer's CD-ROM drive.**

   A window appears with the following options: HTML Interface, Browse CD, and Exit.

2. **Choose one of the options, as follows:**

   - **HTML Interface:** Click this button to view the contents of the CD in standard For Dummies presentation. It'll look like a Web page. Here you'll also find a list of useful Web links from the book.

   - **Browse CD:** Click this button to skip the fancy presentation and simply view the CD contents from the directory structure. This means you'll just see a list of folders — plain and simple.

   - **Exit:** Well, what can we say? Click this button to quit.

If you do not have the Autorun feature enabled or if the Autorun window does not appear, follow these steps to access the CD:

1. **Insert the CD into your computer's CD-ROM drive.**

2. **Click the Start button and choose Run from the menu.**

3. **In the dialog box that appears, type** d:\start.htm.

   Replace *d* with the proper drive letter for your CD-ROM if it uses a different letter. (If you don't know the letter, double-click My Computer on your desktop and see what letter is listed for your CD-ROM drive.)

   Your browser opens, and the license agreement is displayed. If you don't have a browser, Microsoft Internet Explorer is included on the CD.

4. **Read through the license agreement, nod your head, and click the Agree button if you want to use the CD.**

   After you click Agree, you're taken to the Main menu, where you can browse through the contents of the CD.

5. **To navigate within the interface, click a topic of interest to take you to an explanation of the files on the CD and how to use or install them.**

6. **To install software from the CD, simply click the software name.**

   You'll see two options: to run or open the file from the current location or to save the file to your hard drive. Choose to run or open the file from its current location, and the installation procedure continues. When you finish using the interface, close your browser as usual.

Note: We have included an "easy install" in these HTML pages. If your browser supports installations from within it, go ahead and click the links of the program names you see. You'll see two options: Run the File from the Current Location and Save the File to Your Hard Drive. Choose to Run the File from the Current Location and the installation procedure will continue. A Security Warning dialog box appears. Click Yes to continue the installation.

Using the CD with Mac OS

To install items from the CD to your hard drive, follow these steps:

1. **Insert the CD into your computer's CD-ROM drive.**

   In a moment, an icon representing the CD you just inserted appears on your Mac desktop. Chances are, the icon looks like a CD-ROM.

2. **Double-click the CD icon to show the CD's contents.**

3. **Double-click** `start.htm` **to open your browser and display the license agreement.**

   If your browser doesn't open automatically, open it as you normally would by choosing File⇨Open File (in Internet Explorer) or File⇨Open⇨ Location in Netscape and select *Java 2 For Dummies*. The license agreement appears.

4. **Read through the license agreement, nod your head, and click the Accept button if you want to use the CD.**

   After you click Accept, you're taken to the Main menu. This is where you can browse through the contents of the CD.

5. **To navigate within the interface, click any topic of interest and you're taken to an explanation of the files on the CD and how to use or install them.**

6. **To install software from the CD, simply click the software name.**

Running the Java Code That's in This Book

The CD-ROM has all the code from the listings in this book. It also has some helper files — images, data files, and other things that you need to make the most of all the listings. I've tried to organize the code so that copying it is painless. Then, you can get it running right away. I thought a long time and came up with the following scheme:

- ✔ The code from the book is all on the CD-ROM, in the Author directory.

- ✔ In the Author directory, each chapter has its own subdirectory. For instance, the third chapter has a subdirectory named *Chapter03*.

- ✔ In each chapter's subdirectory, each listing has its own sub-subdirectory. For instance, the code from Listing 3-1 is its own little directory named *Listing0301*.

✔ As a rule of thumb, when a listing's code begins with `class SomeName` (or `public class SomeName`), the code is in a file called `SomeName.java`.

If you're a Windows user, you can quickly copy all my listings from the CD-ROM to your computer's hard drive. Just click the Install Author Files link in the HTML interface. Clicking this link copies my entire Author directory to a Java 2 For Dummies directory on your computer's hard drive. For your convenience, clicking the link also adds an item to your computer's Start menu.

Now, to top off this grand list of rules about directories, you may want to note a few exceptions, quirks, and other things. Here's a list of such things:

✔ **Some listings aren't Java programs. They're not meant to be copied and run.**

There's no harm in copying Listing 3-2 from the CD-ROM to your hard drive. But the code in Listing 3-2 isn't real Java. It's fake. (A Warning icon about this appears right after the listing in Chapter 3.) So you don't need to go out of your way to copy that particular listing or other fake listings like it.

✔ **Many directories have helper files in them.**

Take, for instance, Listing 5-1. This listing defines the GuessingGame class. Now, the GuessingGame class calls on a method from a separate class — namely, the DummiesIO class. So, to make things easy, I put two files in the Listing0501 directory on the CD-ROM. That directory has files `GuessingGame.java` and `DummiesIO.java`. Just copy them both to your hard drive, and you'll be all set.

I use the same DummiesIO class over and over again in the examples in this book. So, many, many copies of `DummiesIO.java` are on the CD-ROM. All these copies are identical to one another. If you've copied `DummiesIO.java` once and don't feel like copying it again to run a different example, that's just fine.

✔ **Sometimes, a directory includes code from more than one listing.**

Taken together, Listings 8-1 through 8-3 make up one big example. You can't run the code in Listing 8-2 without having the code from Listing 8-1. And you can't run anything without having the data that's in Listing 8-3. So, if you look at the CD-ROM, you see three separate directories — Listing0801, Listing0802 and Listing0803. Each directory has the same three files in it. The files are: `Employee.java`, `DoPayroll.java`, and `EmployeeInfo` — the code from Listings 8-1, 8-2, and 8-3.

What is this? A big waste of CD-ROM space? Well, not really. The way I figure it, you may crack the book open to Listing 8-3, see the EmployeeInfo data file, and say to yourself, "I'd like to run some Java code that uses the data from this listing." Okay, no problem. Just copy everything that's in the Listing0803 directory on the CD-ROM, and you'll be on your way.

Freeware, Shareware, and Just Plain Ware

The following sections provide a summary of the software and other goodies you can find on the CD. If you need help with installing the items provided on the CD, refer to the installation instructions in the preceding section.

Shareware programs are fully functional, free, trial versions of copyrighted programs. If you like particular programs, register with their authors for a nominal fee and receive licenses, enhanced versions, and technical support. *Freeware programs* are free, copyrighted games, applications, and utilities. You can copy them to as many PCs as you like — for free — but they offer no technical support. *GNU software* is governed by its own license, which is included inside the folder of the GNU software. The distribution of GNU software is not restricted. See the GNU license at the root of the CD for more details. *Trial, demo,* or *evaluation* versions of software are usually limited either by time or functionality (such as not letting you save a project after you create it).

Adobe Acrobat Reader

Commercial version

For Windows and Mac. Talk about value added! This book has three extra chapters on its CD-ROM. The chapters are

> Bonus Chapter A: Responding to Keystrokes and Mouse Clicks
>
> Bonus Chapter B: Writing Java Applets
>
> Bonus Chapter C: Using Java Database Connectivity

To view these chapters, you need a program called Adobe Acrobat Reader. That's no problem, because a free copy of the Reader is on the CD-ROM.

For more information, visit www.adobe.com/acrobat.

Note: For you Web fanatics out there, you can also read the bonus chapters on the Web at www.dummies.com/extras/Java2/.

JBuilder

Trial version

For Windows. Quoting from *JBuilder For Dummies*, "JBuilder is a visual development environment for Java. Want the user to see a list and a button? Just drag these items onto a Designer window — JBuilder writes your program for you automatically."

For more information, visit `www.borland.com/jbuilder`.

Kawa

Evaluation version

For Windows. Kawa is a slick development environment for Java. First, organize your Java files into projects. Then click Kawa's Build button and watch as all the files are compiled. To find Java API classes, you can search Kawa's visual hierarchy tree, or type part of a class name and have Kawa find the class for you. Kawa even has a built-in debugger, with steps, breakpoints, and the whole works.

For more information, visit `www.macromedia.com/software/kawa/trial/`.

IBM WebSphere Studio Entry Edition

Trial version

For Windows. WebSphere is a high-powered development environment that's aimed specifically at Java for Web servers. Create a project with WebSphere and then put it on your host so that the whole world can use it.

For more information, visit `www-4.ibm.com/software/webservers/appserv`.

CSE HTML Validator

Freeware version

For Windows. I discovered this little gem while I was writing Chapter 2. Imagine that you're creating a Web page with a Java applet on it. Your page has lots of HTML code, and that HTML code needs to be perfect. Just run the code through the CSE HTML Validator. The Validator scans your code and tests the code for conformance with rigorous HTML standards.

For more information, visit `www.htmlvalidator.com`.

DJ Java Decompiler

Freeware version

For Windows. Great stuff! Somebody hands you a file named `Mystery.class`. Like all .class files, the file `Mystery.class` is a big mumbo-jumbo collection of zeros and ones. You don't have `Mystery.java`, so you can't use the .java file to find out what's inside `Mystery.class`. So, what do you do? It's easy. You run the .class file through the DJ Java Decompiler. The Decompiler does the opposite of what the javac command would do. The Decompiler digs through your .class file and uses it to reconstruct a .java file. This new `Mystery.java` file may not be exactly the same as the original, but it's close enough. You can read and edit the .java file just like any other piece of Java code.

For more information, visit `members.fortunecity.com/neshkov/dj.html`.

FileQuest

Shareware version

For Windows. Years after the release of Windows 95, the Windows Explorer interface is still the same. It's still cumbersome to deal with more than one folder at a time. You can find dozens of shareware replacements for Windows Explorer. However, most have their own user interface quirks, and many of them are buggy. After trying a bunch, I judged FileQuest to be the best. It's stable, reliable, and intuitive. It has many features that you don't find in Windows Explorer. It uses a multipane interface, which makes moving files from folder to folder easy.

For more information, visit `www.piquest.com/filequest.htm`.

HTMLib

Freeware version

For Windows. When you work with Java applets, you use a mix of Java source code and HTML tags. To do this, you need some complete, reliable reference materials. The HTML Reference Library (also known as HTMLib) has everything you need to know about the HyperText Markup Language. Its point-and-click navigation tools enable you to find the information that you need quickly and easily.

For more information, visit www.htmlib.com.

Internet Explorer

Commercial version

For Windows and Mac. Do you develop Java applets? Most of the people who visit your Web site use Internet Explorer. So, to see your work as these visitors see it, you should install Internet Explorer on your computer. This book's CD-ROM has a copy of Internet Explorer.

For more information, visit www.microsoft.com/ie.

JDataConnect Standard Edition

Trial version

For Windows. As this book goes to print, the world is using three different versions of Sun's Java Database Connectivity API. The older version 1 is still the only version implemented by many database software vendors. The newer version 2 supports scrollable result sets and other goodies. And an even newer version, version 3, is just beginning to emerge.

To run version 1, you can use the JDBC-ODBC Bridge that comes with Sun's Java Development Kit. But, the JDBC-ODBC Bridge hasn't kept pace with the times. If you want to run JDBC version 2, you have to hunt for software that implements the standard. That's when JDataConnect enters the scene. With JDataConnect, you can use older version 1 features as well as features implemented only in the newer JDBC version 2.

For more information, visit www.j-netdirect.com/JDataFeatures.htm.

PasteLister

Shareware version

For Windows. I searched high and low for a good clipboard replacement before I found this gem. For copying and pasting snippets of code, the standard operating system clipboard is much too limiting. The shareware Web sites have dozens of clipboard replacement programs, but most of them are so complicated to use that you're better off retyping text by hand. With PasteLister, you get the flexibility to manage several categories of clips, and the ease-of-use that makes copying and pasting worthwhile.

For more information, visit www.progency.com/pastelister.html.

MetaPad LE

Freeware version

For Windows. Even for jotting down a quick sentence or two, Windows Notepad is much too primitive. In Windows 9x, Notepad doesn't have a Replace feature, a recent documents list, or a way to change printers. The list of inconveniences goes on and on.

In contrast, MetaPad is a real workhorse. MetaPad supports all the features that you wish Notepad supported and more. Along with all this, MetaPad is lightweight. It doesn't consume megabytes on your hard drive, and it doesn't take tens of seconds to open. When I have text to edit and want to work simply and quickly, I use MetaPad.

For more information, visit www.liquidninja.com/metapad.

NetCaptor

Freeware version

For Windows. Talk about cool software! When I use someone else's computer and have to surf without NetCaptor, I feel terribly inconvenienced. NetCaptor uses tabs to keep track of several open Web pages. These tabs replace the need to open several browser windows. So, when I visit a search engine, I keep the results page open while I investigate some of the page's entries. When I do Java development, I keep the API documentation open while I visit one or more of my own documents. Without NetCaptor, I can open several browser windows. However, the interface isn't as seamless, and the stress on my computer's RAM and CPU is greater.

For more information, visit www.netcaptor.com.

TextPad

Shareware version

For Windows. As a Java programmer, you do tons of text editing. Forget the word processor that makes documents look pretty. You need a solid editor that lets you move quickly and easily through plain text.

For writing programs and working with sizable programming projects, my favorite editor is TextPad. It does all the things I want an editor to do. Among my favorite features is the ability to add color highlighting for keywords in any programming language. (To add color highlighting for Java, just visit `www.textpad.com/add-ons/` and download one of the many .syn files that you find at that site.) TextPad even has hotkeys for compiling and running Java programs.

Other useful features include a document selector, the ability to define workspaces, an option to view line numbers, and searching that cycles automatically through an entire document.

For more information, visit `www.textpad.com`.

ZipMagic

Trial version

For Windows. City governments should pipe this program in through the water supply. Install ZipMagic, and you'll never need to think about unzipping a file again. It's absolutely seamless. With ZipMagic, a Zip file appears to be just another folder on your computer's hard drive. Double-click the folder, and it opens like any other folder in Windows Explorer. You can add files, copy files, move files, do anything with files in the folder, and not think at all about the folder's really being a Zip file. When I download shareware, I don't bother unzipping it. I just install straight from the zip folder. That's the beauty of working with ZipMagic.

For more information, visit `www.ontrack.com/zipmagic`.

And, If You Run into Any Trouble . . .

I tried my best to find shareware programs that work on most computers with the minimum system requirements. Alas, your computer may differ, and some programs may not work properly for some reason.

If you have problems with the shareware on this CD-ROM, the two likeliest problems are that you don't have enough memory (RAM), or you have other programs running that are affecting installation or running of a program. If you get an error message such as Not enough memory or Setup cannot continue, try one or more of the following suggestions and then try using the software again:

- ✔ **Turn off any antivirus software running on your computer.** Installation programs sometimes mimic virus activity and may make your computer incorrectly believe that a virus is infecting it.

- ✔ **Close all running programs.** The more programs you have running, the less memory is available to other programs. Installation programs typically update files and programs; so if you keep other programs running, installation may not work properly.

- ✔ **Have your local computer store add more RAM to your computer.** This is, admittedly, a drastic and somewhat expensive step. However, if you have a Windows 95 PC or a Mac OS computer with a PowerPC chip, adding more memory can really help the speed of your computer and allow more programs to run at the same time. This may include closing the CD interface and running a product's installation program from Windows Explorer.

If you still have trouble installing the items from the CD, please call the Hungry Minds, Inc. Customer Service phone number at 800-762-2974 (outside the U.S.: 317-572-3993) or send e-mail to techsupdum@hungryminds.com.

Index

(continued)

(continued)

Notes

Notes

Notes

Notes

Notes

Notes

Notes

Hungry Minds, Inc.
End-User License Agreement

READ THIS. You should carefully read these terms and conditions before opening the software packet(s) included with this book ("Book"). This is a license agreement ("Agreement") between you and Hungry Minds, Inc. ("HMI"). By opening the accompanying software packet(s), you acknowledge that you have read and accept the following terms and conditions. If you do not agree and do not want to be bound by such terms and conditions, promptly return the Book and the unopened software packet(s) to the place you obtained them for a full refund.

1. **License Grant.** HMI grants to you (either an individual or entity) a nonexclusive license to use one copy of the enclosed software program(s) (collectively, the "Software") solely for your own personal or business purposes on a single computer (whether a standard computer or a workstation component of a multi-user network). The Software is in use on a computer when it is loaded into temporary memory (RAM) or installed into permanent memory (hard disk, CD-ROM, or other storage device). HMI reserves all rights not expressly granted herein.

2. **Ownership.** HMI is the owner of all right, title, and interest, including copyright, in and to the compilation of the Software recorded on the disk(s) or CD-ROM ("Software Media"). Copyright to the individual programs recorded on the Software Media is owned by the author or other authorized copyright owner of each program. Ownership of the Software and all proprietary rights relating thereto remain with HMI and its licensers.

3. **Restrictions On Use and Transfer.**

    (a) You may only (i) make one copy of the Software for backup or archival purposes, or (ii) transfer the Software to a single hard disk, provided that you keep the original for backup or archival purposes. You may not (i) rent or lease the Software, (ii) copy or reproduce the Software through a LAN or other network system or through any computer subscriber system or bulletin-board system, or (iii) modify, adapt, or create derivative works based on the Software.

    (b) You may not reverse engineer, decompile, or disassemble the Software. You may transfer the Software and user documentation on a permanent basis, provided that the transferee agrees to accept the terms and conditions of this Agreement and you retain no copies. If the Software is an update or has been updated, any transfer must include the most recent update and all prior versions.

4. **Restrictions on Use of Individual Programs.** You must follow the individual requirements and restrictions detailed for each individual program in the Using the CD-ROM appendix of this Book. These limitations are also contained in the individual license agreements recorded on the Software Media. These limitations may include a requirement that after using the program for a specified period of time, the user must pay a registration fee or discontinue use. By opening the Software packet(s), you will be agreeing to abide by the licenses and restrictions for these individual programs that are detailed in the Using the CD-ROM appendix and on the Software Media. None of the material on this Software Media or listed in this Book may ever be redistributed, in original or modified form, for commercial purposes.

5. **Limited Warranty.**

    (a) HMI warrants that the Software and Software Media are free from defects in materials and workmanship under normal use for a period of sixty (60) days from the date of purchase of this Book. If HMI receives notification within the warranty period of defects in materials or workmanship, HMI will replace the defective Software Media.

    (b) **HMI AND THE AUTHOR OF THE BOOK DISCLAIM ALL OTHER WARRANTIES, EXPRESS OR IMPLIED, INCLUDING WITHOUT LIMITATION IMPLIED WARRANTIES OF MERCHANTABILITY AND FITNESS FOR A PARTICULAR PURPOSE, WITH RESPECT TO THE SOFTWARE, THE PROGRAMS, THE SOURCE CODE CONTAINED THEREIN, AND/OR THE TECHNIQUES DESCRIBED IN THIS BOOK. HMI DOES NOT WARRANT THAT THE FUNCTIONS CONTAINED IN THE SOFTWARE WILL MEET YOUR REQUIRE-MENTS OR THAT THE OPERATION OF THE SOFTWARE WILL BE ERROR FREE.**

    (c) This limited warranty gives you specific legal rights, and you may have other rights that vary from jurisdiction to jurisdiction.

6. **Remedies.**

    (a) HMI's entire liability and your exclusive remedy for defects in materials and workmanship shall be limited to replacement of the Software Media, which may be returned to HMI with a copy of your receipt at the following address: Software Media Fulfillment Department, Attn.: *Java 2 For Dummies*, Hungry Minds, Inc., 10475 Crosspoint Blvd., Indianapolis, IN 46256, or call 1-800-762-2974. Please allow four to six weeks for delivery. This Limited Warranty is void if failure of the Software Media has resulted from accident, abuse, or misapplication. Any replacement Software Media will be warranted for the remainder of the original warranty period or thirty (30) days, whichever is longer.

    (b) In no event shall HMI or the author be liable for any damages whatsoever (including without limitation damages for loss of business profits, business interruption, loss of business information, or any other pecuniary loss) arising from the use of or inability to use the Book or the Software, even if HMI has been advised of the possibility of such damages.

    (c) Because some jurisdictions do not allow the exclusion or limitation of liability for consequential or incidental damages, the above limitation or exclusion may not apply to you.

7. **U.S. Government Restricted Rights.** Use, duplication, or disclosure of the Software for or on behalf of the United States of America, its agencies and/or instrumentalities (the "U.S. Government") is subject to restrictions as stated in paragraph (c)(1)(ii) of the Rights in Technical Data and Computer Software clause of DFARS 252.227-7013, or subparagraphs (c) (1) and (2) of the Commercial Computer Software - Restricted Rights clause at FAR 52.227-19, and in similar clauses in the NASA FAR supplement, as applicable.

8. **General.** This Agreement constitutes the entire understanding of the parties and revokes and supersedes all prior agreements, oral or written, between them and may not be modified or amended except in a writing signed by both parties hereto that specifically refers to this Agreement. This Agreement shall take precedence over any other documents that may be in conflict herewith. If any one or more provisions contained in this Agreement are held by any court or tribunal to be invalid, illegal, or otherwise unenforceable, each and every other provision shall remain in full force and effect.

FOR DUMMIES
BOOK REGISTRATION

Register This Book and Win!

We want to hear from you!

Visit **dummies.com** to register this book and tell us how you liked it!

✔ Get entered in our monthly prize giveaway.

✔ Give us feedback about this book — tell us what you like best, what you like least, or maybe what you'd like to ask the author and us to change!

✔ Let us know any other *For Dummies* topics that interest you.

Your feedback helps us determine what books to publish, tells us what coverage to add as we revise our books, and lets us know whether we're meeting your needs as a *For Dummies* reader. You're our most valuable resource, and what you have to say is important to us!

Not on the Web yet? It's easy to get started with *Dummies 101: The Internet For Windows 98* or *The Internet For Dummies* at local retailers everywhere.

Or let us know what you think by sending us a letter at the following address:

For Dummies Book Registration
Dummies Press
10475 Crosspoint Blvd.
Indianapolis, IN 46256

™

BESTSELLING BOOK SERIES